The Lecturer's Guide to Quality and Standards in

To my mother with love and thanks.
K.

The Lecturer's Guide to Quality and Standards in Colleges and Universities

by

Kate Ashcroft

with contributions from Lorraine Foreman-Peck

RoutledgeFalmer
Taylor & Francis Group

LONDON AND NEW YORK

First published in 1995
By Routledge Falmer
11 New Fetter Lane, London EC4P 4EE

Transferred to Digital Printing 2004

A catalogue record for this book is available from the British Library

Library of Congress Cataloging-in-Publication Data are available on request

ISBN 0 7507 0338 5 cased
ISBN 0 7507 0339 3 paper

Jacket design by Caroline Archer

Typeset in 9.5/11pt Bembo by
Graphicraft Typesetters Ltd., Hong Kong.

Contents

Contents

Contents

Chapter 1

Introduction

My aim in this book is to provide a basic handbook for lecturers concerned with quality and standards in the post-compulsory education sector with an emphasis on an entrepreneurial climate, but at the same time retaining a clear educational philosophy. This philosophy is based on the model of the lecturer as a reflective practitioner. Reflective in this sense is more than 'thinking about', it also includes collecting data about practice and analysing it in the light of the social, moral and political context.

Even inexperienced lecturers can no longer ignore the quality context in which they work. Questions of quality and standards are the business of all those who work in educational institutions. All are concerned with maintaining standards and in documenting quality control processes. If they are to further the interests of students, lecturers have to play a role in defining what 'quality' might look like, what standards might be appropriately set and how they might be measured.

This book rests on the premise that 'quality' and 'standards' are highly problematic; that they may be examined from a number of alternative viewpoints; that these viewpoints and the power each exerts are highly political matters; and that these definitions cannot be separated from the values that underpin them and from the way that they are applied in institutional and individual practice. For this reason I consider several different definitions of quality and standards and intend that the whole book will help you develop an understanding of what 'quality' and 'standards' mean to you, and how what you do may be influenced by these definitions. My intention in writing the book is to make sense of the changing climate of quality control and academic standards.

I cover teaching, learning and management issues, specifically focused on the concerns of the lecturer. Lecturers manage the work of others, usually students, and thus could be said to have an equivalent role to that of middle managers in industry or commerce. They usually have little management training for this role. I focus on the development of key management skills and understandings necessary to understand, develop and monitor standards and quality in further and higher education, focusing especially on the role of lecturers and course leaders. I also explore ways of looking at the interests of the various 'audiences' for this activity (mainly students, but also external assessors, institutional managers, employers, funders and so on). The model of reflective practice I use within this book assumes that professional development will result from a willingness to define the quality of teaching and students' learning and an interest in issues of standards and their relationship to those of differentiation and individual development and learning.

Background

Reflective practice cannot be divorced from its context, requiring you to deepen your understanding of the institutional and wider political context for your work. I hope to stimulate your interest in these matters and to encourage greater effectiveness within these structures, so that you can use them to the benefit of students and teaching. For instance, in the new climate of further and higher education, staff development, especially as it relates to your teaching and your students' learning will be given a higher profile. The development of appraisal has been increasingly linked to performance-related pay for the individual and more indirectly to performance indicators for the institution. These assessments are likely to be increasingly related to funding. For example, in the UK, the new division of Quality Audit, which is part of the Higher Education Quality Council (HEQC), will focus exclusively on the quality of the management of teaching, learning and assessment in each institution.

The HEQC and the Higher Education Funding Council for England (HEFCE) have agreed to work more closely (HEQC, 1994) on such matters as documentation requirements; exchange of reports between the two councils; notes of guidance; training of auditors; scheduling of visits; and evaluation. Data from the auditing process will feed into the quality ratings and affect HEFCE funding for individual colleges and universities.

The Further Education Funding Council (FEFC) has instigated similar quality-assessment processes and funding arrangements for further education colleges. It has set up a committee to assess the quality of provision through a system of performance indicators, external inspection and audit of the college's own systems of quality control. The FEFCE Quality Assessment Committee and its inspectorate will work closely with HEFCE, the Office for Standards in Education (OFSTED) and Local Authority Associations (LAAs) to ensure consistency of standards, develop clear divisions of responsibility and minimize disruption to institutions which would be caused by multiple inspections (Further Education Funding Council, 1994). The operations of these organizations are described in more detail in Chapter 2.

The emergence of the UK funding councils' concern with issues of accountability and quality assessment are related to a move from an elite to a mass system of post-compulsory education. Barnett (1994) sees this as resulting from a change in the relationship between education and society and, in particular, the incorporation of post-compulsory education into society's mainstream. Education has become an economic good, and therefore the concern of Government, employers and education's 'customers', rather than a cultural good, with quality defined by the cultural elite (and academe in particular). This change in the perceived value of post-compulsory education has in turn led to new definitions of 'quality' that focus on competence, outcomes, skills and transferability, rather than knowledge, truth, objectivity and the integrity of the discipline.

The discussion of quality and standards is located within a context of education that embraces entrepreneurial activity, in which issues of consistency, fitness for purpose and value for money become as much a part of the quality framework as absolute notions of 'excellence'.

Ways of Using the Book

You may wish to use the book in various ways. You might use some of the enquiry tasks to collect evidence for an appraisal interview and ideas within the text to analyse the evidence according to your own and institutional criteria for quality. You might wish to work through the book as a professional development text or use it as a reference book to provide another way of looking at a particular problem. In the last case, you may find the synopsis at the end of each chapter is a useful starting point.

Practical exercises intersperse the text, some of which invite you to collect data from within your institution. These are designed to help you understand and use the concepts and to reflect upon the operation of ideas introduced by the text in the context of your own institution and in relation to your own values. Values tend to be so much part of our 'taken for granted' view of the world, that it is sometimes hard to examine them without help. For this reason, I suggest that you may need to involve a trusted colleague in some of your enquiry. The entry for the reflective diary at the end of each chapter is designed to enable you to interact with the material presented and analyse your developing ideas.

Because of the broad scope of the book, I am able to introduce only some of the possible perspectives and ideas which may stimulate your thinking and provide a 'language' for your analysis. I include an annotated reading list at the end of each chapter, so that you can target your reading and take forward those issues of particular relevance to you.

The Quality Context

With the introduction of a rapid expansion of the system of post-compulsory education in Britain, first in higher education and then in further education, fundamental changes in approach to the problems of teaching and learning have become necessary. Various bodies, such as the Committee of Scottish University Principals (1993), see the solution to problems presented by the new mass system in terms of innovative approaches to the delivery of the curriculum and to the structures needed to support these approaches. These structures included the development of systematic ways of monitoring and enhancing 'quality' of provision, in order to ensure that 'more' did not mean 'worse'. The mass system could not easily be monitored through *ad hoc* systems which have sometimes existed in the past.

One of the most significant features of this debate is the emphasis on the quality of teaching and learning. This is sometimes presented as unproblematic and uncontroversial, as if there were no problems in defining what might be meant by 'quality'. Alternatively, the notion of 'quality' may be presented as in some way synonymous with the elaboration of systems by which it is monitored.

The British Conservative Government of the 1990s introduced terms borrowed from the industrial sector, such as 'quality control', 'quality audit' and 'quality assessment', as if the intention to replace the gentler language and more evolutionary approach suggested by the culture of 'evaluation' and 'critical review' was part of a politically neutral agenda about 'getting value for money'

(DES, 1991). This signalled more than a change in rhetoric and has led to real changes in systems and procedures and their relationship to funding. The question of who should assess the quality, who should define it, and so on is now largely determined by the Government and justified in terms of free-market development. This takes place in a market that is essentially not free, where resources are strictly limited, and institutions can be rewarded in one year for responding enthusiastically to student 'demand' and penalized in the next.

The direct involvement of Government in the definition of quality clearly has had an effect on the relationship between universities and colleges and the State. This relationship is under great strain at the moment. The tensions are set up by the underlying conflict between the legitimate authority of Government and legitimate academic freedom. In a parliamentary democracy, the Government may properly exercise great authority over the institutions within the State. On the other hand, traditionally, the further and higher education systems have had considerable freedom, and so, in practice, have attained some degree of power. This subsidiarity has come to be valued as a useful check on the centralizing tendencies of Government.

The increasing direction of further and higher education by Government has also affected the lecturer's relationship with the institution. The academic freedom that has been a traditional feature of the British educational system is sometimes in direct conflict with the interests of the institution, and may even threaten its financial viability. Difficult questions are being asked about the rights and responsibilities of institutions and lecturers and the legitimacy of limitations to academic freedom.

'Quality' issues have become more central to institutional concerns. New committees and senior posts have been created as institutions and departments become subject to 'quality audit', as wise institutions prepare themselves for teaching and learning to be subjected to a similar rating exercise to that which determines research funding allocations to individual institutions. In any case, the creation of league tables for results (such as 'A' Level results from further education colleges) has affected recruitment in some areas, and so certain definitions of 'quality' are already having a real influence on resources. In some cases, the debate had focused on issues of institutional self-protection, accountability and control, and deeper issues about criteria for good practice have been neglected.

Quality, Standards and the Reflective Practitioner Model

The model of the Reflective Practitioner underpins the analysis of approaches to quality and standards in further and higher education within this book. I have previously outlined this model (Ashcroft and Foreman-Peck, 1994), which draws on Dewey's (1916) description of reflective thinking, as developed by Zeichner (1982) and others (Carr and Kemmis, 1986; Isaac and Ashcroft, 1986; Ziechner and Teitlebaum, 1982). The model sees professional development as progressing through a process of critical enquiry and problem-solving, that is in turn dependent upon the development of key qualities: openmindedness; responsibility; and wholeheartedness.

Openmindedness refers to the ability to seek out and evaluate alternative viewpoints. This is seen as a deliberate, and sometimes systematic enquiry into the behaviour and feelings of others which will yield data for the lecturer to assess. This assessment should not be an automatic acceptance of the viewpoints or a rejection of those notions which do not immediately chime with your own, but rather an honest assessment of what they mean for you, for the individuals holding them and for action and development. Openmindedness therefore implies a certain humility in the face of alternative interpretations of practice and context, tempered by a rigorous analysis.

Responsibility involves the willingness to look at both the immediate and the long-term consequences of action for all concerned. This implies that you wish to move beyond a consideration of 'what works' in order to ask essentially moral questions of worthwhileness. Again, questions of worthwhileness require you to examine and sometimes systematically collect evidence of the effects of action from the point of view of various parties.

Wholeheartedness requires that you take openmindedness and responsibility as your aspiration for your 'life position' (aspiration, because it will never be wholly achieved). This means that you are willing to eschew instrumental considerations of personal advantage; that you are willing to take the risks entailed in examining your practice in the light of your values and in examining what those values themselves imply; and that openmindedness and responsibility are not stances for part of your professional life, that can be abandoned in certain circumstances (for instance in the context of entrepreneurial activity).

These qualities imply a willingness to undertake certain kinds of action and to develop certain prerequisite skills. For instance, openmindedness requires you to examine your action from the point of view of others. To achieve this you will need a range of interpersonal skills (such as empathy), communication skills (such as listening skills), research skills (in order to collect systematic data) and analytical skills (in order to organize the data for evaluation). Responsibility and wholeheartedness require similar skills and actions in order that you can investigate the real effects of your action and evaluate the results. Thus, in addition to the list above, responsibility requires qualities of imagination and for you to know and to care about what will happen in a future which may not involve you. Wholeheartedness depends upon perseverance and an optimism about your own and others' ability to change.

Reflection does not take place in a social, political or economic vacuum. It does not require perfect circumstances. Rather the contrary, it may help to make sense of the context for practice and examine actions and values in the light of adverse circumstances in order that practice will improve. I am talking here about a process of professional development in which your practice is explored in the context of the political and social issues and values. This examination may result in changes to values and/or practice. This process should empower you to understand and operate differently within your context, and, perhaps in the longer term, to change that context.

One of the centrally important features of reflective action is its relatively public nature. Reflection as defined in this book is much more than a 'collecting, organizing and thinking about evidence' (although it does include this). It also requires that you share thinking, interpretation of events, and successes and failures with others. This process of sharing encourages the articulation of developing theories of teaching and learning and exposes them to critical examination. This can be a surprising and sometimes painful process (especially when your most basic, taken for granted assumptions are challenged); but it is probably essential for real professional and personal development. The very process of articulating values and the way they might be actualized tends to refine them. It may challenge you to look at issues in new ways and to look for and confront transformational resolutions (solutions that transform the nature of a problem) to the dilemmas inherent within education.

Enquiry Task

Talk to:

* a small group of students
* a trusted colleague

to find out how they would define quality in teaching and/or learning.

What do the definitions of the students and the lecturer have in common and how do they differ?

Perspectives on Quality and Standards

Openmindedness, responsibility and wholeheartedness require you to look at the alternative perspectives on quality and standards of each of those groups involved in the educational process. These groups include lecturers, students, parents and the community, employers, the academic community represented by your 'discipline', institutional managers and funding bodies. Ways of exploring these perspectives are considered in the chapters which follow. Each of these groups may be considered to have some kind of interest in education that constitutes an entitlement. You can therefore only act in an openminded way and with responsibility if you seek out these groups to explore their viewpoints, values and the effects of your action upon them. As Elliott (1993) states, enquiry into action must embrace your own and others' values, since these are part of educational reality. There is no value-free, objective context for 'insider research' (or enquiry into real practice) within education.

Institutions are introducing new models of quality and standards which seem to be defined in terms of quality assurance systems: that is, by the measures taken to check that processes conform to defined policy. Standards may be defined in terms of quality indicators. These refer to measures taken to check on outcomes. Thus, in a context of quality control, you may be involved in predetermined processes of monitoring. These may be mechanistic and fail to take account of the moral and political values implied within them. As a reflective teacher you will be willing to explore the meanings behind the systems, and to allow that it may be irrational to ignore feelings in your assessment of quality. You will see assumed knowledge about quality and standards as highly problematic, and recognize the need for shared discussion and meanings in this area. Entitlements can be defined, for instance, in terms of the services and curriculum which students can expect.

The notion of entitlements can be a starting point for quality, but they only provide a base-line that you should be aiming to go beyond. Aspirations need to be articulated also.

Enquiry Task

Think about a course that you teach.

Identify some 'entitlements' you should ensure for each of the following groups:

	Entitlement
Students	e.g: to have work marked and returned within fourteen days
Other lecturers	e.g: to have a planning meeting two weeks before the course starts
The 'discipline'	e.g: to develop students' understanding of the 'fair test' as part of the scientific process
The institution	e.g: to receive an evaluation report within one month of the course finishing
Employers	
The Funding Body	
The Community	

What problems did you find in defining 'entitlement'?
What limitations do you see to this approach?

The Context for Teaching and Learning

Brown *et al.* (1993) point out that the quality of teaching can only be assessed if it is part of a process and a context that include the whole teaching environment. Therefore, the observation of teaching in individual sessions may be of some value but it cannot tell the whole story. For instance, the quality of the teaching the student receives also depends on the quality of the learning environment, including learning equipment and library provision, as well as how well the lecturer uses these resources.

The quality of the teaching is also dependent upon the congruence of that teaching with your own and institutional aims, for instance, whether you wish to cater better for people from particular ethnic groups, or women; whether the institution is interested in a competency-based approach to learning; or whether you or the institution define 'quality' learning in traditionally academic or other terms. In each of these cases, particular teaching styles may be more or less appropriate.

The balance of skills within the institution depends in part on the recruitment policy of the institution. For instance, research experience may be prized over teaching experience and competence. Alternatively, the institution may be interested in recruiting 'cheap' staff who may be relatively inexperienced. How these

7

kinds of priorities are handled may affect the quality of teaching and learning. The possibility of linking resources to quality in the management of teaching, learning and assessment has led to a developing interest in each of these areas at institutional level.

The institutional knowledge required for effective management of the teaching and learning process is underestimated by many lecturers. Because most of us are interested in people, we may underestimate the importance of systems and structures. As you develop as a reflective practitioner, it is almost inevitable that you will wish to change things. If you do not have an understanding of the committee and executive structures of your institution and the principles of strategic and financial planning, you will lack much of the basic data which might enable you to come to wise decisions. At the most basic level, if you lack this information you are less likely to succeed. Perhaps more importantly, the educational, economic and political climate of the institution where you work, and its relationships to the wider educational, economic and political context, are part of the alternative viewpoints sought out by openminded lecturers who take responsibility for their actions.

Enquiry Task

How well do you understand the institutional framework for your teaching and the students' learning?
Do you know the following:

- Who to go to if you have a student with a severe personal problem?
- Who to go to next if the student's problem is not solved?
- Who to go to if you have a student presenting you with a discipline problem you cannot handle?
- Who to go to next if the problem is not solved?
- What processes should a revision to an existing course go through?
- What is the system for approving a new course?
- What is the institution's equal-opportunities policy as it relates to students and to staff?
- How would you get a new item into next year's budget?
- What does the institution's mission statement contain?
- What are the major items within the institution's strategic plan for the next three years?
- What are the major sources of funding for your institution?

Discuss the answers with a colleague you trust. What do they imply about the way quality is perceived in your institution and its priorities?

Outline of the Content of the Book

This book is intended to inform the teacher in further and higher education about issues in quality and standards as they affect them. In this context, I have used the term 'lecturer' throughout. This does not imply that the main job of the teacher in colleges and universities is 'lecturing'. Indeed, it should become clear to the reader that I take the responsibilities of the lecturer to include among other things: teaching in all its modes, managing learning, sustaining the learning environment, personal support of student, research and scholarship and contributing to institutional management.

In writing this book I am trying to provide you with the tools for understanding and developing your practice within a framework of quality control, quality audit and the maintenance of academic standards. In Chapter 2, I explore the external context for this process: financial, political and moral. I look at the ways in which these external factors commonly influence the internal committee and executive systems within colleges and universities, so that you can start to analyse the relationships between these systems and the micro-political culture of the institution. I believe that such an understanding is important because of the influence that people, systems and management perspectives have on course delivery, and thus on the learning experience of your students.

In Chapter 3 Lorraine Foreman-Peck focuses on the students' learning itself, and in particular its relationship to issues of quality and standards. She looks at the models of quality which are implied by certain definitions of learning, and in particular, the competency model that underpins the standards introduced by the National Vocational Qualifications (NVQs). She looks at institutional definitions of quality in the student learning experience, and their relationship (if any) with lecturers' definitions, particularly in the area of group size. She explores the learners' perspective on quality and standards and focuses on the needs of adult learners and the quality control system.

In Chapter 4, I explore the relationship between formal and informal systems of student support and the maintenance of quality and standards. I look at the problems and opportunities that the new climate and definitions of quality and standards offer for management, teaching and student support, taking assessment, and monitoring of equal opportunities as a starting point.

Staffing and staff development are central to many quality issues. In Chapter 5, I explore the appraisal system as a starting point for such a focus. I examine the problems inherent in certain definitions of appraisal and the conflict between the bureaucratic, political and developmental purposes of appraisal. I look at the role of research, scholarship and professional updating in maintaining quality, and the link between management issues and quality, particularly team working, time management and the change process. I also explore the role of institutional and management style in promoting teaching effectiveness.

In Chapter 6, Lorraine Foreman-Peck and I explore models of assessment and their role in monitoring standards. We look at student appraisal and issues in self-assessment, especially its relationship to formal systems of assessment. We discuss different models for the assessment of performance and how they relate to issues of equal opportunities. We examine the role and purposes of evaluation and how these relate to formal systems and course and personal development.

Chapter 7 deals with the principles of course design. I make distinctions between aims and objectives, processes and outcomes. The importance of mapping consistency between rationale, aims, objectives, content and assessment is considered. Institutional issues, such as the maintenance of academic standards, committee systems and the relationships between committee systems and executive processes are analysed. The role of the committee within the micro-political culture of the institution is explored. I finish by looking at course design as a process that involves systems, people and the management perspective on course delivery.

Chapter 8 examines issues within resource management. I look at what the lecturer needs to understand about funding and the macro systems of post-compulsory education. I provide material that may assist you in applying for funding within your institution or for outside funds, especially researching and writing bids for different audiences. I describe how you might find out about what sources are available and ways in which you might access them.

In Chapter 9, I explore marketing and recruitment as a human process that involves researching 'client' perspectives. I look at admissions procedures and interviewing as part of the induction process and the ways in which the quality of teaching and learning are related to marketing perspectives. I explore ways of pricing and costing new developments and ways you may use pricing as part of a marketing strategy.

In Chapter 10, I examine research as a public activity that is central to further and higher educational purposes. I explain the Government mechanisms for research rating and the impact of various research traditions on values in research. I explore criteria for assessing the quality of research and mechanisms for monitoring it. I consider the impact of insider research on the development of practice and locate research activity within an ethical framework, that includes entitlements for researchers, research students, research assistants and the subjects of research.

Finally I draw the threads of the book together. In Chapter 11, I link each of the issues explored in the book to the Reflective Practitioner model. I look at the ways in which this can operate in a climate that sometimes appears hostile to the exploration of values. I explore transformational ways of understanding quality perspectives, which encompass all aspects of the life of an institution, the community and the wider educational context, in order that these may be drawn into a holistic model of development, that has at its heart the quality of the student's experience.

Summary

The aim of this book is to provide a handbook for lecturers from any discipline concerned with quality and standards in post-compulsory education. The book is based on the Reflective Practitioner model, with its concern for evidence, context and moral issues.

Quality and standards as they apply to teaching and learning are complex, problematic concepts with many interpretations. They are becoming central concerns of the funding councils for post-compulsory education. An institution may focus on definitions of quality in practice and/or the specification of systems of control. An overemphasis on control tends to lead to a neglect of the debate about alternative audiences and interests within the educational process and an exclusive focus on the concerns of funders.

I discuss critical enquiry as a means of defining and developing quality in education, based upon the development of attitudes such as:

- openmindedness;
- responsibility; and
- wholeheartedness

and certain enabling skills and qualities such as:

- empathy;
- communication skills;
- research skills;
- imagination; and
- perseverance.

The Reflective Practitioner model allows for professional development in sub-optimal circumstances. It involves a process of exploration of practice and values, in which each may be changed. The development of a theory of quality in practice is facilitated by the consideration of evidence and perceptions with others and an understanding of the institutional, practical and political context of action. This includes the institutional aims, systems for quality assurance and human and other resources available.

In the book, I explore issues of quality and standards as they apply to:

- the external context;
- institutional committee and management systems;
- models of teaching and student learning;
- student support;
- staff development and research;
- assessment;
- course design;
- resource management;
- marketing and recruitment; and
- research.

Entry for the Reflective Diary

Write about your own experiences of good and poor quality education.
Write down the definitions of quality in teaching and learning implied by these descriptions of experience.
Was there a direct link with the standards achieved?
How do the definitions of quality relate to the issue of standards?
List ways you might assess your own performance as a teacher in the light of these definitions.

What difficulties might such an assessment present?

Notes
Annotated List of Suggested Reading

Quality Assurance in Education, Bradford, MCB University Press.
This is a new journal which looks as if it will be of interest to lecturers as well as institutional managers. The early articles are focused largely on higher education, but there is a commitment to broadening this. The editorial policy emphasizes a broad interpretation of quality. Papers are to be included which explore the debate about alternative definitions of quality, perspectives on quality and the bridging of theory and practice. To this end, early articles include case studies of innovative experience and some more conceptual papers.

Ashcroft, K. and Foreman-Peck, L. (1994) *Managing Teaching and Learning in Further and Higher Education*, London, Falmer Press.
This handbook provides a practical guide to the development of teaching, learning and assessment methods within a framework provided by the Reflective Practitioner model and provides a background to many issues of relevance to the quality debate as experienced by lecturers.

References

ASHCROFT, K. and FOREMAN-PECK, L. (1994) *Managing Teaching and Learning in Further and Higher Education*, London, Falmer Press.
BARNETT, R. (1994) *The Limits of Competence: Knowledge, Higher Education and Society*, Buckingham, SRHE/Open University Press.
BROWN, S., JONES, G. and RAWNSLEY S. (Eds) (1993) *SCED Paper 79: Observing Teaching*, Birmingham, SCED.
CARR, W. and KEMMIS, S. (1986) *Becoming Critical: Education, Knowledge and Action Research*, London, Falmer Press.
COMMITTEE OF SCOTTISH UNIVERSITY PRINCIPALS (1993) *Teaching and Learning in an Expanding Higher Education System*, Edinburgh, SCEF.
DES (1991) *Higher Education: A New Framework*, London, HMSO.
DEWEY, J. (1916) *Democracy and Education*, New York, The Free Press.
ELLIOTT, J. (1993) 'Towards a methodology of insider research', Invitational Lecture Oxford University, November.
FURTHER EDUCATION FUNDING COUNCIL (1994) *Council News*, 12, 15 February, FEFC.
HEQC (1994) *HEQC Update: March 1994*, London, the Higher Education Quality Council.
ISAAC, J. and ASHCROFT, K. (1986) 'A leap into the practical', in NIAS, J. and GROUNDWATER-SMITH, S. *The Enquiring Teacher: Supporting and Sustaining Teacher Research*, London, Falmer Press.
WATSON, D. (1994) 'Games of high stakes for cool hand players', *The Times Higher*, 7 January, pp. 12–13.
ZEICHNER, K.M. (1982) 'Reflective teaching and field-based experience in teacher education', *Interchange*, 12, 4, pp. 1–22.
ZIECHNER, K.M. and TEITLEBAUM, K. (1982) 'Personalised and inquiry oriented curriculum for field-based experience', *Journal of Education for Teaching*, 8, 2, pp. 95–117.

Chapter 2

Processes in Quality and Standards

In this chapter I distinguish between and discuss competing definitions of quality and standards and begin the process of exploring their implications for the lecturer. I look at models of quality assurance and consider their relationship to committee processes and academic standards. I take the view that lecturers will be disadvantaged in their work if they do not understand how executive, committee and political processes work within their institution. I provide a framework for understanding these systems so that you can use them to further your aims and create more appropriate conditions for student learning.

In order to avoid using too many conditional clauses I have described a management structure with institutional, departmental and course levels. I use these terms throughout the book. If you work in an institution which organizes itself differently (for instance, around faculties, programme areas or programme levels rather than departments), you will probably find that many of the same issues arise and similar systems will be needed. Most institutions will have a management structure which includes senior, middle and junior managers, each with specific areas of responsibility.

Similarly, most institutions will have some central committees which deal with major policy issues and with quality assurance and academic standards. I have termed these the 'academic board' and its subcommittees. The functions described will usually be achieved through some sort of representative system, although it may be termed differently. Similarly, there will usually be a middle level management group or committee. I have termed this the 'departmental board'. There are also likely to be more or less formalized groups around the day-to-day work which lecturers have in common. I have termed these 'course teams', although in your institution, they may be given a formal status such as 'course or field committee'.

I have described a minimal system: you may experience a more elaborate one, for instance, a faculty board between the department and academic board or various subcommittees at the senior or middle level, which deal with specific issues such as interdisciplinary work, learning resources or research.

Definitions of Quality and Standards

Harvey and Green (1993) point out that quality may be viewed as a bench mark, an absolute like 'truth', that allows no compromise. Alternatively it may be discussed in terms of thresholds of minimum performance that a 'quality' education should exceed. Finally, it may be seen as a relative matter, related to the extent that processes result in desired outcomes.

Part of the confusion that sometimes occurs in discussions about whether standards have fallen may result from differing interpretations of quality and its relationship to standards. Harvey and Green's analysis provides a useful starting point for this discussion. Quality can be discussed in terms of perfection, excellence, fitness for purpose, value for money or transformation.

Perfection implies both faultlessness and that 'standards' are checked to achieve consistency. Excellence implies notions of reputation and a high-class operation. It is perhaps not surprising that a broadening of access and a movement away from curriculum-based learning, towards experiential and problem-based learning, has led to these notions being less prominent within today's quality debate.

Fitness for purpose is discussed in more detail below. It can be used to validate learning that takes place outside of colleges and universities and allows for the definition of quality from the point of view of other stakeholders in education, in particular: students, employers and the wider community. Barnett (1994) points out that, off-site working may be cheaper (lecturing costs and institutional overheads may be lower), and problem-based learning renders learning tasks open to external influence. This may explain why the idea of fitness for purpose has come to be favoured during a time of greater external accountability and reducing unit resources.

Value for money is a natural preference of governments committed to lowering or controlling taxation. It is therefore not surprising that notions of value for money underpin many of the definitions of quality that are emerging from the funding councils in the UK. These include the use of resource-based performance indicators and charters with targets for performance (DFE, 1993a and 1993b).

Quality can also be defined in terms of the transformational experience of students. In this model, the aim is to create the conditions where students can experience a qualitative change that enhances them and empowers them as participants in education. It is compatible with the view that education is about 'adding value'. The notion of the 'value-added' relates to the amount that student achievement is 'changed', or added to, by an educational programme.

It is important to be able to spot when incompatible ideas are being used in the quality debate. For instance, Harvey and Green point out that a 'standards' approach to quality assumes that standards are in some way objective and that they can be checked. It rests upon the notion that if standards are raised, higher quality is produced. This assumes that standards are measurable and that these measures can, indeed that they *should*, stay the same. Such an idea is certainly incompatible with the transformational view of quality and may also be inimical to notions of fitness for purpose.

Quality Audit

The present arrangements for quality assurance within Britain stem from the 1991 White Paper *Higher Education — A New Framework* which distinguished between quality audit and quality assessment. Quality audit was defined in the paper as external scrutiny to determine that institutions have quality control mechanisms in place. Quality audit is one of the functions of the HEQC. It is in effect a 'users' club' set up by the universities. Audit was conceived of as a one-off 'event' when a team of auditors visit an institution to enquire into its quality control systems.

During this process, no attempt is made to observe teaching or learning or to assess quality itself. Quality auditors rely on verbal reports and paperwork to establish whether the systems are in place for assessing quality and acting on that assessment.

Audit covers systems that serve both publicly and privately funded activity. The aim is to provide public information and reassurance about the suitability of methods used by institutions to assure the quality of their operations and to help them improve by suggesting areas for development. The auditors achieve this by looking at the mechanisms and structures that are in place to 'monitor, assure, promote and enhance academic quality and standards in the light of their stated aims and objectives' (HEQC/HEFCE, 1994, p. 3).

Quality audit is essentially a sampling operation. The auditors will usually find some aspect of the institutional mission, aims or objectives (such as a commitment to equal opportunities), pursue a line of questioning related to this aspect with groups of people involved in the institution at various levels. They will then compare the responses of these groups with information in background documents provided by the institution. For example, if the institution claims a commitment to the development of 'employability skills', the auditors might examine the extent to which this commitment is reflected in a sample of institutional, departmental and course documents. They might question members of the academic board, departmental boards, course leaders, lecturers, students and so on to discover how employability skills affect course design, approval and review; what bearing it has on teaching, learning and assessment; whether it features within staff development programmes; and whether it is mentioned in evaluation reports and promotional material.

From time to time particular issues arise as a matter of general concern at government level or the media. These may be reflected in audit trails. For instance, the recent charters for further and higher education (DFE, 1993a and 1993b) have led to an increasing emphasis by auditors on the claims made in institutional prospectuses. Before that, the growth of franchise arrangements between further and higher education institutions led to close attention being given to ways quality and comparability were monitored and the extent to which the franchisee was adhering to the stated aims of the provision.

Quality Assessment

Barnett (1992) points out that the desire to reduce unit costs is inevitable in an expanding system. This gives rise to assessments of efficiency and effectiveness. Tensions become inevitable when 'quality' becomes a criterion in funding decisions. Assessments of quality have tended to focus on institutional mechanisms to assess it. Four main kinds of system for this assessment have been developed: independent inspection; the use of performance indicators; market forces; and peer review.

Independent Inspection

Under Section 70 (1) (a) of the Further and Higher Education Act (1992) funding bodies (HEFC and FEFC) are required to ensure that the quality of education in institutions they fund is satisfactory (or to ensure it is remedied if it is not). They are also charged with improving the quality of education through the publication of assessment reports and an annual report (HEFCE, 1993; FEFC, 1993) and with the role of informing funding strategies, with a view to rewarding 'excellence'. The connection between publication and incentives for improvement appears to be stated as unproblematic. HEFCE (1994) assessors will visit every institution.

Excellence also is not stated as difficult to assess: it seems to be defined as a mixture of the institution's statement of self-assessment; various statistical 'indicators' (again, the validity of these 'indicators' is not stated as problematic); the analysis of these by assessors; and (sometimes) the direct assessment of teaching and learning, for instance through an inspection by the Office of Standards in Education (OFSTED) or the FEFC inspectorate. The final assessment takes into account achievement of funding targets (indicator of institutional effectiveness); student-enrolment trends (institutional responsiveness); student continuation (programme effectiveness); learning goals and qualification (student achievement); contribution to national targets and average levels of funding (value for money). (See, for instance, FEFC, 1993; FEFC, 1994a). The funding councils are intending to investigate ways of measuring 'value added' — the extent that the institution students attend enhance their development above that normally expected. The assumption seems to be that outcomes are reliable and valid indicators of the quality of teaching.

Both audit and assessment use the institution's statement of self-assessment and mission as their starting point. HEFCE (1994) now provide specific guidance on preparing this statement. Auditors may decide their priorities and the audit trails they will follow. Quality assessors on the other hand are required to work in a defined framework and examine particular aspects. These include the relationship of the teaching, learning and assessment methods to the aims, their effectiveness, appropriateness, variety and the comparability of standards with other institutions. In higher education, quality audit focuses at institutional level, quality assessment focuses on a subject. Within further education, the distinction is less marked, since both functions come under the FEFC Quality Assessment Committee remit. Neither of these systems can in themselves maintain and enhance the quality of provision in colleges and universities. This has to be the main task of the institution and of the people within them.

Market forces

Government policy favours performance indicators but has tended to use the language of the market. One of the performance indicators for FEFC funding is that of student enrolment. This is defined as growth in response to student and employer demand (FEFC, 1994b). An element of funding may be held back to reward 'demand-led' expansion. Responsiveness also becomes an element in the assessment of quality (FEFC, 1994c).

The use of market systems in education raises the problem that the consumer of education (the student) does not pay its whole cost and consequently the volume of demand has no 'natural' ceiling. Local conditions may impose a ceiling (for instance, the cost of living may make study in the new London universities less attractive), but these tend to be extraneous market mechanisms, unrelated to quality considerations. The market may be defined as anarchic, and to that extent, value-free. In education, the emphasis on market forces as a determinant of educational priorities is not, in fact, value-free in operation. Its anarchic nature means that what emerges may not be 'good' for the student, society or the institution in the longer term. In particular, it is likely to benefit the economically and socially powerful at the expense of others.

Performance Indicators

Performance indicators have usually been introduced to meet the bureaucratic needs of the Government. For instance, they enable institutions to be ranked and funding decisions to be made and justified in numerical terms. The supposed objectivity of numerical indicators makes decisions easier to justify.

An additional benefit of performance indicators for government is that they provide the means for steering policy without the need for a close inspection of the values underlying that policy. For instance, the FEFC (1994c) include among their indicators of quality the contribution of an institution to national targets. These are expressed in terms of National Vocational Qualifications (NVQ) and are steering institutional policy away from promoting traditional courses (even where these are of proven quality), towards the Government's preferred style of qualification. Barnett (1992) points out that in the last few years performance indicators have enabled the British Conservative Government to change the higher education system from an élite to a mass system through the use of performance indicators related to recruitment.

Performance indicators, by their nature, relate to what is measurable. It is easier to measure simple and immediate evidence, such as financial performance and scores, rather than complex issues such as changes in attitudes and long-term benefits. This tendency fits well with government policy that emphasizes 'value for money' and immediate vocational outcomes. For instance, the FEFC (1994c) include among their performance indicators, the average unit funding of students in individual institutions. This might be interpreted as an encouragement to ever lower unit funding or as a check against norms. In the second case, a very low unit of resource might be seen as a cause for concern. The emphasis on equity or economy is likely to be influenced by the values of the political party in power.

The use of performance indicators has led to a shift in values in further and higher education, which now emphasize economic rather than cultural preparation, and the good of society as a whole at the expense of personal development. To some extent this emphasis on generic vocational skills required in the workplace may be a counterbalance to what was seen at one time, certainly in government circles, as an overemphasis on personal development (Foreman-Peck, 1993). The important thing is to realize that definitions of success that emphasize certain forms of performance are not value-free, and that you will need to assess the underlying values against your own.

It appears that performance indicators more often focus on efficiency than effectiveness. The recent FEFC announcement of the performance indicators of quality which will influence funding confirms this tendency (FEFC, 1994c). College effectiveness is seen in terms of the achievement of the strategic plan and FEFC agreements. There is little assessment of whether the planning is well conceived or agreements are educationally defensible. Similarly, responsiveness is measured in terms of percentage changes in student enrolments and the numbers continuing to the end of the college year. The value of what is provided and its appropriateness in the short- or long-term are not considered. Student achievement is assessed according to the proportion of students achieving their primary learning goals, with no consideration that a good education might cause a proportion of students to change direction.

Where effectiveness is a consideration, this tends to be expressed in inputs and outcomes. The notion of 'value added' as an indicator of effectiveness (the idea that quality could be measured on the degree of change in the level of performance of students between start and finish of a course of study) has been mooted at various times (FEFC, 1994c), although at the time of writing it has not been put into operation by the UK Government. The processes involved in teaching and learning are not features of performance indicators. Thus, education itself is generally seen in instrumental terms, rather than as a good thing in its own right.

Peer Review and Inspection

Peer review is favoured by some universities and colleges. The 'quality audit' form of assessment enables quality to be assessed in terms of the values of the academic community. These may or may not reflect those of the Government. Both peer review and inspection systems can be inward-looking. Lecturers and institutions may wish to seek outside and dissenting voices if they are to develop qualities of openmindedness necessary for reflective practice.

Barnett (1992) points out that there are a number of other interest groups that are from time to time involved in assessing quality in further and higher education. These include lead bodies in various vocational areas, students and potential students, employers and professional bodies. You may have to reconcile competing concepts of quality as each of these interest groups defends its values and its idea of further and higher education.

Since quality audits are based on institutional self-assessment, there may be scope for lecturers to influence the self-assessment. The problem here is in connecting your ideas and feelings with those of the institution. To achieve this, you will need to understand how your institution works and how decisions are made. Alternatively, you can seek to use your own expressed values to inform your own definition of educational values and quality. However, judgments of quality should not be merely matters of individual preference. In any institution or discipline area there are likely to be competing definitions, for instance, in English studies, those provided by Marxism and by liberalism.

In order to establish monitoring systems for quality, it is necessary to establish a collective view within the institution or department. This process is difficult and complex. Its importance, and its problematic nature, is a continuing theme of this book. Definitions of quality need discussion and some consensus, so that they can inform decisions and prioritization. They usually include notions of accountability. It should be noted that education is accountable to a variety of interests: to society in the shape of the Government; to consumers, especially students; to the subject discipline including colleagues; and the professions and employers.

Enquiry Task

Are you familiar with your institutional mission statement and departmental aims and objectives?

List ways that these aims and objectives relate to each of the following:

- pre-entry guidance for students;
- selection of students;
- programme information for students; and
- staff development policies.

Models of Quality Assurance

Models of quality assurance in further and higher education should be primarily directed at improving the quality of teaching and learning. Concern should focus on how results are achieved as well as on the results themselves. This implies that the process involves all those whose efforts contribute to the student experience in planning and evaluation. The model needs to be flexible and responsive to a changing environment, but also have a basis in a clearly expressed and relatively stable set of values in education. It may be important to subject externally imposed and internally generated innovation and change to critical analysis. The process of critical analysis requires some stability in the frame of reference used for the assessment of quality and standards. The quality of openmindedness requires that the frame of reference is actively created and developed in the light of evidence. This suggests that the frame should be open to critical scrutiny, subject to evolutionary change but that definitions of quality should not change to fit each new trend in education. Analysis has to be based within a clear theoretical framework that is related to basic educational values.

Total Quality Management

Total Quality Management (TQM) is a model that seems to embrace some of these concerns. It is a concept that originated in industry, but that is increasingly adapted to an educational context. It describes a process that is designed to realign the culture and working practices of an institution in order to create a constant search for quality improvement. Individual effort, supported by extensive training or coaching for people at all levels of the organization, is seen as the key to this process. The focus of this effort is the improvement of 'inputs', 'processes' and 'outcomes'.

TQM typically includes five guiding principles (FEU, 1991): the creation of an appropriate climate; focus placed on the 'consumer'; management by data; people-based management; and continuous quality improvement. You may find that some of these principles adapt relatively well to the educational context. For instance, the creation of an appropriate climate could involve a constant process of research, analysis of student needs, requirements and expectations and feedback of results and effectiveness. Placing the focus on the 'customer' is more problematic. It may not be clear who the customer is, since someone other than the students may be paying for the service.

Management by data rests on the assumption that data are 'facts'. In education, this cannot be assumed. TQM talks in terms of 'proof' of success or improvement. You may feel that any proofs you would be able to supply were at too trivial a level to be the main evidence that informs your action. It may be more useful to develop intelligent hypotheses, based on carefully collected evidence, perhaps related to course processes. If so, you may need to develop arguments for this being the most valid basis for development and the assurance of quality. The challenge for teaching teams is to find creative ways to respond to the demand for quality and accountability, that effect a transformational resolution of dilemmas. There is always a danger that long-term consequences of action may be masked by short-term and instrumental consideration.

The interpretation of TQM can be very individual and can be subverted so as to relate more to the pre-existing style and the fundamental values of senior management than to TQM's underlying principles. Thus, its application may result in very different institutional climates. For instance, an authoritarian college principal may focus on management by data, and see accountability and control as being at the heart of TQM. According to the TQM model, definitions of quality and standards should be agreed by those operating it in the institution, but in institutions with autocratic managers, in practice they may be determined from the top. Such an emphasis is unlikely to empower lecturers to influence quality assurance. The successful introduction of a TQM system, involves everyone in seeking and sharing definitions of quality in practice, would seem to be enhanced by a prior commitment to reflective practice and a pre-existing open management system.

The Further Education Unit (FEU, 1994a) has expressed the central idea in TQM, that of continuous quality improvement, in terms of systems and processes within colleges. This model includes a focus on the institutional mission and a needs analysis (finding out what people want and need from the institution and comparing this with current provision), in order to produce a vision of the kind of organization that is desirable and the values that will underpin this structure.

The process of continuous quality improvement is underpinned by the development of a culture of improvement that starts with the example of senior managers, especially with regard to aspects of behaviour such as: communication; respect and listening; openness to praise and criticism; and the encouragement of staff at all levels to identify barriers to achievement and solutions to problems. Within this culture, criticism is seen as an opportunity for improvement and not an attack or act of subversion. It is clear that developing such a culture requires a clear strategy. This is likely to include staff training and the establishment of a quality infrastructure (perhaps through quality councils) to monitor quality and standards.

The FEU suggests the establishment of quality-initiative groups to look at specific services. Unlike the quality control system, these groups would not be responsible for the ongoing maintenance of quality, but rather their task would be to analyse a service and bring about improvements. The FEU recommends that these groups work through a number of identified steps, including: identifying the gaps between current and required practice; setting quality standards for particular features of the service; redesigning processes to reduce problems that inhibit desired features; implementing the new processes; and, finally, evaluating the results and reporting them to the quality control system.

British Standard 5750

Increasing numbers of colleges and universities are considering or pursuing accreditation under British Standard 5750 (BS5750). This is part of the British Standards Institution system which is mainly applied to the products of commerce and industry. The system sets standards for each step of a business process (for instance, communication) to ensure efficiency. This does not imply that the products are of high quality, it is not a 'kitemark', but rather that processes are standardized, and that the standard is defined.

In educational institutions, this system typically guarantees that staff are aware of the quality assurance system in operation and that it is monitored and documented. Colleges and institutions can opt for all or parts of their operation to be covered by the standard. The BS5750 mark therefore does not necessarily relate to the whole of a student's experience. Neither does it imply standardization across colleges and universities. Institutions may want to explore accreditation for the new programmes they are developing, even if other areas are not involved in accreditation under BS5750.

The British Standard implies a procedural approach to quality. This approach has some relation to that of the Higher Education Quality Council (HEQC) Quality Audit Division. Processes and procedures have to conform to a given framework. In the case of the HEQC, this framework is devised by the individual institution. In the case of BS5750, it is externally imposed. BS5750 guarantees the capability of a system. HEQC also audits its operation. Under both systems definitions of 'quality' as far as outcomes are concerned remain to be defined by the individual institution. Both systems *should* empower and promote critical analysis in terms of an institution's mission, but there is a danger that paperwork becomes the focus of attention, rather than the improvement of provision.

Investors in People

A number of further and higher education institutions are seeking accreditation under the Department of Employment's 'Investors in People' initiative. Again, this is a model derived for industry, but this time the metaphor focuses more on people rather than systems in the first place.

The basic idea is to help employers to improve performance by linking the setting and communicating of business goals with staff development to match these needs. It does not imply that staff development need be worthwhile in any terms other than instrumental outcomes defined by the institution. If 'Investors in People' is being interpreted correctly, these outcomes should enhance the institution's mission, but they may or may not enhance the career or personal development of the individual lecturer or the education sector in general.

'Investors in People' is underpinned by the assumption that people will be more motivated and able to work to institutional goals if they are properly prepared for full participation in processes that further these goals. The process is underpinned by adherence to the National Standard for Effective Investment in People. This is a benchmark against which an institution can measure its commitment and performance. This standard includes principles and performance indicators that provide the basis for determining whether or not it has been achieved.

The local Training and Enterprise Council (TEC) has the responsibility for providing systems that determine whether or not an organization can be recognized as an 'Investor in People'. The TEC can also provide financial assistance to support activities directed at the achievement of the award. The number of 'Investors in People' awards made is a performance indicator for TECs. This may lead to a clash of interests, with the possibilities of TECs encouraging institutions, over whom they may have considerable power (see Chapter 4), to use this model of quality assurance, when another might be more appropriate.

The 'Investors in People' scheme has a number of attractions for institutions. It can help marketing and recruitment by advertising a commitment to staff development, and it can help ensure that staff development is structured and targeted. If the individual lecturer believes that the scheme will necessarily ensure a greater commitment to staff as individuals, or a more humane working environment, they may be disappointed. The investment is not in people as individuals, but rather in staff training for the benefit of the institution. For this reason, in some circumstances, such training could be instrumental and might not inspire critical questioning. Of course, there are many occasions when institutional and personal or career goals coincide, for example where a member of staff obtains personal satisfaction and growth from such training.

The 'Investors in People' scheme is essentially concerned with local benefits. It does not necessarily imply commitment to an individual's career progression, to educationally or morally defensible values nor to the wider academic or industrial community. Where institutional goals and those of the institution coincide, 'Investors in People' can be empowering and may encourage fewer talented staff to leave to seek employment elsewhere. On the other hand, the rationale for the scheme implies that, should the training provided encourage the ambitions of a 'good' lecturer and lead him or her to seek a job elsewhere, it has probably been 'unsuccessful'. Thus, it is evident that the definition of quality implied is a somewhat narrow one, tied to the means and ends of a particular institution.

Fitness for Purpose

Another way of defining the quality of educational provision is in terms of 'fitness for purpose'. This implies one of two things: firstly that each activity within an institution should have defined *aims and outcomes* against which performance may be judged; and secondly, that each *process* should be assessed as fit or not for its purpose.

The first notion is attractive at first sight, but has a number of hidden difficulties. Firstly, there may be problems of narrowness, difficulty or even fraudulence in the definition of aims and outcomes. The question of whose purposes are to count may be ignored. The purposes of individual students, of lecturers, of institutions and employers may be in conflict with each other or those of the main funder, for instance, the TEC or the funding council. Although 'fitness' should be defined in terms of the institution's mission, in practice it is likely to be defined in terms of the most powerful groups.

The idea of fitness for purpose does not necessarily require a consideration of the moral dimension. For instance, a situation might exist where institutional purposes include acquiring more students and resources by devising a course in terms required by an accrediting body, even though there are no jobs in that particular area for the graduating students. In this case, definitions of 'fitness' related to employability outcomes could give way to more immediate institutional priorities. On other occasions, an institution may be tempted to develop courses that conform to the prevailing orthodoxy about 'state of the art' course design (for instance, in the early 1990s, courses that involve modularity, open learning, technology, competency-based assessment and enterprise skills). These may be developed because they are the kind of programmes that are most likely to be funded, without a proper consideration of either the skills and knowledge available in the institution to undertake this kind of course or whether they will in fact meet the purposes of the potential students.

Institutional purposes can also lead to certain courses or departments becoming 'cash cows', that can be asset-stripped when it is convenient to the institution. I have observed a further education college where every department was required to 'create at least £10,000 worth of self-funded courses'. In another, staff were required to sign up for specially created short courses in order to fulfil institutional quotas for part-time students. Resourcing must remain part of quality assessment, but the kind of institutional purpose that focuses on the acquisition of resources at the expense of the appropriateness and morality of their allocation has very little to do with quality.

It may be that the notion of 'fitness for purpose' can be in part redeemed by redefining it as 'fitness for educational purposes'. This requires the institution to define what its educational purposes are, but it still begs the question of whose purposes should be paramount. For instance, the institution may decide that it wishes to contribute to the creation of a flexible workforce. It still has to decide who shall benefit from this flexibility. If it is employers, they may wish to have a workforce that is multi-skilled, uncritical of change and essentially conservative in their political thinking. The student, on the other hand, might benefit from an education that emphasizes knowledge and skills that can be used to analyse and critically assess a workplace (so they know when to leave the sinking ship). Some may need skills that enable them to negotiate changes in the workplace to make it more compatible with their needs (rather than fitting them for the needs of workplaces as they exist now). Others will need skills for dealing with leisure and self-employment.

The notion of fitness for purpose, rests on the assumption that purposes can be defined in terms of predetermined and intended antecedents, processes and outcomes. This is more problematic than appears at first sight. Problems with definition may occur at any stage. For instance, in terms of antecedents, students may not be as expected. Their purposes may vary or conflict. Processes may not yield expected outcomes. Some outcomes may be valuable but unintended or impossible to measure.

Another definition of fitness for purpose, implies that the notion can be used to examine each process or system to determine whether it is fit for its intended purpose. This shift of emphasis from outcomes to processes allows for the idea that 'more' is not necessarily better. For instance, an elaborate quality control system may not be fit for its purpose, because its bureaucratic nature may distract

23

lecturers' attention from teaching and learning. (On the other hand, if its real purpose is to demonstrate to outside auditors that the institution takes quality control seriously, it may fit its purpose.)

The notion of fitness for purpose as it applies to processes rather than outcomes may appeal to lecturers. They can ask questions that are of relevance to them, such as 'If I want students to learn X, which teaching method would be most appropriate?', or 'If the course aims to develop Y skill, what form of assessment will test whether they have succeeded?' Of course, this notion of fitness for purpose does not necessarily embrace higher-order moral and educational questions about definition and defensibility of purpose and the relevance of particular purposes for the various actors in the education process. It is possible to focus purely on the instrumental question of 'What works?' Important as this question is, as a reflective lecturer you will want to go beyond this to ask questions such as 'How worthwhile is it?', 'Is it conducive to excellence?', and 'How does it relate to my developing theory of quality in teaching and quality in learning?'

As a reflective lecturer you will be interested in considering the short- and long-term consequences of your actions. Most assessments of 'fitness for purpose' are essentially short-term (for instance, whether the students find jobs on graduation, or whether assessment methods are getting at particular skills). Long-term goals might include providing an education that nourishes the individual throughout her or his career, up to and including retirement, or providing an education that equips the student for change. Such goals may be difficult, or even impossible to measure, but they are not irrelevant to quality.

All quality measures and definitions seem to have distinct limitations. Some of these have been described above. This should not be taken to mean that attempts should not be made to define and measure quality, but rather, that these attempts cannot be seen as value-free. Unless institutional and personal values are well thought out and clearly articulated, and unless they are morally and educationally defensible, quality measures are unlikely to have real meaning.

Enquiry Task

Investigate what systems of quality audit exist in your institution and what data is collected at each level:

	Data collected	*System operating for analysis/evaluation*
At course level		
At departmental level		
At institutional level		
By external bodies		

Discuss your list of systems of quality audit and data with a senior colleague and refine it.

Whose purposes does each of these systems serve?

Finally, it is important to realize that there are some areas where the language of quality is entirely inappropriate. Products can be defined as of poor quality. In educational terms this can refer to the products of research or educational materials. Educational processes, teaching, the arrangements for learning and assessment, may be of poor quality. On the other hand, *people* should not be referred to as of poor quality, since this opens the way for a number of abuses. For instance, the powerful can define inferior outcomes for those they regard as of lesser quality. For this reason, I believe that those quality assessments which focus on intake standards as an absolute measure lack a moral basis.

Standards

There are a variety of definitions of standards. Part of the problem with the use of the term is that it is sometimes used as a synonym for quality. For instance, I may describe a hamburger as being of poor quality or of a low standard and mean the same thing. Standards are an aspect of quality, but quality must include aspects that go beyond the consideration of standards.

The terms 'quality' and 'standards' each have a benchmark of acceptability embedded within them. Both therefore require explicit criteria for assessing that acceptability. The maintenance of standards implies that, whatever the aims, purposes and processes of education, its products reach an acceptable, measured level. In terms of education, quality also includes the notion that the aims, purposes, processes and products of education are morally and educationally defensible. Thus quality is the superordinate concept and is closely related to excellence. It is therefore possible to have a low-quality course with high standards, but not to have a high-quality course with low standards.

The debate about the distinction between quality and standards is related to that about fitness for purpose outlined above. An extreme example may illustrate this. In Mahfouz's (1990) novel set in Egypt during World War I, the hero's wife and daughter have received an education that had appropriate standards to fit them for the life it is anticipated they will lead. To the western eye, this life seems to consist of life-long domestic slavery under conditions of house arrest. According to western notions, this education is extremely impoverished and morally indefensible. Therefore, I would not say it was of a high quality. On the other hand, an education that had led to these women acquiring enquiring and questioning minds, would have rendered them unfit for their defined purpose.

In this novel, the powerful defined what education was 'fit' for what Western women would consider inferior beings. The education provided had appropriate standards from the 'consumers' point of view only if the consumers were defined as the masculine community (the mother in the story was desperate for more knowledge). In the UK, it is sometimes possible to see parallel situations, where government or employer purposes have been met by the provision of an impoverished educational or training provision experienced by the student.

The advantage of a clear distinction between quality and standards is that it enables us to separate the moral and educational discussion from the technical one. The technical discussion (about standards) is likely to be the easier to resolve. The moral and intellectual questions (about quality) are much harder, but need to be debated if students' educational experiences are to be fundamentally improved. It may be that fundamental differences in values and ideologies will be revealed and their resolution may be very problematic. However, I believe that this resolution is fundamental to the practice and the experience of students and lecturers.

This may go some way to explaining why quality control systems that focus exclusively on academic standards are sometimes experienced as restrictive and baffling by lecturers. Perhaps the many 'academic standards committees' in colleges and universities need to be renamed and given a new remit if they are to influence the quality practices and debates in institutions at the heart rather than the margins of student and lecturer experience.

Sometimes the term 'standard' is used to denote the level that should be achieved by students at a particular stage of their education. Standard in this sense is an *apparently* value-neutral concept that has the idea of norm-referenced standardization at its heart (i.e., the notion that a student's performance should be judged against a cross section of that of his or her peers). Standards in this sense are built around normal expectations and ideas of average and above and below average. Both students and courses can be judged against these norms. On the other hand, standards can be defined in terms of a minimum 'threshold' of performance. This suggests that students' performance is judged against some kind of competency (perhaps defined in terms of the course aims and purposes), and is therefore criterion-referenced.

These two views of standards have sometimes been pitched against each other, for instance in the debate about the value of a liberal education versus a competency model. A transformational resolution to this argument may enable courses to include an academic and intellectual orientation and also good vocational preparation. This may require us to find new ways of defining standards which embrace both traditions. Technical questions about reliability (i.e., are tests 'fair', would one assessor come to the same conclusions about the level of performance, or the achievement of a competence as another?) tend to dominate discussion about standards. It may be that the debate should shift to questions about validity (i.e., whether we are measuring and exploring what we think we are, and if so, whether there are other things we should be measuring and exploring which we are neglecting at the moment).

The Further Education Unit (FEU, 1994a) explores the idea of quality standards. These may be applied to any aspect of the service supplied by a university or college. The idea is that the levels of performance which can be expected for any given feature of a service should be specified. This specification should be in terms of measures which define the ways in which actual performance is monitored. From the analysis of quality standards it may be possible to prioritize particular areas and to create agreed improvement targets to be achieved over a given period. This notion of quality standards and improvement targets clearly have much in common with performance indicators and have similar problems and disadvantages.

Criteria, Standards and Quality

There has been evidence of a growing concern about falling standards resulting from the expansion of the further and higher education systems. Moodie (1986) points out that it is not always clear whether these concerns centre around the difficulty of teaching larger groups, or whether there is a fear that the additional students are in some way of lower quality than those taught in the past. However, there seems to be little evidence that 'standards' have fallen. An increasing number of students achieve worthwhile qualifications at all levels. It may be that the standard for assessment has fallen, but there is little solid evidence that this is or is not the case.

It is now routinely expected that course-development teams consider criteria, standards and quality. It is important that you develop an explicit and shared definition of each. Criteria and standards are intimately related, but they are not the same thing. A standard is the measurement and criteria are the means of measuring and indeed as Moodie points out, some criteria are unrelated to standards (for instance, staff–student ratios) and so the terms must be used with precision. For instance, 'A' Level is not a standard for entry into higher education, but rather an imperfect criterion for assessing the student's ability to benefit. One of the difficulties in determining whether standards are being maintained is that the criteria for making such a judgment are problematic.

Confusions also exist between quality and standards. Again, they are not the same thing. Indeed, conventional standards may work against quality. The controversy over the revised specification of National Curriculum English in the UK resulted from a disagreement about the definition of 'standards' in terms of levels of knowledge about the structure of language that could most easily be achieved by a return to highly traditional English teaching at the expense of more creative and exploratory work.

Criteria for judging each of quality and standards may diverge. For instance, Moodie suggests that the timeliness of an intervention may be important in judging quality but not standards. The level of a programme is related to standards, but not to quality. For instance a degree programme is at a higher level than a GCSE programme, but not necessarily of a higher quality.

Enquiry Task

Ask the following people how they would define 'standards in education':

- yourself;
- a colleague;
- a student;
- a departmental head;
- a member of the senior staff of the institution.

Compare these definitions:
What have they in common?
How do they differ?
How do they fit with the models of:

- norm-referenced standardization?
- a minimum threshold of performance presented in this chapter?

How might each of them be measured or monitored?
What criteria or systems would be needed?

Committee Processes

In this section I will describe a typical committee system within a university or college and explain the usual rationale for such a system and how it normally works. Most institutions have a committee system which ends with an academic board. This committee is often advisory to the principal. It will usually have terms of reference that require it to advise the principal on overall policy direction. In smaller institutions, it might be the body that also advises the principal whether an outline proposal for a major change should be supported and a course-planning group set up.

Principals of institutions vary greatly in the extent to which they are willing to ignore the advice of the academic board. If you are in an institution where the principal regularly overrules the advice he or she has been given, or determines that a number of policy issues are outside of its remit, you are likely to find staff disillusioned with committee processes. The academic board should be a major safeguard for lecturers and students from management by whim and whimsy. This is one reason why you might take an interest in the way it operates. It also should have a major voice in policy decisions which affect the academic programme or the academic experience of students. If you are interested in instigating institutional change, the academic board is usually the key committee to influence, or to which to get elected.

The committee process is one of the means by which an institution assures itself that quality is being maintained within academic area. Quality in this sense usually focuses on the development of new courses and the monitoring of teaching, learning and more especially assessment and evaluation on existing ones. The academic board in universities commonly delegate this responsibility to a subcommittee. This subcommittee of academic board may be given terms of reference which requires it to examine individual proposals for change to the academic programme, or alternatively to assure itself that appropriate procedures have been followed in the approval of a proposal. In this second case, the job of examining proposals in detail are usually delegated to a subcommittee, often the departmental board or the faculty board.

The academic board may receive individual course reports in a smaller institution. In a larger one, this is likely to be delegated to the departmental board or the faculty board and the academic board may restrict itself to examining the procedures to ensure that the subcommittee has explored aspects such as the management of the change, its rationale, resource implications and so on. Thus if you are interested in the development of programmes, it will be important for you to understand the committee process for approval and to know what should be included in your documentation about the programme itself and the process of development. If you have an opportunity to become a member of an institutional committee, you should consider it very carefully. It is likely that you will learn a great deal from the experience about the official political systems within the institution, and also about its micro-politics.

In a well-designed committee system that is working well, each layer should have a distinct job to do. Thus, broad approval for a development might be given at one level, another might monitor that correct procedures have been followed and that the proposal fits institutional guidelines and yet another might look at the details of proposed changes. What should not happen is that the details of a proposal are explored at a variety of levels by different sets of people, each with their own prejudices and some with no knowledge of the subject area or its context.

Similarly with monitoring and review, it should be the duty of a higher-order committee to set up guidelines and policy for monitoring of programmes and their review and to assure the institution that these have been adhered to. It is usually the responsibility of a lower layer to examine the details of evaluation or review reports. Again, it is an inefficient use of committee time for course reports and so on to be examined in detail at a variety of levels by people who may not know the context. Such a system is likely to lead to perverse decisions and policy.

Lecturers who do not experience this crucial distinction can sometimes become impatient with committee systems. I have observed a large and bureaucratic institution, where a member of staff had to rewrite a document ten times as it went through the course committee, through a departmental board and a faculty board, to a modular management committee, to a subcommittee of the academic board and finally to the institutional executive. At each stage the document was looked at in detail, by people increasingly removed from knowledge of the context and practice. The third version of the document was probably the best, and certainly there were a number of errors and inconsistencies introduced into the document by the end of the process.

It is my opinion that, in most institutions, there is probably no need for more than the three layers of committee described above. Most other work, such as the detailed planning, costing, resource management and so on, is probably better carried out by a mixture of permanent and *ad hoc* working parties of lecturers and managers.

If you are interested in joining the committee system, it is important that you think about the responsibilities of each layer and attempt to join at the level which suits you. If you are interested in influencing global quality, the academic board may be the place to aim for. If your interest is in the way systems work, you may enjoy the work of the various subcommittees of academic board that deal with this aspect at different levels. If you are interested in influencing the ways in which policies are actualized in terms of the details of courses and programme change, the departmental or faculty board may be stimulating.

Enquiry Task

Find out one or more of the following decision making routes:

- the route for determining the amount of money you have to spend on a course you teach;
- the route by which a new post is approved;
- the route by which the decision is made to buy a piece of capital equipment; and
- the route by which a major modification to a course is approved.

Committees and the Lecturer

Your relationship with the committee system is likely to be fundamentally affected by your understanding of its purpose. You can use the committee system to obtain formal approval for desirable change; to test ideas in a democratic forum; to cross-examine others who are proposing change or a lack of change (in particular, you can call managers to account for their actions); and finally you can use committees to cover your back. The last point can be particularly useful in institutions where the management has a dictatorial style, or a tendency to reverse decisions or policy. The committee minutes often provide the definitive statement of policy and approval.

If you develop the kind of political 'nose' that I believe is important for a lecturer who is interested in the quality of teaching and learning, you may develop a deeper understanding of the institutional functions of committees. For instance, it is hard to see how the institution or department can be defined to outside bodies and to themselves except through the committees. This is in part because the committee meeting is essentially a collective event expressing a collective will and mission. It is part of the social life of the institution that formally brings people from various areas with different interests together to share experience and define direction. It also sets boundaries and limits to management decisions.

Farr (1994) states that the committee defines the institution or department because it brings things (for instance, courses, projects and departments) into existence and keeps them there. He sees the system as central to communication. It makes things visible to other entities that exist at the same level (for instance, departments) through the publication of minutes, but also makes the action and policy of one level visible to another. Indeed it is difficult to see how else different levels can have access to the various realities that exist within the institution.

He believes that part of the function of the committee is a micro-political one, especially in relation to the establishment of a pecking order. This jostling for position will happen with or without the committee system, but the committee provides a legitimate and rule-bound setting for it to occur. This makes it unlikely that such jostling will become personalized and damaging to the participants' sense of 'self', but it does imply that, as a member of a committee, you have a duty to seek to 'win' or those you are responsible for representing will 'lose'. It also implies that those outside of the committee systems are resigning themselves and their students to being the ultimate peckees!

Various models of committee operation stress their function in terms of managing conflict or consensus. Nevertheless, whichever model is applied, the committee system is the main location for lecturers to influence the definition of mission, the development of policy and the approval of actions which flesh out the mission and policy of the institution or department. This is the reason that outside organizations interested in assessing or auditing quality and standards often start with a description of the committee system.

An astute lecturer will be aware that the committee can also be an organ for illegitimate political activity. Committees can be used to make things 'legal' but invisible. For instance, a manager who has a particularly unpleasant issue to deal with, may set up a series of working parties to consider it, in the knowledge that by the time they report it, it will be too late for action. Alternatively, managers can use committees to shoulder responsibility for unpopular decisions which should properly rest with the executive.

Lecturers and students are affected by the decisions made by committees. They also create the need for these decisions. Therefore, committees are an integral part of teaching and learning. It is useful to know how decisions are made and to monitor how minutes are written and kept. Committees create the teaching environment and determine the resources. The lecturer's work starts in the committee where the course is described, the resources allocated and the framework of policy approved. If you have made no efforts to argue for them through the appropriate channel, perhaps you have no right to expect that resources will be available or complain if policies are unhelpful. You might wish to consider whether lecturers who take no interest in the committee system are parasitic, insofar as they depend on others who are active for opportunities within their own practice.

Executive Processes

The extent to which the committee system can temper management power varies between institutions. Definition of the role of the committee system can be broad or narrow. If managers within an institution are inclined to define it narrowly, they will increase their power and field of decision-making at the expense of that of the wider academic community.

However terms of reference are defined, in practice there are always some decisions which must be made by managers throughout the system. I am calling the system of non-committee decision-making, the executive system. In the final analysis, if the management process is to mean anything, there must be some areas of accountability which are the responsibility of named individuals. The executive process describes what happens within this system of management authority and accountability.

Management systems have become more sophisticated in institutions of further and higher education since they became largely responsible for their own management. The 1988 Education Reform Act set up the Polytechnic and Colleges Funding Council and provided the polytechnic and higher education college sector with independence from local education authorities and the self-governance that universities had previously enjoyed. It also allowed further education colleges in England and Wales a considerable freedom over the management of their own affairs. Northern Ireland and Scotland received similar freedoms under the 1989 Draft Order in Council for Education Reform (Northern Ireland) and the Self Governing School etc. (Scotland) Act. These acts set up governing bodies (called college councils in Scotland) and charged them with considerable delegated financial and management control. The Further and Higher Education Act of 1992 allowed colleges of further education to take full control of their own affairs and granted university status to the polytechnics. In April 1993, the process became complete, the FEFC came into being and further education colleges became corporations entirely independent of the local education authority.

Touche Ross (1992) pointed to the enormous changes in responsibilities implied by these developments. Colleges and universities have had to learn to plan and manage finance, fulfil personnel responsibilities and maintain appropriate premises. They have had to develop new management skills, including the establishment of financial procedures. They have had to develop expertise in personnel legislation and policy-making, record keeping and contract law. They now have to manage whole new areas of responsibility including security, energy management, maintenance, insurance and space utilization.

In most institutions the executive system has a variety of layers. Typically these include course leaders or programme area managers, departmental or faculty heads, the institutional managers and the governing body. Each should be involved in the fundamental decisions affecting the institution in a variety of ways. Members of the executive system should be absolutely clear as to the extent and limits of their authority, the nature of their accountability, and of their rights and duties as far as consultation is concerned. Where duties, lines and modes of accountability and the extent of delegated authority are not clearly laid out, it is almost inevitable that conflict will result. These executive processes should not only be transparent to those who are responsible for them, but also to those who work within them. If this is not the case in your institution, you may end up feeling confused, frustrated and cynical about the way management works. Your efficiency and effectiveness as a lecturer will almost inevitably be affected. You are likely to waste time seeking management decisions and your ability to influence change for the better may be curtailed.

Thus, the course leader must have some delegated authority or his or her effectiveness and job satisfaction will suffer, and you, as a member of the team, may find it too complicated to effect beneficial change. Such authority is usually limited to decisions which do not create changes beyond those allowed by the course document and/or those which do not require additional resources. This does not mean that the course leaders should not consult with others when making decisions which are within their remit. The course leader should also be clear about the ways in which he or she is accountable for the decisions taken and the form that accountability takes (for instance, through the course report).

Similarly, the departmental head will need considerable delegated authority to do his or her job properly. This authority will usually include the right to use the resources allocated to the department in a variety of ways, to decide departmental policies and priorities (as long as these remain within the framework of the institutional policies, strategic plan and mission) and to determine staff deployment and programme development within certain parameters. Generally speaking, departmental managers cannot make decisions which commit the institution to continuing expenditure (such as the appointment of staff) without the approval of the senior management.

Among operational areas which must in the final analysis be within the Senior Managers' remit, are those concerned with drawing up the strategic plan (the major direction that the institution will take over the next few years in terms of such matters as student numbers in various programme areas, major development work, and so on) and the allocation of resources to departments and other areas, including staffing. These plans are usually drafted by the senior management, but must be ratified by the governors.

The governing body will have responsibility for determining the institutional mission, the appointment of senior academic staff and approving the budget and the strategic plan for the institution. The Education Reform Act of 1988 broadened the representation of the local community, ensuring a range of perspectives and expertise, and gave the governors a clear responsibility to promote higher standards and better performance. Under the Further and Higher Education Act of 1992, colleges were released from local education authority control and former polytechnics achieved university status. Governing bodies of further education colleges, like those of higher educational institutions, are now responsible for the conduct of their institutions, including the employment of staff and the management of institutional assets.

The Further Education Unit (FEU, 1994b) states that governing bodies should be responsible for:

- the strategic direction of the (institution) including setting and overseeing its mission and general policies;
- ensuring within the (institution) a climate for creativity, change and responsiveness to the external environment, the local community and customers;
- ensuring the effective and efficient use of resources and the solvency of the (institution) and the corporation;
- monitoring the performance of management in meeting targets, carrying out policies and maintaining adequate management information systems;
- ensuring the corporation gives a proper account of its activities;
- selecting and evaluating the principal and senior managers;
- supporting and advising the principal. (FEU, 1994b, p. 15)

This implies that the governors should scrutinize all aspects of college life, but it does not imply that they should be active in managing them. The governing body has a broadly strategic role and the principal and other managers, a broadly operational one. This does not mean that the principal and other managers should not involve themselves in strategic planning, but rather, that governors must be the final arbiters of such planning.

Each layer of management has a responsibility for overseeing and ensuring quality and assuring standards within its area of responsibility. Part of this responsibility involves establishing agreement throughout the institution on purposes and methods of various forms of practice (including those that the lecturer is likely to be most interested in, such as teaching, learning and assessment) and establishing feedback loops to inform and improve the quality of provision. If, as stated by the HEQC (1994):

An effective quality assurance and control system is underpinned by wide participation, effective channels of communication, the collection of acceptable evidence, the acceptance of responsibility by staff and students and an institutional commitment to staff development and training. (HEQC, 1994, p. 45)

it must be the responsibility of named individuals to ensure that this happens within their particular area.

The executive process may vary in different institutions. In an open institution, this may be highly political and involve a round of 'bidding' from various areas for resources and the inclusion of development priorities within the strategic plan. Managers at various levels may put forward structured arguments, backed up by numerical and qualitative data. This is expensive in terms of the time taken to allocate resources and determine the institutional strategy, but may lead to more satisfactory results in the end. (I explore management processes in the allocation of resources in more detail in Chapter 8.)

Farr (1994) states that there is a tendency to assume that management styles that emphasize authority rather than power; shared goals; consensus; stability; and staff motivation are in some way 'good', but they may lead, in fact, to stagnation. For instance, a set of shared goals which becomes embedded in a mission statement may lead to a 'word-based' authority, that stamps out ideas and activity which might be usefully explored but which fall outside of its remit. This word-based authority can lead to a stable organization, committed to certain goals over a period of time. This can, however, lead to a certain inflexibility, where strategic goals become impossible to change.

Farr believes that in reality all institutions have diverse goals, and a consensual management style will, of necessity, stifle alternative ideologies and questions of 'who owns the goals'. It is possible to conceive of an institution that embraces a diversity of goals, set up in competition with each other (for instance through the creation of relatively autonomous units).

The problem with this approach is that values are unstable and exist only for so long as opposing ideologies retain an equilibrium in terms of power. Even at the level of 'working', such competitive systems seem likely to lead to particular forms of inefficiency unless particular areas have no need to cooperate. It can only work where areas have equal incentives for cooperation or where there is a debate and at least a temporary consensus about values and direction. Clearly this model raises questions about what is it to be an institution, and what is the institution's purpose.

The culture of academic administration in the UK is generally premised on a concensual model. Indeed, it is my experience that institutions can only function if there is some attempt to find consensus. The process of reaching a common view has sometimes been described as a democratic one, perhaps drawing on the idea of universities and colleges as self-governing entities, republics of citizen-scholars, along the lines of the classical Greek democratic state. In this sense, democracy refers to consensus about what constitute fair and effective procedures.

Enquiry Task

Create a diagram of the management structure of your institution. Find out the extent and limits to the authority of managers at each level.

	Authority	Limit of that Authority
Course leader e.g.,	Spending within a defined budget	Individual items costing more than £200
HoD e.g.,	Employment of temporary staff within budget	Employment of tenured staff
Senior manager e.g.,	Approval of replacement of existing staff within budget	Creation of a new post

---

In modern western societies, democracy involves an organized opposition and regular shifts of political power between competing ideologies. It is alien to consensus (consensus would lead to one party rule). In this sense, democracy does not seem to me to represent an appropriate management model for the educational institution. Rather, I believe that a political system in Crick's (1982) terms is perhaps a more useful notion: that is a rule-bound and open system of negotiation.

The Micro-political Culture of the Institution

If you develop an understanding of the formal decision-making systems of the institution, but neglect the informal, micro-political culture, you may end up confused by your inability to influence events.

In any institution there are influential individuals and groups, who may be within or outside of the formal decision-making systems. These often understand both the formal and informal systems and may be very helpful in facilitating changes in which you are interested. Systems are often defined in operation. However terms of reference and job descriptions are set out, there will always be areas of ambiguity. Some people are able to exploit these areas by deciding on the route for decision-making that will present the fewest obstacles and then defining the problem or decision in terms appropriate for this route.

If the committee system falls into disrepute, subversion of educational purposes is likely to occur. Jockeying for position will take place outside of accepted conventions. The lecturer can experience conflicting signals from the committee, management and micro-political systems. For this reason, I believe that it is in everyone's interests to be concerned and vigilant about the ways that committee and executive systems are used to set institutional agendas, how 'legitimate' concern is determined and what is excluded. The committee can be an arena for gladiatorial games, for secret plotting or for cooperative activity. It is up to lecturers to work for their preferred option.

Equally, micro-politics is likely to operate in the management system. This may be more comprehensible if you understand some common concerns of managers at different levels. For instance, senior managers may have an interest in restricting the middle manager role to operational rather than strategic decision-making. Similarly, middle managers may wish to restrict the influence of the junior managers on policy issues. The resolution of these tensions is important to the delivery of teaching and learning in the classroom. Unless restrictions on the role of middle and junior managers are successfully challenged, it is likely that senior managers will make uninformed decisions and policy-making will appear to them to be unproblematic.

Summary

There are a number of competing definitions of quality, some of which focus on systems for quality assurance and others on teaching and learning processes and products. It is possible to distinguish between quality audit and quality assessment.

Quality may be assessed through:

- independent inspection (for instance through HEFCE, OFSTED, by BS5750 inspectors);
- the operation of market forces;
- the use of performance indicators; or
- peer review and inspection.

Each of these methods implies a particular ideological standpoint.

Quality audit focuses on systems for quality assurance. There are a variety of models of quality assurance. These include:

- models based on systems determined by the individual institution;
- Total Quality Management;
- British Standard 5750;
- the 'Investors in People' initiative; and
- notions of fitness for purpose.

Each of these has advantages and limitations and none are value-free.

Standards are included within the notion of quality but quality is the superordinate concept. Standards may relate to the appropriateness of levels achieved and the idea of norm-referenced standardization or to the idea of a minimum threshold of achievement. The debate about standards relates closely to that relating to the reliability and validity of assessment. The definitions of quality and standards require explicit criteria but are not co-synonymous.

Committee processes are central to the life and purpose of the institution and to the teaching function. Thus the lecturer's job begins in the committee room. Most institutions have committees functioning at academic board, academic standards and departmental levels. Each level has its own functions and each influences the quality of students' experience. Lecturers who come to understand and use the committee system can affect the quality of the teaching environment and the experience of students, by influencing overall policy direction and by making direct proposals for change.

The overall function of the committee system may include:

- assuring the quality of educational provision;
- defining the institution and its work;
- developing policies and procedures;
- making one level and area of work visible to another;
- bringing new areas of activity into being;
- establishing the institutional pecking order;
- legitimatizing dubious political activity; and
- tempering the power of the executive system.

A narrow definition of the role of the committee system increases the power of the executive within the institution. The executive system is the means by which areas of authority and accountability become the responsibility of named individuals. Each layer of management should have clearly defined roles and duties within an overall system of quality assurance and control, and authority compatible with those duties.

The governing body has responsibility for determining the institutional mission, key staff appointments, the strategic plan and the budget.

Different models of management emphasize creative conflict or consensus. I believe that quality is likely to be enhanced within a system of involvement at all levels in a rule-bound, but open, system of negotiation, where fair and effective procedures for discussion and decision-making have been agreed. Ultimately the quality framework of the institution will be determined by the extent and resolution of tensions within the formal and informal decision-making and accountability systems operating within the institution.

Entry for the Reflective Diary

- Write about your definitions of quality.
- List the actions you might take to enhance the quality of your practice according to these definitions.
- Decide what areas implied by your definition depend on the cooperation of others in your institution.
- List ways that you might use formal and informal systems within your institution to exert influence.

Notes
Annotated List of Suggested Reading

Freeman, R. (1993) *Quality Assurance in Training: How to Apply BS5750 (ISO 9000) Standards*, London, Kogan Paul.
This book includes a step-by-step guide to setting up a quality system within education and relates this to BS5750 requirements. It also contains a short overview of the concepts underlying 'Total Quality Management'.

Further Education Unit (1991) *Quality matters: Business and Industry Quality Models and Further Education*, London, FEU.
A short and easy to understand summary of industry-derived models of quality assurance, including total quality management and BS5750 together with some analysis of their appropriateness in the educational setting.

Further Education Unit (1994a) *Continuous Improvement and Quality Standards*, London, FEU.
A short, easy to read guide to setting up systems of continuous quality improvement at college level, identifying priorities, setting up quality groups and using quality standards, measures and improvement targets.

Further Education Unit (1994b) *Further Education Governors: Supporting the Curriculum*, London, FEU and The Staff College.
This is probably the clearest and most succinct account of the duties of governing bodies and good practice in relation to those duties. The vast majority of the recommendations made within the booklet apply equally to higher education. The main points are summarized in five pages contained in a pocket at the back of the booklet.

Higher Education Quality Council (1994) *A Briefing Paper from the Higher Education Quality Council: Checklist for Quality Assurance Systems.*
A very short (three pages), fairly comprehensive and easy to follow paper that lists aspects that should be included in a quality control system.

References

BARNETT, R. (1992) *Improving Higher Education: Total Quality*, Buckingham, Society for Research into Higher Education/Open University Press.

BARNETT, R. (1994) *The Limits of Competence: Knowledge, Higher Education and Society*, Buckingham, SRHE/Open University Press.

CRICK, B. (1992) *In Defence of Politics (2nd Edition)*, Harmondsworth, Penguin.

DEPARTMENT FOR EDUCATION (1993a) *Further Choice and Quality: National Charter for Further Education*, London, DFE.

DEPARTMENT FOR EDUCATION (1993b) *Higher Choice and Quality: The Charter for Higher Education*, London, DFE.

FARR, B. (1994) 'Committee Systems and Processes', an invitational seminar held at Westminster College, Oxford, June.

FOREMAN-PECK, L. (1993) 'Enterprise education: A new social ethic for higher education?', *The Vocational Aspects of Education*, 45, 2, pp. 99–111.

FURTHER EDUCATION FUNDING COUNCIL (1993) *Press Release*, 16 April, FEFC.

FURTHER EDUCATION FUNDING COUNCIL (1994a) *Council News*, 17, 12 October, Coventry, FEFC.

FURTHER EDUCATION FUNDING COUNCIL (1994b) *Guidance on the Recurrent Funding Methodology 1994/5*, February, Coventry, FEFC.

FURTHER EDUCATION FUNDING COUNCIL (1994c) *Circular 94/12: Measuring Achievement*, Coventry, FEFC.

FURTHER EDUCATION UNIT (1991) *Quality Matters: Business and Industry Quality Models and Further Education*, London, FEU.

FURTHER EDUCATION UNIT (1994a) *Continuous Improvement and Quality Standards*, London, FEU.

HARVEY, L. and GREEN, D. (1993) 'Defining quality', *Assessment and Evaluation in Higher Education*, 18, 1, pp. 9–34.

HIGHER EDUCATION QUALITY COUNCIL (1994) *Guidelines on Quality Assurance*, London, HEQC.

HIGHER EDUCATION QUALITY COUNCIL/HIGHER EDUCATION FUNDING COUNCIL FOR ENGLAND (1994) *Joint Statement on Quality Assurance*, Bristol, HEFCE.

HIGHER EDUCATION FUNDING COUNCIL FOR ENGLAND (1993) *Circular 3/93: Assessment of the Quality of Education*, Bristol, HEFCE.

HIGHER EDUCATION FUNDING COUNCIL FOR ENGLAND (1994) *The Quality Assessment Method from April 1995*, Bristol, HEFCE.

MAHFOUZ, N. (1990) *Palace Walk* (English Language Edition) London, Anchor Books.

MOODIE, G. (Ed.) (1986) *Standards and Criteria in Higher Education*, Guildford, SRHE and NFER/Nelson.

TOUCHE ROSS (1992) *Getting Your College Ready*, London, Touche Ross/DES.

Chapter 3

Quality in Teaching and Learning

In this chapter I outline the major changes in government policy in the UK since the mid 1980s which have led to a particular concern with the quality and standard of teaching and learning in further and higher education.[1] Ideas of quality and standards in teaching and learning are explored and you are invited to elaborate your own views. Institutional ethos and student satisfaction measures and their links to the quality of teaching and learning are discussed. The last section of the chapter discusses one particular threat to quality, increased class size. By the end of the chapter you should be able to use your ideas of quality and standards in teaching and learning to evaluate your own courses, institutional arrangements and some quality assurance measures.

Background

The drive towards wider access to higher and further education and towards new forms of public accountability in the UK has led to urgent questioning of quality and standards in provision. The opening up of opportunities to students with a diversity of backgrounds, a reduced unit of resource in higher education, together with financial incentives to accredit further education students with National Vocational Qualifications (NVQs), has led to serious concern about the quality and standards of educational qualifications. Old assumptions about our learners' backgrounds are no longer valid. Problems that greater numbers bring threaten previous conceptions of what was considered good practice. These factors have led to a focus on quality and standards in teaching in relation to the effectiveness and efficiency of delivery. In the UK during the early 1990s, there has been a significant shift in thought about the aims and processes of education forced by Conservative Government policy. There is a new emphasis on preparation for employment, even in traditionally academic subjects, that is forcing a reappraisal of the role of the lecturer in higher and further education.

Since Prime Minister James Callaghan's Ruskin speech (1976) there has been continuing pressure for education in general to be more relevant to society's needs. From the middle of the 1980s there has been a continuing political assumption that all sectors of the education 'industry' have failed to deliver that which is good for 'economic health' (DFE, 1985). Higher education in particular had failed to make enough of a contribution to wealth creation. Weiner (1981) and Ball (1990) blame Britain's industrial decline on the 'gentrification' of the curriculum. Dale (1985) reports that a significant factor was thought to be the autonomy of lecturers, who developed their own professional interests at the expense of wider society.

Whilst there is a variety of ways of conceptualizing the purposes of higher and further education, the demands of industry or more generally the workplace, have come to override other possible ways of construing the purposes and values of education (Atkins *et al.*, 1993). In the stark language of the market-place rhetoric that has come to dominate educational discourse, educated or trained people may be viewed as commodities produced to a certain specification, for a customer. The customer, or at least the paymaster, is often the British Government, and the Government's concern is to get the best 'value for money' and to be assured that educational products are 'fit for their purpose': that is, are of a good enough standard and quality suitable for the workplace.

The White Paper, *Higher Education — Meeting the Challenge* (DFE, 1987), proposed 'teaching quality' as an important factor in judging quality in higher education as a whole. This has led to the introduction of staff appraisal, systematic institutional quality audits, and the assessment of teaching quality carried out by Office for Standards in Education (OFSTED) and Higher Education Funding Council for England (HEFCE) inspectors.

The Government has also tried to influence the criteria by which the quality of teaching is assessed in further and higher education, by introducing, in 1987, a new emphasis on enterprise competences and dispositions through the 'Enterprise in Higher Education Initiative'. Personal transferable skills and dispositions which are claimed to be useful to employers include communication skills, problem-solving, leadership, team work, negotiation and persuasion, decision-making, creating opportunities, risk-taking, flexibility and being pro-active, numerate and computer literate. These are of particular interest as they concern the processes of education and have implications for judgments of standards and quality of teaching and learning.

In further education the Government has promoted the idea of National Vocational Qualifications (NVQs) as a way of systematizing and controlling occupational preparation for employment. The Government's target of establishing NVQs to cover 80 per cent of the workforce was achieved by the end of 1992. Targets set for 1995 are set to cover 90 per cent of the workforce, including new awards at the equivalent of degree level. NVQs involve the close specification of competences. There is an emphasis on what students must be able to do to demonstrate competence, rather on what they know. Early critiques of NVQs have centred around this omission, since a knowledge component is not always an unproblematically inferred from behaviour (Bartram, 1992). More recent criticism of NVQs has been concerned with the integrity of assessors and the feasibility of a training system driven only by assessment specifications.

From 1992 many colleges in the UK will have been involved in delivering General National Vocational Qualifications (GNVQs) which are intended as preparation for broad occupational areas. These have been introduced to provide an alternative to 'A' Levels, and are intended to carry 'parity of esteem'. It is anticipated that GNVQs will eventually be available in at least fourteen occupational areas. The GNVQ qualification is intended to be the equivalent of two 'A' Levels. They entail a high degree of coursework and a high degree of assessment. On the whole, universities have agreed to accept the qualification and, at the moment, there is a high take-up rate. However, there is a continuing debate and questioning of standards (see Chapter 6).

Recent research supports the view that the vocational and instrumental purposes of education are more valued by employers and students than intrinsic general purposes (Otter, 1992). However, there is continuing tension and debate at government level and in the press between those lobbyists who want to see a thorough-going vocationalism extending to the 14-year-old age group, and those who wish to maintain the academic sixth form and, by implication, the élite tradition of higher education (see for instance, MacLeod's *Guardian* Report, 1994). It is against a decade or more of radical and, for many, unwelcome, change in higher and further education that various views of quality and standards in teaching and learning are considered.

Quality and Standards in Relation to Teaching and Learning

This section is concerned with how we arrive at judgments of excellent or of inadequate teaching and learning where those judgments come from, what assumptions underpin them and how they accord with our own ideas.

'Quality' in teaching and learning is a value-laden term and refers to the purposes, processes and standards of education. Teaching and learning of high quality, necessarily have morally, epistemologically, and educationally defensible aims and processes and reaches high standards according to the criteria which define those aims. It has been argued in Chapter 2 that it is not sufficient to define the quality of teaching and learning in terms of effectiveness, efficiency, or even fitness for purpose, since these purposes may be immoral. Indeed poor-quality teaching, defined in terms of indefensible aims and processes, is not education at all but indoctrination. Poor quality teaching may also be poorly resourced, poorly conceived or fail to meet student needs.

Judgments about the excellence or mediocrity of teaching and learning have traditionally depended on evaluative criteria, drawn from authorized sources who have been given the right to make judgments: for example Her Majesty's Inspectorate (HMI). Traditionally, Her Majesty's Inspectorate was drawn from a body of people with long experience and excellent reputations. The credibility of OFSTED and HEFCE the newly restructured and privatized inspectorate, now depends on a draconian training process that seeks to ensure that judgments of quality and standards are as standardized as is humanly possible. However, other participants also have the right to define quality, not least practitioners themselves and students. The National Union of Students (1993) has recently produced its own charter that outlines what good quality in teaching and learning means from the students' view point. Their demands include that teaching staff be trained to teach, compensation for 'bad quality' teaching, and students' maximum choice over the content of their courses through increased use of modularization and semesterization.

The term 'standards' is often used to mean 'a high quality' or 'high standards' as in the phrase 'standards in teaching have risen'. In both uses there are unarticulated descriptions of what exactly is meant by high standards and high quality. I am using the term *quality* to refer to value-laden descriptions of what we and others mean by good teaching. These are contestable and are likely to be different for different people. Because they are contested they have to be argued for. For example, assessments of quality based on the match between the published aims and processes and content within a course may be challenged if it is held that spontaneity is at the heart of good teaching, leading the enthusiastic and committed teacher in unpredictable directions.

It has been stated in Chapter 2 that the term 'standards' has 'yardstick' connotations, independent of the dimensions that are being assessed or evaluated. The argument that high-quality teaching may involve expertise in subject matter is contestable, but not in the same way as arguments about how to assess a lecturer's security in his or her knowledge base. Deciding how to assess an attribute is not the same as deciding which attribute constitutes (or ought to constitute) good or high-quality teaching. 'Standards' in teaching and learning may be used in the more neutral sense of a measure referring to processes, performances and outcomes that can be graded, as is OFSTED and HEFCE inspectors' current practice.

Judging the quality of teaching on a course or degree is complicated because the achieved standards of students may be high but we can only *infer* that the course processes led to that achievement. Many independent learners, such as Open University students, learn without much teaching in the formal sense.

Enquiry Task

The following table is taken from Tate (1993, pp. 291–292).

The items are intended to represent a continuum of extreme positions between lecturers who are wholly teacher-centred and lecturers who are wholly student-centred.

Plot your own values on each continuum.

Teacher-centred	*versus*	*Student-centred*

- Focus on content
- Emphasizes knowing that
- Students work as individuals often in competition with each other

- Students highly dependent
- Learning objectives imposed
- Assessment by written exams
- Knowledge is handed down from subject to novice

- Lectures predominate as mode of curriculum delivery
- Teachers role is that of expert

- Focus on process
- Emphasizes knowing how
- Students work in groups and teams, collectively and cooperatively
- Students work independently
- Objectives negotiated
- Assessment varied
- Students actively generate and synthesize knowledge from many sources
- Teaching sessions flexible and not always classroom-based
- Teacher is facilitator and a resource for students' learning in partnership

Ask a colleague to plot their values.
Discuss those areas where his or her values differ from yours.

Looking at standards on student assessments is only a partial way of judging the relative quality of teaching. Similarly student appraisal of teaching cannot constitute complete evidence, since students are not usually in a position to judge the whole situation.

Judgments of quality about teaching and learning incorporate fundamental views about the nature of learning and teaching, and tend to be matters of ideological conviction rather than reasoned discourse based on evidence. Competing positions may polarize staff, especially if they hold fundamentally different views about their roles as lecturers. Such differences may not be settled easily by reference to the small amount of empirical research available. Other complicating factors include the relationship of research to teaching, professional identity, the ethos of the institution and the wider political climate. However, the nature and quality of student learning should be the base of most judgments about the quality of teaching, since judgments about teaching a subject well are logically dependent on what it is to learn that subject and to be a learner of that subject. This is a philosophical rather than an empirical point.

The enquiry task below sets out the relevant dimensions to do with teaching that may enter into our judgments of quality.

Judging Quality in Teaching

Many commentators have held that it is not possible to judge the quality of teaching since judgments in this area are subjective (Loder *et al.*, 1989). Part of the problem is that lecturers have their own intentions and priorities when they teach, which may not be acceptable to all. Even the vocabulary they use to describe what they think they are doing may have different connotations for different people (Lewis, 1993). This makes simple observation problematic and begs the issue of how we know what counts as quality in teaching. It is dependent on contested points of view and we lack agreed terms. Our judgments about quality are dependent on our prior beliefs about learning and what is worthwhile. These are often tacit and unexamined. However, if 'good quality teaching' consists of an explicit and operationalized concern for students' learning, students should be aware of their learning processes and the ways that their learning is facilitated. This notion does not privilege some teaching methods over others and allows for the possibility of empirical inquiry into effectiveness. This view is encapsulated in the idea of the student as a reflective practitioner that we have developed elsewhere (see Ashcroft and Foreman-Peck, 1994).

There have been other attempts to make the evaluative criteria underlying judgments of quality in teaching and learning explicit. They are also informed by implicit beliefs and values. At Secondary School level, OFSTED (1993) have their own criteria for judging quality in learning and teaching which informs their direct observations in the classroom. These are presented in modified form in the Enquiry Task below.

OFSTED has also developed evaluative criteria for the judgment of quality in teaching and learning in higher education. The prime concern is with the standard of learning (Heythrope Park, 1989). Judgments about other aspects of further and higher education provision, such as resources and teaching, are based on their perceived 'impact upon learning'. In the view of OFSTED the term 'quality' only has a meaning when related to function such as in the phrase 'fitness for purpose'. 'Fitness for purpose' is seen as involving the assessment of non-quantifiable variables which call for professional judgment based on wide experience. The judgment involved is collective rather than individual and draws on a knowledge of national as well as regional and local standards. In carrying out judgments of this kind the inspectors examine aims and objectives, assess whether the management and resources are adequate for the aims to be achieved. They explore how courses respond to information from assessments and whether the assessments are well matched to the skills and understandings encapsulated in the aims and objectives. When this has been done, they compare the aims and outcomes of the course, for example, with similar courses in other institutions.

The quality of learning is also judged by scrutinizing examination papers and scripts, assignment exercises and projects. Inspectors evaluate the level achieved by the students in the light of the nature of the courses studied. In the view of the OFSTED inspectors, good courses have well-conceived objectives, are well organized and include purposeful teaching programmes, lucid lecturer exposition at a

---

Enquiry Task

Assess the relevance of the following criteria for judging the quality of your own teaching and your students' learning:

Teaching

- Teachers have clear objectives for their lessons, students are aware of these objectives.
- Teachers have a secure command of the subject, lessons have a suitable content, activities are well chosen to promote learning of that content.
- Activities are presented to engage, motivate and challenge all students, enabling them to make progress at a suitable pace.

(Evidence should include, observation, planning of work, such as lesson plans and notes, discussion with teachers and pupils, samples of work, including assignments, marking, comments and follow-up, individual education plans for students with special educational needs.)

Learning

- Most students respond readily to the challenge of the tasks set, showing a willingness to concentrate on them, demonstrating progress in learning.
- The students adjust well to the demands of working in different contexts, selecting appropriate methods and organizing effectively the resources they need.
- Work is sustained with a sense of commitment and enjoyment. Students are sufficiently confident and alert to raise questions and to persevere with their own work when answers are not readily available.
- They evaluate their own work and come to realistic judgments about it. Where appropriate, students readily help one another.

---

challenging level and well judged sharply focused student assignments. Students respond intelligently and diligently and show evidence of secure learning and progression. Students are provided with regular indications of their progress and can build on the advice and guidance derived from assessment.

Elton (1987) has argued that judgments about the quality and standard of teaching of a lecturer are unproblematic and can be based on evidence such as students' work, exam scripts, theses, prepared teaching materials, papers at conferences on teaching and learning, publications on teaching and learning, willingness to experiment and innovate, willingness to accept feedback from students and willingness to cooperate with colleagues. This suggests a developmental view of the lecturer and usefully emphasizes professional development. Such development can be recorded and evaluated by the use of a teaching profile (Gibbs, 1993). This may be a major and complementary step to appraisal in encouraging good quality

---

Enquiry Task

Brown (1978) found that university lecturers agree on characteristics that define a good lecturer.
Such lectures are:

- well organized;
- well prepared;
- interested in the subject;
- friendly;
- flexible;
- helpful;
- creative
- clear;
- enthusiastic;
- interested in students;
- open;
- systematic; and
- committed.

Moses (1985) found from an analysis of student questionnaires that good teaching resulted from:

- competence in subject matter;
- communication skills;
- commitment to facilitating student learning; and
- concern for individual students.

It could be argued that these lists, while being desirable and necessary characteristics of good lecturers are not sufficient descriptions of good teaching.

List any additional criteria that you would employ to judge good teaching in your subject or discipline area. Discuss these with a colleague who teaches in the same area.

---

teaching. It does however presuppose an institutional climate that values and fosters professional development.

Other criteria are derived from survey research into lecturers' views and students' preferences (see for instance, Brown, 1978; Elton, 1987). These surveys are interesting in that they highlight certain aspects of student–lecturer relationships, but make no value judgments about the quality of the learning.

The Institutional Context and the Quality of Teaching and Learning

Judgments about the quality of teaching of individual lecturers may be important to the evaluation of an institution's educational provision but, if that is all that informs judgment of quality then it may be skewed. Tutors are often teaching in a situation where other factors do impinge, yet they may be appraised as if they are not. Teaching a course is often a matter of team delivery and good teaching can often depend on how that team works. Being a good lecturer is sometimes a matter of being allowed to be a good lecturer. There are many stories about the tyranny of some departmental cultures and their hostility to taking professional concerns seriously.

Judgments about teaching may be enhanced by expanding quality criteria to include collaboration and support for the professional development of colleagues. This would at least go some way to acknowledging that teaching is something that is learned and that lecturers need support in self-evaluation and deliberation on their experiences. Even experienced lecturers should be concerned with the improvement of their practice (Mitchell, 1985). However, creative and innovative teaching does not flourish in a vacuum. There is a growing body of research that suggests that a traditional university education, with its lack of concern for professional issues and the competitive individualism of lecturers does not necessarily provide a good learning climate.

The HMI reported in 1989, that typically 10–20 per cent of higher education teaching has shortcomings such as over-dependence on one mode of teaching and learning (often the formal lecture) so that students do not develop a range of skills appropriate to higher education. They found evidence of spoon-feeding in lectures, seminars and practical work so that students become over-dependent on information selected and provided by the lecturer. They found some seminars lacking clear objectives, in which students were inadequately prepared to make a full contribution and inadequate comment from lecturers on students work, particularly their writing-assessment methods which placed too high a premium on the ability to recall factual information.

The claim that certain course arrangements and teaching and learning models facilitate a better quality of learning only carries weight if it can be argued for and demonstrated, and lecturers accept that they have a responsibility for helping students to learn. Traditionally this has not always been the case. For instance, in higher education, creative effort and reward has been directed towards research. In further and higher education, heavy teaching loads have sometimes been seen as 'punishment' for not producing research or undertaking administration. Good quality teaching requires an inordinate amount of preparation that is to some extent 'invisible' and taken for granted.

Dependence and passivity in learning are not values that further and higher education admits to, yet research indicates that this is the effect of traditional patterns of organizing teaching and learning. A few institutions have sought to redress the balance. For instance, London Guildhall University has created new promoted posts equivalent to Readerships for staff with proven excellence and contribution to teaching.

Innovations in teaching and learning, and the associated risks (such as student confusion), that they entail should not be the sole responsibility of the individual lecturer. Unilateral decisions to depart from custom and practice, however justifiable and seemingly small scale, may lead to trouble with colleagues and students. Quality in teaching is generally a matter of departmental and institutional policy.

Enquiry Task

The following is a policy statement on Teaching and Learning in Higher Education taken from the Brighton Polytechnic's (now The University of Brighton) Handbook (1990) *Teaching and Learning in Higher Education.*

The University has a commitment to:

- Developing students' competence and capability for their personal and professional lives.
- Promoting approaches to teaching and learning which recognize the importance of learning to learn.
- Developing students' responsibility for their own learning.
- The active involvement of students in the learning process, as a primary requisite for effective learning.
- Recognizing the prior knowledge and experience of learners as a valuable resource in their learning.

Write a policy statement that you recognize operating in practice at your institution. Is it one you could subscribe to?

Research into learning indicates that successful learners do approach their learning in ways which differ significantly from less successful learners. It is these aspects which I suggest should become part of our criteria for judging good quality teaching and assessing practices. Students who are successful learners are able to approach their learning with a range of learning approaches. They can utilize a 'deep approach' or a 'surface approach' as appropriate. Less successful learners can only utilize a surface approach. There is also evidence to show that a dysfunctional learning climate can be caused by teaching and assessments which require students to take a surface approach (Ramsden, 1992).

I argue that teaching should be so designed as to encourage as far as possible a deep approach where that is appropriate. While a concern to foster a deep approach to learning is not synonymous with my idea of good quality teaching, it is a crucial part of it. Encouraging a deep approach is not unproblematic. Marton and Saljo (1984) indicate that, even when assessments are structured to encourage learners to take a deep approach, surface learners distort the task, so that it

Enquiry Task

Discuss with a colleague how you might monitor quality in learning, with reference to a course you teach on, using the distinction between deep and surface approaches as characterized below.

Students utilizing a deep approach do the following:

- Intend to understand. Student maintains structure of task.
- Focus on 'what is signified' (e.g., the author's argument, or the concepts applicable to solving the problem).
- Relate previous knowledge to new knowledge.
- Relate knowledge from different courses.
- Relate theoretical ideas to everyday experience.
- Relate and distinguish evidence and argument.
- Organize and structure content into a coherent whole.
- Internal emphasis; 'A window through which aspects of reality become visible, and more intelligible'.
  (Entwistle and Marton, 1984, cited in Ramsden, 1992, p. 46)

Students utilizing a surface approach do the following:

- Intend only to complete task requirements. Student distorts structure of the task.
- Focus on 'the signs' (e.g., the words and sentences of the text), or unthinkingly on the formula needed to solve the problem.
- Focus on unrelated parts of the task.
- Memorize information for assessments.
- Associate facts and concepts unreflectively.
- Fail to distinguish principles from examples.
- Treat the task as an external imposition. External emphasis: demands of assessments, knowledge cut off from everyday reality.
  (Ramsden, 1992, p. 46)

becomes a surface task. The real challenge for lecturers interested in quality in higher and further education is to provide the opportunities for deep learning in the way that the teaching and learning is managed. Deep learners are already competent learners and it can be assumed will learn adequately under any regime that allows them access to resources. Raising overall standards in education means being committed to the interests of those students who do not yet know how to learn optimally. The intention behind many recent attempts to revise curricula and teaching methods in further and higher education (driven by increased numbers, reduced resources and non-traditional students) has been to enable the majority of students to achieve as well as the minority who did well on traditional degree programmes.

Judging the Quality of Learning

I have argued so far that good-quality teaching consists in a combination of reasoned value judgments about various aspects of the lecturers role in delivering courses, in a subject or discipline specific commitment to the quality of learning, a commitment to continual development and improvement of courses and course delivery, and a commitment to a collaborative climate in which innovatory work can be supported. The quality of student learning is also a matter of making value judgments about how students ought to be encouraged to learn in order to become the kind of person that the institution values. The 'Enterprise in Higher Education Initiative' had as its ideal a notion of the 'enterprising graduate', a person who is able to communicate well, adopt appropriate leadership roles, and who can collaborate with others (Foreman-Peck, 1993). This kind of profile is a challenge to traditional arrangements for teaching and learning, where the content and methodology of a subject dominated, or obliterated concern with such competences and dispositions.

The values embodied in the list from the University of Brighton above are partly justified by research into learning by Marton and Saljo (1984) that has shown that successful learners operate in substantially different ways from less successful learners. Successful learners actively seek to make meaning. Less successful learners tend to memorize material that they believe will be assessed. Certain features of course design and delivery can promote or discourage more fruitful approaches to learning. Teaching methods can encourage initiative and original thinking or they can encourage dependence and derivative thinking. Therefore, there is a strong case for basing judgments about the quality of teaching on the quality of the learning that is being encouraged through the design of the course. For example, we could ask whether the assessments promote the development of higher-order skills such as synthesis and evaluation, whether the course design encourages problem-solving and initiative. It is unlikely that these qualities or competences will be encouraged by a reliance on lecturers' enthusiasm for their subject matter alone.

Assuring the Quality of Learning: Performance Indicators for Standards in Teaching

Peformance indicators have been defined by Ball and Halwachi (1987) as objective and usually quantitative measures of achievement. Indicators, like much quantitative data, reduces the complexity of a situation to a simple measure and so the application of quantitative measures has to be carefully thought through. A recent controversy highlights this problem. The UK Government recently required schools to keep a record of pupil's unauthorized absences from school so that each school's truancy rate could be published. There has however been differences of opinion between schools about what constitutes unauthorized absence.

Loder *et al.* (1989) identifies four sorts of institutional performance indicators which may be isolated from the literature: input measures, market performance, process measures, and output measures. Process measures include progress rates, student choices of electives, student appraisal of staff, peer appraisal of courses, variety, effectiveness, suitability of teaching methods and opportunities for learning, amount and relationship of research and scholarship to teaching and learning and effectiveness of validation and review. Perhaps the indicator of most interest to the lecturer concerned with the quality of teaching and learning in the classroom, is student appraisal of staff, since it could be argued other indicators are to some extent dependent on student satisfaction.

Student Appraisal of Staff

Student appraisal of lecturers, against standardized criteria of teaching performance, can be used for judgmental purposes, informing decisions about promotion or tenure. Students' views can also be sought for developmental purposes. With these purposes in mind, information can be collected by the lecturer from students, in order to help make a case for promotion, or in order to make decisions about the improvement of teaching or course delivery. In some institutions, notably in the USA questionnaires are administered without prior consultation with lecturers concerned. The design of these questionnaires is often standardized and crude, since they may be used to elicit student opinion without reference to the aims and intentions of the course or the teaching. As such, they give an indication of 'consumer satisfaction'. Where evaluation is used for developmental, as opposed to bureaucratic purposes, the lecturer has usually designed the evaluation instrument with a view to taking action to improve some aspect of teaching.

A performance indicator that has been used for a long time is the extent of student satisfaction. The questionable assumption underlying this performance indicator is that high student satisfaction equates with high quality and standards. While at first sight this seems a reasonable assumption, it oversimplifies the way in which educational transactions should be construed in several ways. This will be explored later. Here suffice it to say that, if you regard learning as in some crucial respect the creation of the student, who is as responsible as the lecturer for the learning they achieve, and the fact that students come with different orientations to their studies, then the idea of a simple customer satisfaction model is inadequate. This does not mean that students should not be given certain rights. They are in some respects our customers in the sense that we are providers, and other means of trying to monitor good quality and standards (assurance procedures such as peer review of courses, external examiners, validation exercises), do not give 'power' to the student as customer. Without giving real power to students there is the problem that the providers become a 'providers' club'. If this happens there is a real danger to quality and standards since the beneficiaries of the transaction have no real voice and no real 'teeth'.

These measures of student satisfaction are problematic. On the other hand, they may be the main way that students can influence the quality of teaching and course provision.

Strengths and Limitations of the Provider–Customer Model of Education

A strength of the use of the 'provider–customer' model of education is that it can encourage a certain amount of explicitness about students' entitlements and providers' obligations. Another strength is that it suggests ways in which the quality of education can be guaranteed, or assured, through accountability mechanisms. However, students, unlike OFSTED inspectors, are not trained to make judgments based on a foundation of reflection on experience. This does not mean that students cannot express preferences or indicate the presence of serious problems, such as failure to understand course content. The problem lies in deciding what weight to give to student ratings or qualitative feedback.

Like all analogies the provider–customer image simplifies. It leaves implicit certain crucial dimensions of the student–lecturer relationship, which are not analogous to the provider–customer relationship. If we are unclear about these differences, certain performance indicators may lead to a decrease in the standard of education provided. This has already happened in the USA, with the emergence of 'grade inflation' as a way of keeping student ratings high. Popular lecturers are not necessarily providing a high quality of education. They are caught by the need to show high student satisfaction in order to increase their chances of full tenure and to alleviate anxieties felt by students in an educational system that encourages grade dependency.

A crucial factor in the measurement of performance is the way in which the substantive content of an education is thought about. In the customer–provider model, this is an unspecified and unproblematic commodity. Commodities can be transferred between people in a relatively straightforward way. The act of transference in an educational context is complex, since learning is dependent on many interacting variables. Students bring with them different levels of experience and expertise and possibly out-moded expectations. With the UK Government's initiatives on access and the expansion of student numbers, this may be particularly pronounced at the moment. Taylor *et al.* (1981) point out that students also come with marked differences in their orientation to learning.

Ironically, none of this might matter if the content of education were an unproblematic commodity, where it was up to the student to take or reject what was on offer. However, once you accept that it is part of the lecturer's responsibility to match the learning to individual needs and differences, to allow students elements of choice, and to use professional judgment in providing challenges (which might promote dissonance rather than satisfaction), then the relationship (at least at classroom level) is distorted by the use of the provider–customer relationship as a model.

The provider–customer relationship does not require that the provider know the customer in any depth, except as a representative of the target market group. In an education of good quality, the student has a right to be known and treated as an individual. The model more appropriate to this relationship is the conversation or debate. Here, student evaluations or appraisals can be used as part of the dialogue between lecturers and students to enhance the quality of provision. In order to be effective, student evaluation has to be invited at intervals during the course and acted upon. Tutors should be supported and encouraged in this activity. Present arrangements for appraisal are inadequate to this purpose and could be more fruitfully supplemented by the idea of stewardship, as in some industry models (for instance, within Austin Rover) or supervision (as in the Social Work Profession). Summative negative appraisals serve only to demoralize lecturers and encourage timid, safe approaches to teaching.

The provider–customer model reinforces the view that education is something that is handed over, rather than something that is created and owned by individuals. This is in conflict with the Government's own desire to see higher education transformed. If education is no more than the transmission of information, attitudes, and skills, then it is, according to the Government thinking, a poor-quality education, since it has sold students short. A good-quality education is one that not only provides a good knowledge base but also enables students to become knowledge creators or reflective practitioners. Transmission techniques, which require the student to be a passive recipient, where that is *all* that the student receives, encourages dependency, risk averseness and an emphasis on individual competitiveness. The UK Government's recent 'Enterprise in Higher Education Initiative' was driven by the needs of industry for graduates who showed initiative, could work in groups, and had other transferable personal skills. These qualities can be encouraged without sacrificing academic qualities such as rigour and depth (Foreman-Peck, 1993). However, they require new methods of teaching, which may be unfamiliar to some of the student body. The requirement to work in groups, for example, can generate bewilderment and hostility in students who do not see a place for collaboration in learning. Rating schedules which reflected negative views on this dimension would need careful interpretation. The danger is that worthwhile innovations become blocked because of student resistance to change.

The language of the market-place is not value-free. The attempt to assure quality and standards means that the need to be clear about values is urgent, since what counts as quality and standards is evaluated in terms of them. The idea of customer satisfaction can only take us so far. The UK Government's and employers' needs have to be weighed up as only one part of the picture (albeit an important part). The need for effectiveness and efficiency have to be balanced against the need for those conditions that research has shown leads to the optimal conditions for learning, including lifelong learning. It may be that the drive for efficiency, value for money, and customer satisfaction results in some of these optimal conditions not being met. As an educator you may feel quality in education should be uncompromised. The dilemma is how to maintain quality and standards in the face of reduced resources and student diversity.

Enquiry Task

- Collect two or three examples of course evaluation questionnaires.
- Identify (possibly implicit) assumptions that are being made about learning.
- With a colleague, design an evaluation questionnaire that would give you feedback about the way in which students perceived the learning demands of your course.

Threats to Quality and Standards in Further and Higher Education

Student numbers in higher education have increased substantially ever since the Robbins report (University Grants Committee, 1963) pronounced the principle that there should be higher education places for all who are qualified and want it. There has also been a steep rise from the 1970s in the staff–student ratio. Between 1970/71 and 1988/89 the Association of University Teachers reported a rise from 1:8.5 to 1:11.5 (Gibbs and Jenkins, 1992). The position in former polytechnics and colleges of higher education is worse. Her Majesty's Inspectors report staff–student ratios in the humanities and social sciences of between 1:15 and 1:20 (DES, 1991). Further education colleges have been encouraged to expand similarly. The Government's aim is to continue rapid expansion at lower unit costs. So rapid has the expansion been in some years that, in some institutions, students have had to be accommodated in makeshift dormitories in church halls; students have been unable to fit into classrooms designed for smaller numbers, and basic equipment, such as the number of chairs, have been inadequate. The increase in numbers and in the diversity of students' prior experience are challenging assumptions underlying traditional methods of teaching and assessment especially where it no longer seems possible to get to know each student as an individual and the burden of assessment has become almost intolerable.

In countries where large undergraduate classes are the norm, high failure and drop-out rates are expected. There is also an assumption that standards are lower than in Britain. Another taken-for-granted aspect of mass educational systems is that contact with a teacher or professor will be minimal. These features of mass education are opposed to some criteria defining quality, especially the criterion of a collaborative partnership with a lecturer who knows students individually. 'Concern for individual students' appears in the research into good teaching carried out by Moses (1985) and Brown (1978) and as one of the values underlying the competences required of lecturers in higher education described by Baume (1993).

Students need to feel that their individual learning needs are being met. Traditional approaches have involved discussion reflection and guided reading, where students can clarify ideas and follow up enthusiasms. This model of a good educational experience is a powerful one and one that you may feel is even more important now that there is such diversity in student background. Students who feel that they are anonymous 'faces in the crowd', unknown to lecturers and fellow students alike, are likely to feel frightened and dismayed. Gibbs and Jenkins (1992) point out that this is the antithesis of a good educational experience.

Tutors too can feel dismay and low morale when they are forced to change practices which they see as fundamental to an education in their discipline. There needs to be an institution-wide policy on teaching and learning that recognizes the difficulties that have to be faced by lecturers and that supports them through a re-evaluation of their practices and a climate that welcomes and supports innovation in the management of teaching and learning.

Another important change is in the role the student is called upon to play as a learner. This role is radically different from the traditional experience of being an 'A' Level student or an 'access' student, where very small teaching groups used to enable frequent intervention by the teacher, pupils know one another well and dialogue is a possibility. Such experience of learning is not likely to be a good preparation for being taught in very large groups. Traditionally taught students may be ill prepared for a new approach to managing their learning.

Gibbs (1992) has argued that it is a mistake to assume that the traditional pattern of higher education was an efficient and effective model. He argues that

---

Enquiry Task

The following list comes from a planned institutional response to teaching large classes by Booth and Watson (1992, pp. 157–8).

List action taken by your own institution under each item.

- Promote a culture of innovation.
- Show a realistic concern for the problems facing lecturers in making change.
- Develop course monitoring and review procedures which foster rather than block innovation and diversity.
- Give local discretion to course teams to decide how to deliver course.
- Build in incentives to greater efficiency.
- Raise the status of teaching.

List further action you could recommend to your institution. Discuss your list with a trusted senior colleague.

---

the typical pattern of lectures and small tutorials, regular feedback and end-of-course assessments seemed to work because of the frequency of informal contact between staff and students. Poor lectures could be compensated for by explanations to individuals as could lack of clarity of course expectations and aims. Any difficulties students were experiencing could be quickly identified and dealt with. As course size increased it became impossible to maintain this frequency of contact. This has meant that the weaknesses inherent in the traditional way of managing teaching and learning have become exposed.

Gibbs (1992) argues that it is not possible to achieve acceptable quality in teaching and learning by relying on conventional methods. Although there is some evidence drawn from research at school level to show that class size does not have a major effect on final grades achieved by pupils (Andresen, 1991), in the new circumstances, unadapted methods may cause the nature of the educational experience to deteriorate. In smaller classes there is an attempt to individualize instruction (Smith and Glass, 1980). We need to find other ways to preserve the development of critical ability through dialogue. Gibbs argues that to continue with conventional methods is to accept (if not to publically acknowledge) a lowering of aims.

What is needed is a radical reconsideration of how those aims can be achieved in the light of increased numbers. It may be possible to retain the conventional values of discussion and reflection if much of this work is delegated to students. The challenge is in coming to see how this could be possible, given that we ourselves most probably lack experience in learning in this way. How, we might ask, could an education of quality substitute students for experts and still be a 'quality education'? Furthermore, an implication of such approaches is that there will be less emphasis on course, or subject content and more on managing course processes and on enabling students to become independent learners. This entails a major identity switch for those lecturers who think of themselves as experts in subjects rather than experts in managing students' learning. It also requires students to accept a radical redefinition of what it is to learn.

The kind of problems students face in large courses and the consequences for their learning has been discussed by Gibbs (1992). These range from students being unable to ask questions in large lectures, to fewer books per student to fewer assessments being required leading to less writing practice and so on. To meet some of these problems Gibbs has suggested a variety of control and independence strategies. Control strategies are tightly defined and lecturer-initiated. Independence strategies allow the student some freedom and independence. For example, one problem associated with a large course is that students often feel that they do not know where the course is going or what is expected of them. A 'control' strategy would involve detailed description of what should have been achieved on completion of the course. This can be described in terms of behavioural objectives or in terms of learning outcomes. Both make what is to be learnt very explicit. Behavioural objectives are used to structure Business and Technical Education Council (BTEC) courses. Statements of competences can also be regarded as behavioural objectives, although competences may define job related behaviours rather than learning behaviours. Each part of a course and its relation to other parts can also be described.

An independence approach to this problem would involve students specifying their own purposes. This can be facilitated by the use of learning contracts. A learning contract is an agreement between the lecturer and the student, about the learning they will undertake. It can specify resources to be used, actions to be taken, criteria by which the learning will be assessed. It can be used for substantial parts of degree courses, or for structuring work placements. It makes the goals of study explicit and at the same time ensures that the goals are appropriate to each student.

To compensate for lost opportunities for discussion in large classes, a control strategy could be to introduce short discussion activities for pairs or threes. (Jenkins, 1992) In large seminar groups of between ten and thirty students, it is possible to structure discussion so that everybody is actively engaged. Syndicates groups, brainstorming, pyramids, line ups are some of the methods that can be used (Gibbs, 1992). However, all these methods still entail lecturer control over topic and direction of the discussion. Independence strategies involve students discussing in groups without being lecturer-led, or more formally in giving seminars or working on assignments together. Although the interaction between students is not controlled, the activities and assignments, ground rules and assessments have to be meticulously prepared and understood by the students.

Competences as Statements of Teaching Quality

Competences have been described for many occupations since the advent of NVQs. They have also been described for secondary school teachers in initial training. These are made out in terms of subject knowledge, subject application, class management, assessing and recording pupils' progress, and foundational knowledge that will enable them to continue their professional development after qualifying in such areas as working with professional colleagues and parents, being aware of individual differences, recognizing different learning needs and so on.

While these lists clearly specify various aspects of a teacher's job they do not constitute a set of competence statements in the NVQ sense: that is, they are not closely specified in terms of standards and elements.

Similar competences have been described for lecturers in higher education by the Staff and Educational Development Association (SEDA) (Baume, 1993) as describing the minimum performance requirements of the job. Both sets of competences have values within them, implicitly in the case of school competences, explicitly in the case of the SEDA competences: for instance, a commitment to equal opportunities and knowledge about the learning needs of individuals.

This raises the question whether the competences are a sufficient description of what we would like to mean by quality in teaching. They go some way to describe and make explicit what lecturers are expected to do in the workplace but not what they are expected to know or the kind of moral behaviour that is required by the profession. This is true whether we use a narrow definition of competence, such as the ability to perform to recognized standards for a particular role in a particular job, or a wider notion of a repertoire of skills, knowledge and understanding that can be applied in a range of contexts and organizations (Jessup, 1991).

Professional competence in teaching has often been seen as more like the definition put forward by MacLure and Norris (1991), where competence is situationally specific, and depends on the value judgments of the practitioners present at the time. In this view, competent practice cannot be defined in advance. This approximates more closely to the view of professional competence underlying the reflective practitioner model.

Eraut (1989) argues that teachers need a wide repertoire of methods, approaches and ideas. These are best developed in the company of others, where awareness of alternatives and possibilities may be enhanced. Planning and decision-making may be supported through discussion about practice. Teachers also need to develop interactive skills. Many aspects of these cannot be worked out in advance. They may need help in thinking about their experiences after the event, to understand what happened, why it happened, and whether things could have been managed differently. This is the process basic to the reflective practitioner model. This model does not attempt to destabilize routines established in order to get by, but it does encourage the development of the ability and commitment to find better ways of teaching, so that learning is improved for students. It lays the foundation for continuing professional development. There is also that element of professional development concerned with curriculum development and pastoral care which have become particularly pressing in the present climate of constant change. The quality of teaching also depends to a great extent on the individuals personal development. We have seen, in this chapter that there is a great premium placed on a lecturer's personal qualities. Qualities such as enthusiasm and creativity have to be valued and fostered. There is a real danger that in a competence-led model of lecturer development, the quality of teaching may be impoverished since the non-work-based elements of it will not be made out.

Summary

Since the mid-1980s there have been a number of government initiatives which have intensified demands on the UK system of further and higher education. This has led to a concern for the quality and standard of teaching and learning in these sectors.

Views of quality and standards in teaching and learning are:

- related to purposes;
- often derived from authoritative sources;
- depend on viewpoint and are contestable; and
- related to subject or discipline specific concerns.

Judging quality in teaching may involve:

- evaluating the quality of student learning;
- evaluating qualities of educational thinking, planning and course design;
- evaluating classroom interaction, communication and management skills;
- evaluating published work on teaching and learning;
- personal qualities, such as friendliness, enthusiasm;
- giving students choice over course content;
- adequate and suitable resources; and
- well-designed activities, assignments and feedback designed to promote learning.

Judging quality in learning may involve:

- variety in assessments calling for appropriate learning strategies;
- the opportunity to question and debate; and
- assessments calling for higher-order thinking, creativity, initiative, and collaboration.

Assuring the quality of teaching and learning may involve:

- student feedback;
- appraisal;
- a developmental teaching profile; and
- an institutional climate that fosters and rewards excellence in teaching.

There are many threats to quality of teaching and learning in the current situation. In this chapter I have discussed the problem of very large teaching groups. Finally I have discussed the recent trend to try to guarantee quality in teaching through the specification of teaching competences.

Entry for the Reflective Diary

What do you understand by:

- quality in education;
- quality in learning; and
- quality in teaching?

Write about the implications of your definitions for your professional development.

Notes

1. This chapter is by Lorraine Foreman-Peck.
2. **Annotated List of Suggested Reading**

Bartram, D. (1992) 'A framework for Analysis and Assessment Methods in Competence-Based Approaches to Human Resource Development', *Competence and Assessment*, Issue 18, Employment Department.
This is the quarterly journal of the Employment Department's Standards Methodology Branch. It contains discussion articles and debates on latest developments in training.

Gibbs, G. and Jenkins, A. (Eds) (1992) *Teaching Large Classes in Higher Education: How to Maintain Quality with Reduced Resources*, London, Kogan Page.
Gibbs, G. (1992) *Discussion With More Students*, No. 3 in the series: 'Teaching More Students', Oxford Polytechnic, Oxford Centre for Staff Development.
These publications bring together many ideas and suggestions for innovatory teaching for lecturers faced with large classes.

Ramsden, P. (1992) *Learning to Teach in Higher Education*, London, Routledge.
Excellent introduction to thinking about quality in teaching and learning.

References

ANDRESEN, L. (1991) *The Influence of Class Size on Teaching and Learning Law at the University of New South Wales*, Professional Development Centre, University of New South Wales.
ASHCROFT, K. and FOREMAN-PECK, L. (1994) *Managing Teaching and Learning in Further and Higher Education*, London, Falmer Press.
ATKINS, M.J., BEATTIE, J. and DOCKRELL, W.B. (1993) *Assessment Issues in Higher Education*, Sheffield, Employment Department.
BALL, C. (1990) *More Means Different*, London, RSA.
BALL, R. and HALWACHI, J. (1987) 'Performance Indicators in Higher Education', *Higher Education*, 16, 4, pp. 393–405.
BARTRAM, D. (1992) 'A framework for analysis and assessment methods in competence-based approaches to human resource development', *Competence and Assessment*, 18, Employment Department.
BAUME, C. (Ed.) (1993) *SCED Teacher Accreditation Year Book*, Vol. 1.
BIGGS, J. B. (1992) Teaching: Design for learning higher education research and development, cited in ENTWISTLE, N. (1992) *The Impact of Teaching on Learning Outcomes in Higher Education*, Sheffield, Employment Department.
BOOTH, C. and WATSON, D. (1992) 'Teaching large classes: The institutional perspective', in GIBBS, G. and JENKINS, A. (Eds) *Teaching Large Classes in Higher Education: How to Maintain Quality with Reduced Resources*, London, Kogan Page.
BROWN, G. (1978) *Lecturing and Explaining*, London, Methuen.
CALLAGHAN, J. (1976) 'Towards a National debate', Ruskin College, Oxford, 18 October, *Education*, 22, pp. 332–3.
DALE, R. (1985) *Education, Training and Employment: Towards a New Vocationalism*, Milton Keynes, Open University Press.
DEPARTMENT FOR EDUCATION (1985) *The Development of Higher Education into the 1990s*, Cmnd. 9524, London, HMSO.
DEPARTMENT FOR EDUCATION (1987) *Higher Education: Meeting the Challenge*, Cmnd. 114, London, HMSO.

DEPARTMENT OF EDUCATION AND SCIENCE (1991) *Higher Education in the Polytechnics and Colleges: Humanities and Social Sciences*, London, HMSO.

ELTON, L. (1987) *Teaching in Higher Education: Appraisal and Training*, London, Kogan Page.

ENTWISTLE, N. and MARTON, F. (1984) 'Changing conceptions of learning and research', in MARTON, F., HOUNSELL, D. and ENTWISTLE, N. (Eds) *The Experience of Learning*, Edinburgh, Scottish Academic Press.

ERAUT, M. (1989) 'Initial Teacher Training and the NVO Model in Competency Based Education and Training', in BURKE, J.W. *Competency Based Education and Training*, Lewes, Falmer Press.

FOREMAN-PECK, L. (1993) 'Enterprise education: A new social ethic for higher education?', *The Vocational Aspect of Education*, 45, 2, pp. 99–111.

GIBBS, G. (1992) 'Control and independence', in GIBBS, G. and JENKINS, A. (Eds) *Teaching Large Classes in Higher Education: How to Maintain Quality with Reduced Resources*, London, Kogan Page.

GIBBS, G. (1993) *Guide to Submitting Teaching Profiles for Promotion*, Oxford, Oxford Polytechnic (now Oxford Brookes University) Educational Methods Unit.

GIBBS, G. and JENKINS, A. (1992) *Teaching Large Classes in Higher Education: How to Manage Quality with Reduced Resources*, London, Kogan Page.

HEYTHROP PARK (1989) A report on the HMI conference *Quality in Higher Education*.

JENKINS, A. (1992) 'Active learning in structured lectures', in GIBBS, G. and JENKINS, A. (Eds) *Teaching Large Classes in Higher Education: How to Maintain Quality with Reduced Resources*, London, Kogan Page.

JESSUP, G. (1991) *Outcomes: NVQs and the Emerging Model of Education and Training*, London, Falmer Press.

LEWIS, J. M. (1993) 'Teaching styles of award winning professors', in Ellis, R. (Ed.) *Quality Assurance for University Teachers*, Buckingham, OUP.

LODER, C., CLAYTON, D., MURRAY, R., COX, R. and SCHOFIELD, A. (1989) *Teaching Quality in Higher Education: A Review of Research and Literature*, Institute of Education, University of London for the Polytechnic and Colleges Funding Council Committee of Enquiry into Teaching Quality.

MACLEOD, D. (1994) 'Teachers fear diploma could be poor relation', *Guardian*, 25 May, p. 15.

MACLURE, M. and NORRIS, N. (1991) *Knowledge, Issues and Implications for the Standards Programme at Professional Levels of Competence*, Internal Report to the Employment Department.

MARTON, F. and SALJO, R. (1984) 'Approaches to learning', in MARTON, F., HOUNSELL, D. and ENTWISTLE, N. (Eds) *The Experience of Learning*, Edinburgh, Scottish Academic Press.

MITCHELL, P. (1985) 'A view from the bridge', in *The Quality Controllers; A Critique of the White Paper Teaching Quality*, University of London Institute of Education, Bedford Way Papers.

MOSES, I. (1985) 'High quality teaching in a university: Identification and description', *Studies in Higher Education*, 10, 3, pp. 301–13.

NATIONAL UNION OF STUDENTS (1993) *NUS Student Charter*, London, NUS.

OTTER, S. (1992) *Learning Outcomes in Higher Education: A Development Project Report*, London, UDACE.

RAMSDEN, P. (1992) *Learning to Teach in Higher Education*, London, Routledge.

SMITH, M.L. and GLASS, G.V. (1980) 'Meta-analysis of research on class, size and its relationship to attitudes and instruction', *American Educational Research Journal*, 17, 4, pp. 419–33.

TATE, A. (1993) 'Quality in teaching and the encouragement of enterprise', in ELLIS, R. (Ed.) *Quality Assurance for University Teaching*, Buckingham, OUP.

TAYLOR, E., MORGAN, A.R. and GIBBS, G. (1981) 'The orientations of Open University students to their studies', *Teaching at a Distance*, 20, pp. 3–12.

UNIVERSITY GRANTS COMMITTEE (1963) *Report of the Committee on Higher Education*, The Robbins Report, London, HMSO.

WEINER, M.J. (1981) *English Culture and the Decline of the Industrial Spirit 1850–1980*, Cambridge, Cambridge University Press.

Chapter 4

Student Support

In this chapter I discuss the implications of student charters and marketing considerations for arrangements for student support. The involvement of students, the community and employers in the creation of institutional targets is considered. I explore various models for the management of support services and the entitlements implied by the new context that includes new arrangements and criteria for funding, as well as learner-centred and workplace-based learning. I identify a variety of student needs in terms of educational and non-teaching support and explore some of the quality and management questions these raise.

The Context of Student Support

The rapid expansion of higher education and that predicted for further education is causing many of those responsible for the management of quality and standards to take the student viewpoint seriously. Students are seen less as passive recipients of an education which an institution deems is good for them and more as active partners in the creation of systems and programmes which meet their needs and aspirations.

Colleges and universities are increasingly looking at initiatives such as the development of the National Charter for Further Education (DFE, 1993a), The Charter for Higher Education (DFE, 1993b) and the National Union of Students Student Charter (NUS, 1993) to see whether they can change their practice to meet the needs and aspirations of students. These include enabling students to take part in decision-making at institutional and programme level. It is becoming more usual for students to be represented on institutional committees and for students to elect representatives to liaise with course leaders and course-management committees or groups.

While some students may have the will and ability to take an active part in the management of their learning environment, others may need help before they can begin to achieve their potential. The Higher Education Quality Council (HEQC, 1994a) reports that the quality of students' learning experience is fundamentally influenced by the quality of the guidance and counselling available to them during, and on completion of, their course of study. This conclusion must be set in the context of the rapid expansion in student numbers and changes in their financial support. This context may make it more difficult for individual lecturers to supply all the support needs of students.

The HEQC is clear that students in mass systems of further and higher education require impartial, comprehensive and professional support systems. You may wish to consider measures of student satisfaction in assessing the quality of such systems and whether they should be the central criteria. If so, the implication is that the institution may need to divert more resources from other areas to set up systems, provide expert staff and other resources and monitor the operation of a range of student services. These may need to cover guidance and assessment on entry; tutoring and/or mentoring systems; learning support; financial and personal advice; careers guidance; medical services; chaplaincy; and assistance with housing.

The institution will be faced with decisions relating to the definition of the roles of central and departmental support services and the relationships of these to external support systems. For instance, you may consider that an effective student support centre should be underpinned by a variety of systems and processes such as communication systems involving lecturers and students; staff development for admission and academic tutors; induction programmes for staff and students; resource banks of various kinds; and systematic systems for evaluation and feedback.

The decision-making process necessary for determining the form and functions of the student support service may involve a thorough review of existing provision within the institution and locally. If you become involved in this aspect of institutional life, you may wish to enquire into student needs as perceived by actual and potential students, as well as lecturers, in order to guide policy-making and strategic planning. In this analysis, you may need to find ways of drawing on the experience of others, nationally and perhaps internationally, in what is a rapidly developing field.

Student Rights and Quality

Colleges and universities are now required to implement the charters for further or higher education (DFE, 1993a and 1993b). These charters set targets for information provision and student feedback. Students have a clear right to reliable, impartial and timely information about courses, qualifications, facilities and entry requirements and procedures. They should be informed about teaching methods, likely group sizes, assessment requirements and college policies which may affect them (for instance, equal opportunities policies and policies for students with particular learning requirements). Colleges and universities are expected to publish quality reports as well as other information about fees, careers advice and counselling services.

Like further education, each university may end up with its own charter, including precise targets related to National Charter commitments, which will be used to guide quality assessment, and thus funding (FEFC, 1993). In any case, further and higher education institutions would be wise to gear themselves for the new quality assessment criteria as they relate to student services. The charters for further and higher education may provide a useful starting point for exploring good practice. For instance, they suggest that the institution will wish to ensure an efficient and fair application procedure, that includes guidance and counselling as well as the right for the student to see teaching rooms and facilities.

The emphasis in the charters on time management suggests that institutions might set targets for the time taken to turn around applications, marking and so on. In any case, it seems to me that timeliness, almost as much as actual provision, affects the students' experience of quality. As a reflective lecturer, you may be concerned to influence systems of application, assessment and teaching to ensure equal opportunities and the students' right to have learning difficulties taken into account.

For rights to be meaningful, students will need access to a grievance and appeal system that is independent, and perhaps external, to the institution. The Student Charter (NUS, 1993) suggests students should have the right to complain if the quality of a programme of study is inadequate. Systems may need to be established, including information about the systems themselves, to enable complaints to be handled at the appropriate level and recourse to a higher level (and eventually an independent hearing) if the student is not satisfied by the response. Carefully specified student rights and institutional targets with respect to those rights, may go some way towards ensuring that students become part of the quality assurance system. This seems to me right and proper, since further and higher education exists, to a large extent, to serve their interests.

Employer and Community Rights and Quality

The National Charter for Further Education (DFE, 1993a) specifies employer and community rights to involvement in institutional planning and quality assurance. Employers and the community provide part of the support for further and higher education, directly through taxes, by providing work placements and the payment of student fees, and indirectly, by providing a powerful lobby for the furtherance of continuing education and an outlet for the student talents nurtured by colleges and universities.

The charters for further and higher education state that employers and other members of the community have the right to a quick and efficient response to enquiries and to expect colleges and universities, wherever possible, to be responsive to their needs. In meeting these needs, you may become involved in the creation of programmes, information about facilities and charges for them and information related to the suitability of particular students as potential employees. An institution concerned with quality will have systems to ensure that this involvement and programme planning is subjected to the same quality assessment and criteria as those created for a more traditional client group.

The arrangements for funding further education require colleges to go further than this in their community involvement. The FEFC requires colleges to work closely with the Training and Enterprise Councils (TECs) on matters such as meeting local skills-training needs (FEFC, 1994a). The TECs have been given a role in the approval of the college's strategic plan and the duty to comment on the college's past performance. These comments are taken into account when making funding allocations to colleges. This implies a view of quality in post-compulsory education that many lecturers may find alien. It certainly risks a definition of quality that emphasizes instrumental concerns at the expense of more liberal educational values, and emphasizes the interests of a certain section of the community (employers), and a particular aspect of social life (economic activity) at the expense of other interests and activities.

Enquiry Task

- Create a list of those services and standards that an employer client has a right to expect from your institution.
- Discuss your list with someone within your institution who has a responsibility for entrepreneurial activity.
- Add to your list in the light of discussion.
- Discuss the services he or she expects from your institution with a local employer.

Are there any areas of conflict between your perspective and the other perspectives you explored?
What did you learn from this exercise?

Resources for Learning

Funding within higher and further education has depended upon ambitious growth targets in student numbers, largely paid for by a decrease in unit funding. (See Chapter 8 for more details). 'Efficiency' savings will continue to be enforced. Since staff costs account for around 75 per cent of expenditure (FEFC, 1992), either group sizes will become larger, or alternative ways of teaching and learning will be developed.

Shackleton (1991) believes that teaching costs are likely to go down as a proportion of total institutional spending and that material and student services costs will rise. The Government also expects that staff costs will decrease in real terms, but that other costs, including resources for learning will not. FEFC (1994e) has determined the overall allowance for inflation for the year 1994/5 in the funding for further education at 1 per cent, by allowing for an increase of 4 per cent in non staff costs, but no increase whatsoever in staff costs (i.e., a cut in real terms).

Changes in teaching and learning methods and the growth in the availability of information is likely to mean that the institutions' central learning resource facility will become more important to the quality of its work. I am calling this facility 'the library' in the interests of readability, although I recognize that in some institutions, book and non-book information systems are organized differently.

The Follett Report (Follett, 1993) looked specifically at higher education in the UK, but the recommendations of the Review Group apply equally well to further education. They suggest that in the future libraries will play a central part in meeting the information needs of students and lecturers. Recent changes mean that institutions interested in the quality of provision may need to reassess the role and function of libraries and the nature of staffing within them. This reassessment will probably have considerable resource implications. Information now comes through many different media which may be located and accessed in places other than central library facilities.

The management of this information and the strategy for its dissemination has to be coordinated. The role of the 'information manager' has thus become more complicated, and management and teaching skills may be at more of a premium than skills in administration. The technology and information revolution implies that libraries and library staff are becoming as central as the lecturer to the teaching and learning process and to the management and quality assurance systems of the institution. Academic quality assurance systems within institutions may need to develop to encompass an overview of the information needs of students and lecturers and strategies to meet them.

Quality assessment may take account of the performance indicators recommended in the Follett Report. These relate to the integration of library and institutional objectives and the ways in which the library is involved in the planning and evaluation of teaching, learning and research. User satisfaction of staff and students (particularly in relation to support for courses and research and the supply of print and non-print media, study facilities, information-skills tuition and information services) is suggested by the review group as a valid indicator. It also suggests that 'effectiveness' measures can be linked to output measures such as availability and appropriateness of services and material and the time taken to access particular services. Efficiency and value for money may be assessed through the relationship of costs to numbers of loans, photocopying volume, number of enquiries and so on, as well as the overall cost per full-time equivalent (FTE) staff and student member.

Such performance indicators may be useful when comparing the performance of a particular library year-on-year, but they say little about the real quality of the service. For example, a library might lower their FTE cost by providing no outreach or distance-learning service or by an institutional policy that requires students to buy their own computer and copies of many course texts. Such strategies could not be seen as adding to the 'quality' of the service unless the funders', rather than the students' purposes were the prime consideration. Other performance indicators have similar problems of interpretation. For instance, the time or costs of the enquiry service might be a function of the efficiency of the library system or the complexity of the queries made (as more staff are involved in research, the complexity of the enquiries library staff have to deal with may increase). User satisfaction may be high where there is a genuinely fine service or where library staff do the students' work for them (rather than train the students to satisfy their own information needs).

Follett notes that within higher education the proportion of institutional costs allocated to libraries has declined in recent years. This has led to a number of pressures on the service, such as a lack of space. Given the changes to teaching and learning, and the increasing importance of higher levels of staff scholarship and research, institutions may need to review their resource-allocation priorities.

Some increased expenditure will probably be needed to alleviate existing difficulties (for example, to increase opening hours and thus ease some of the pressure on space). Other investment may be needed to contribute to a future where the library manages an information service that is increasingly central to the process of student learning. Providing for the research needs of staff (and students in higher education) will require particular kinds of investment, including investment in information sources and services and in making links with other institutional libraries for mutual advantage. Investment in new technologies is likely to include regular updating of software and hardware, access to databases and networks and the creating of services such as reprographics, online document delivery and desk-top publishing.

Enquiry Task

Find out what systems are in existence for monitoring the quality of the library/ learning resource provision in your institution and the way they operate.

What quality criteria are implied by these systems and the way they operate?

How do these reflect the interests of:

- the full-time students;
- part-time students;
- the lecturers;
- institutional management; and
- funders.

If possible discuss your findings with a member of the library/learning resource staff and between you create a list of positive indicators of quality that takes account of all these interest groups.

What data would need to be collected to monitor performance against these indicators?

The Role of Student Services

Kleeman (1991) points out a variety of services required by students if they are to receive a quality education. Many of these may be organized centrally. Some elements may be better delivered by departments or through particular programmes. Perhaps the main function of student services is to develop an overview and direction for these services, in order to help learners clarify their aims, the routes towards achieving these aims and to minimize barriers to progress. This implies that a student-services function will be involved (directly or indirectly) in activities such as guidance and counselling, accreditation of prior learning, skill enhancement, specialist-advice sessions to staff and students and establishing and managing systems which enable students to identify and overcome learning difficulties.

A quality service will probably go beyond this to become involved with liaison with other sectors of education and in the review and accreditation of programmes. The student-services function may encompass arrangements for students likely to have particular difficulties because of the nature of their programme (such as distance learning and overseas students), or because of the social milieu (such as gay or black students) or because of problems they bring with them (such as specific learning difficulties).

In order to minimize barriers to achievement, the student-services function may undertake research to identify these barriers and the long- and short-term effects of various kinds of remedial action. A variety of database information, such as patterns of recruitment, retention and destination may be needed. It may be necessary to set up a variety of systems dealing with referral to outside agencies, requests for student references and advocacy systems for students in trouble and to establish means of communication through an advice desk, handbooks and lecturer networks.

You may wish to consider whether the student-services function affects the work of all areas of the institution where you work. Kleeman points out that good practice may include the production of material, such as profile guidelines, study-skills packs or induction-resource packs. It is likely to include a careful integration of central and local services and support and training (for instance, case-study groups for lecturers) for aspects delegated to courses or departments. These functions raise a variety of management and quality issues: for instance, the status of staff within support services and the level of training and clerical and other resources available. The physical layout and geographical location of a service will also affect its functioning and reflect its relative status in the institution. Kleeman points out that the success of student services may depend as much on the attitudes of senior managers: their belief in empowerment and willingness to acknowledge and encourage achievement in this area, as on the internal organization of the services themselves.

Enquiry Task

Which of these roles are performed at lecturer, programme and central student-services level:

- pre-entry guidance and counselling;
- accreditation of prior learning;
- study-skill enhancement;
- personal counselling;
- careers advice;
- health education; and
- help with specific learning difficulties.

Where there is overlap, find out what systems are in place to:

- determine the philosophy underpinning provision;
- monitor and evaluate overall provision;
- coordinate work with particular students; and
- ensure all students and student groups have equal opportunities with regard to support for their particular needs.

What criteria for success in student support are implied by the systems presently in place?

Guidance and Assessment at the Point of Entry

The charters for further and higher education state that colleges and universities must have published admissions arrangements and further education colleges should have targets for handling applications. Students have a right to know how their previous experience and learning will be taken into account. They should have access to information about any arrangements for managed learning and about the aims, structure and qualifications in any programme in which they may be interested.

FEFC (1992) includes guidance and admissions among the aspects of learning support that should be adequately resourced. These include marketing and outreach; diagnostic assessment and accreditation of prior learning at the point of entry; guidance and counselling pre-entry, when students are on course and at exit; registration and induction; and assessment and progress records from entry to exit. From August 1994, colleges were funded in part according to the costs they incur in supporting students across three key stages: entry, on programme and exit (FEFC, 1994b).

The Student Charter (NUS, 1993) states that the analysis of needs should start with the students' needs, not with an analysis of what lecturers want to teach. It indicates one of the first needs of students is access to the institution. Students, colleges and universities have a common interest in increasing the participation of particular social groups in further and higher education. (This is discussed in more detail in Chapter 9.) In order to manage this, institutions may need to consider investment in a range of non-teaching provision, including child care, the physical arrangements which might permit the participation of disabled students and dietary and other arrangements for students from religious minorities.

Students who can benefit from further and higher education come with a variety of previous learning experiences and qualifications. One of the first needs of the student is to have his or her qualifications for entry assessed fairly and open-mindedly. For this to happen, colleges and universities may need to set up systems for developing and disseminating a body of knowledge of various types of

---

Enquiry Task

List the elements which should be included in pre-entry contracts specifying student rights and responsibilities.

Discuss your lists with a colleague and a group of students.
Add to your lists in the light of these comments.

List the advantages and disadvantages of such a contract:

- from the students' point of view;
- from your point of view; and
- from the institution's point of view.

Does the pre-entry contract have significant advantages and/or disadvantages over a statement of institutional rules, systems and procedures?

---

qualification and experience and their value as predictors of performance on various types of course.

It is likely that a system for ensuring the quality of the admissions process will include a regular audit of needs and provision from the point of view of staff and students, directed at providing regular recommendations for the improvement of the admissions process. Good admissions procedures are likely to include some sort of pre-entry guidance programme and a system for supported self-assessment as well as more formal assessment of prior learning. Institutions may wish to explore ideas such as a pre-entry contract with students, specifying their rights, and perhaps their responsibilities.

Study Skills

The Student Charter (NUS, 1993) suggests that all students should have a learner agreement with their institution to give them more control over their own learning. Students are not always clear about the relationship of the various components on offer to them in a particular programme of study. In order for students to manage their time effectively and identify study priorities, they need to know the ways in which components and assessments within a programme of study count towards a final qualification. For example, a student studying part-time for a chartered surveyor qualification was told that, in order to avoid having to retake all his examinations in the event of failing in one element, he had to average a 'C' grade in all elements of his assessment. His coursework was given numerical marks, without any indication of their relationship to letter grades, so he was in no position to assess his progress. Students also need to be clear about the objectives of particular courses and components and what they allow them to do next.

Adequate information is an essential prerequisite to the development of a coherent study plan. You may wish to consider what say students should have in the establishment of learning goals if they are to work within a realistic study plan. Some non-traditional groups of students need a flexible approach to study. This flexibility may be built into the programme or relate to the attitudes of lecturers. Ashcroft and Peacock (1993) found that a positive attitude on the part of the lecturer, with some understanding and tolerance of the difficulties caused by family pressures, was central to the success of mature women students. Flexibility in course design may come through modularization, the establishment of credit-accumulation systems to allow flexibility in place and mode of study and the establishment of accelerated and part-time routes to particular qualifications. Flexible systems of study usually require a higher standard of student guidance than traditional linear courses. Institutions which are interested in quality within flexible systems may need to invest more in such guidance, as well as in course management, record-keeping systems and systems for monitoring student progress.

One of the important aspects in the student's ability to develop appropriate study skills is the provision of adequate feedback of their progress. The Student Charter suggests that every student should participate in the creation of a record of achievement, dealing in some detail with their academic attainments and the role that they have played in other aspects of the life of the institution. For such a record to be useful for formative purposes (and also for some summative purposes such as finding a job), the record should be fairly detailed and up to date. For instance, an overall grade for a whole year's work presented at the end of the next academic year is unlikely to be as useful as marks and comments on each component of a course, presented shortly after the work has been assessed.

Learner Support

The term 'student-centred learning' is increasingly being adopted by institutions which wish to encourage student choice in their mode and content of study and emphasize the learner rather than the teacher. In reality, student choice makes particular demands on the student. It relies on skills of self-assessment and attitudes of responsibility towards their own learning.

The Council for National Academic Awards (CNAA, 1992) states that student-centred learning emphasizes the empowerment of the individual. The empowerment requires institutions to create new systems of tracking and accountability. A variety of approaches to choice is open to institutions. For instance, they may decide to emphasize choice in terms of: location; duration; mode of curriculum delivery; content; assessment; or outcome. You may wish to consider the role of language in helping the student to be clear about the precise form and extent of choice, as well as about what various choices imply in terms of costs, benefits and responsibilities.

Each of the various forms of student-centred learning raises its own quality issues. For instance, particular care may be needed in the specification of the role of internal and external examiners in systems which allow negotiated assessment, to ensure that students are being assessed at the right standard and do not unknowingly exceed or fail to meet the normal requirements for a particular award. It is sometimes assumed that success in a set of assessment means that learning has taken place. This is not necessarily the case. For instance, I achieved an 'A' grade in an accountancy module with very little understanding of the underlying principles. It was only when I came to apply the concepts in my work that I fully understood their relevance. Up to that point my success in accounting had relied on my ability to use contextual and semantic cues and good examination and essay-writing technique.

Students themselves are often best placed to judge the quality of their learning. The Further Education Unit (FEU, 1990) states that the institution should include as an indicator of quality in learning, opportunities for students to identify and reflect on what they have learned. Formalizing such opportunities for reflection may support the process. Increasingly, institutions and departments are introducing records of progress and achievement which allow the students' progress to be carefully monitored. This is usually through a process that enables students to agree and subsequently review learning outcomes with a supportive lecturer (FEU, 1993). Action planning and recording achievement are often central to modular and interdepartmental programmes. Without some system of tracking, student learning may be a haphazard business. The movement towards records of progress and achievement implies a shift from a view of the institution as a place that provides teaching to one that provides opportunities for learning.

The basic principles of such systems include the notion that students need recognition and encouragement. Learning and achievement are inadequately captured in marks and qualifications. The process of 'naming' and recording learning helps. Facilitating learning is a management process, which can be aided by management actions such as target setting, progress review and developing systems for tackling specific learning problems.

The introduction and maintenance of such systems requires management time and effort. This may include staff training. Lecturers may need to develop new skills, such as the ability to provide specific rather than judgmental feedback and to turn such feedback into achievable goals. Recording progress and achievement is likely to be time-consuming. If it is not timetabled, deadlines may slip and the system fall into disrepute. It may be necessary to set up systems to monitor the operation of the scheme and to allocate roles and responsibilities (such as whether the lecturer or student is responsible for setting up review meetings), and the action that will be taken if they do not exercise that responsibility.

Once set up, the system should be subject to periodic quality review. Lecturers may be expected to produce summary information about the successes and needs of the students as revealed by their records as part of the review process. Review reports might include statistical information about the rate of success achieved by students against defined outcomes or the rate of take up of personal and group interview. It is likely that review reports will also include qualitative information about student learning achievements and difficulties and the operation and format of the record of progress and achievement itself. If these reports are to be useful, some system for arriving at judgments and conclusions about emerging trends and possible actions will need to be set up. The system for ensuring the quality of the profiling process may also embrace the accuracy of the product (for instance, statements about the level of achievement). This implies evidence to back up assertions and may be particularly important where the document is to be used in the transition to employment or further study.

Quality support for the learner should recognize his or her development and social needs. The FEU suggests that this individuality must be taken into account in the support services which are offered. For instance, you may have to take into account the understandings students bring to tasks. Sometimes, students may need individual help if they are to develop these understandings in educationally desirable ways. This implies that the learner-support service will have a role in helping individuals, but also in developing subject lecturers' ability to interpret learning, distinguish between different kinds of error, use them as diagnostic tools and engage in timely intervention with appropriate resources. You may also wish to consider whether it is part of the support-service role to confront curriculum and institutional issues directly (for instance, by arguing for change on the basis of evidence about actual learner needs).

The need to promote equal opportunities has influenced funding within further and higher education at the margins. For example, when the FEFC wished to introduce funding related to outcomes, they were made aware that lower-achieving students might be excluded and modified their proposals accordingly (FEFC, 1992). The FEFC promotes equal opportunities and to that end it has established a committee looking at learning difficulties. It has started to collect views, particularly students views, on provision for their needs (FEFC, 1994c). The National Charter for Further Education (DFE, 1993a) states that students with disabilities are entitled to information about additional support, accommodation, access to buildings. Since their needs are likely to be diverse, help may be more accessible if there is a named point of contact.

The provisions in the charter for higher education (DFE, 1993b) related to equal opportunities are weaker than those for further education, although they state that institutions should publish the steps they are taking to encourage under-represented groups.

Enquiry Task

- Assess the range of numeracy, literacy and study skills needed for success on a course that you teach.
- Ask a group of students to assess the numeracy, literacy and study skills which they lack.
- Find out how many of them know how to find help in developing the skills they lack.

Do you know how to get them specialist help? What qualitative and quantitative measures might be needed to assess the effectiveness of such help?

Support for Work-based Learning

Many programmes now substantially take place in the workplace. In some programmes, such as many of those based on the National Vocational Qualification (NVQ), it may not be clear who has responsibility for the student. Within higher education there are also programmes, such as initial teacher training courses, where a large proportion of the curriculum must be delivered and assessed in the workplace. Ambiguities about responsibility for the student may be less where the university is the body that awards the qualification, since the student is more clearly a student of the university.

Work-based learning introduces particular problems for student support. Students may be isolated. They may have workplace mentors who have no expertise in the support of learning. The practice they are exposed to may be of a variable standard. Placements may be difficult to find and their quality hard to assess. Since the institution is in no sense responsible for a firm or other organization where it wishes to place students, it is unlikely to be able accurately to assess their quality as learning environments. At the same time, some accrediting bodies may lay this responsibility on them. For example, the Office for Standards in Education (OFSTED) assesses the quality of teacher education in universities to a large extent on the quality of student placements in schools and the support provided by the classroom teachers. This creates a dilemma for the university, since there is no way that the average school will allow the local university to inspect its provision.

Some of the problems of quality assurance in work-based learning involve establishing a satisfactory equivalence in the student-support services provided, compared with classroom-based programmes. Colleges and universities interested in developing and maintaining the quality of work-based learning programmes may have to find ways to ensure that such students are not disadvantaged in terms of access to library and other resources, advice and counselling, opportunities for supported self-assessment, the development of study skills and so on.

Some of the recently funded research and development projects linked to work-based learning, approved by HEQC (1994b), are interesting in what they omit. They imply definitions of quality based on output, assessment methods and issues of reliability and validity. Plans to examine the quality of work-based learning in terms of students' needs and interests or of student rights do not appear much in evidence. This approach seems to have been encouraged by the move to competence-based models of learning and can be interpreted to imply that the *only* valid measure of the quality of a programme is in what students can do at the end of it. It is as if what students know, feel and experience is discounted (or counted only if it affects the final assessment) as part of a quality education.

Enquiry Task

List the essential data which a quality assessment system for workplace learning should have available.

What dilemmas are raised in achieving and measuring quality in work-based learning programmes?

Discuss with a manager of such a programme how some of these might be resolved.

Are there differences in practice between the criteria by which quality is measured in work-based and institution-based programmes?

Personal Support of Students

Much of the following three sections is premised on a post-Robbins model of further and higher education, where the university is a place where students live away from home and colleges and universities contain various support services used exclusively by students and staff. With a move from an élite to a mass system, the costs of this provision is growing. In the long-term, institutions may have to share services with the community, or move to models common in other parts of Europe, where the provision of personal and financial counselling and vocational, medical and accommodation services are not the responsibility of the educational institution.

Meanwhile, the stated expectations of the funding councils make it clear that services should be maintained or enhanced. In any case, a lack of support on these areas can lead to a wastage of resources, and more importantly, human talents, though higher levels of drop-out or underachievement. A couple of examples may illustrate this. A student studying for her first degree was a perfectionist. If she received less than an 'A' grade for any piece of work she was devastated. Not unnaturally, her fellow students, most of whom were satisfied with 'B' and 'C' grades, were unsympathetic. The personal-tutoring system in the institution was very weak. Eventually, rather than expose herself to the possibility that she might achieve less than a first-class honours degree, the student left the course. Another student, a single parent, was on the point of giving up her course because of the perceived attitude of one member of staff to occasional lateness or absence caused by problems with her small child. A short counselling session, followed by a discussion with the staff member concerned, enabled the student to complete her course successfully.

Transitions are difficult and personal growth is often painful. The education process involves transition and growth. Students often experience feelings of incompetence, disappointment, low self-esteem, doubts and so on. The resulting emotional difficulties and stress may cause any number of problems. Therefore it is not surprising that responsible colleges and universities find that they must invest in the personal support of their students. The personal support of students is only partially an individual matter. Quality support requires institutional commitment. Thus, some institutions provide a time allocation for lecturers acting as personal tutors, with structured programmes to build up mutual knowledge and trust, so that problems can be dealt with as they arise.

Civil (1991) reports that too often lecturers have to deal with a wide range of student problems without adequate training or written guidelines. Quality issues arise in these circumstances. In her survey of sixty-six further education colleges, she found a lack of consistent and coherent policies. This was especially true of smaller colleges where many had no staff within student services above the basic lecturing grade (some had no dedicated appointments at all). This inevitably led to a lack of involvement at senior-management level. Civil states that lecturers are key figures in supporting students. You are likely to be assisted in this role if you have an adequate job description and training so that you are clear about the role and the limits to your responsibility. You may need help to distinguish between providing basic information and support and the counselling role.

The quality of personal-support services is crucial to the quality of education an institution provides. Real learning causes change in the individual. Change involves loss and pain. This can lead students to suffer a variety of crises, such as loss of religious or political faith or a loss of self-esteem. Some mature and younger students may be in established relationships. The personal growth which accompanies real education can lead a couple to develop at different paces, so that one partner is left behind and the relationship breaks down.

Some students may experience change and the stresses that it brings because of their stage of development. Younger students may be confronting aspects of their sexuality and identity. Older students may be suffering from the death or illness of parents or other family members. The quality of the students' learning will be affected by such stresses. Without adequate support some of them may suffer permanent damage. Others may decide that the institution is the source of their unhappiness and leave without fulfilling their potential. A source of stress which seems to be increasing is financial difficulty (NUS, 1993). Student grants and loans no longer meet reasonable living expenses. There has been a decline of 8 per cent in real terms in discretionary awards to students within further education between 1990/1 and 1993/4. During the same period, there has been a decline of 50 per cent in discretionary awards for students in higher education (FEFC, 1994d). Temporary vacation work is sometimes hard to obtain. Part-time students may receive no support at all. Institutions are increasingly introducing charges for leisure and other facilities. The costs of study materials continues to grow. Local education authorities are not always as prompt in paying the grant as they should be. Many students are thus under considerable pressure and may require expert and specialist counselling and welfare services.

Enquiry Task

Discuss the skills needed for effective counselling with someone who is a trained counsellor.

Which of these skills are you confident you possess?

In the light of this assessment create a set of guidelines for yourself about:

- the nature of the help you can provide for students with personal difficulties;
- the limits to the help you can give them;
- the limits to the confidentiality you can promise them; and
- the circumstances when you would refer problems to specialist services.

Vocational Preparation

The Further Education Unit (FEU, 1982) suggests that the responsibility of the institution for its students' vocational preparation includes much more than careers guidance and advice. A quality provision may include the development of students' work-related skills, experience and knowledge. Vocational preparation may become part of an integrated process, involving lecturers and course leaders, rather than an event or series of events. You may become involved in a process that helps students to assess their potential and optimize their employability. This does not mean that students coming towards the end of their course of study will not need expert career guidance. For many, a key outcome objective, central to the quality of the programme will not be achieved if they do not find employment or the opportunity for further study. During a programme of study, others may start to wonder whether they are on the right course and may need help to consider other options open to them.

In order to ensure that students are making informed decisions about their study and its relationship to the world of work, careers education and guidance may need to be integrated into a variety of systems and processes from entry to graduation. This implies that career aspirations are discussed at the point of selection, careers education becomes a cross-curriculum theme, affecting every programme within the institution, and that there are expert individuals that students can turn to at key points in their development.

Decisions about careers guidance and advice thus embrace more than whether to have a full-time or part-time careers tutor. They encompass the roles of counsellor, teacher and manager, and the extent that these roles should be separated. If the role of the careers tutor is seen in terms of information giving and counselling, the main activity may be to build a resource centre for students to use independently and to provide problem-centred one-to-one tutoring for a few. If careers advice and education is seen as a teaching function, the careers tutor may work with others to design and pilot core and subject-specific learning modules. If it is seen more as a management role, the tutor may spend his or her time working with colleagues to develop their awareness and work out strategies for integrating careers education into the normal curriculum, managed by the subject lecturer.

An institution may decide to take a multifaceted approach to careers support for students. This may make monitoring of the quality and consistency of the service relatively complex. Accountability will lie partly with the careers tutor, but also elsewhere. Such an approach may require systems of monitoring and review which are similar to those for interdisciplinary or interdepartmental programmes of study.

Enquiry Task

List skills and knowledge related to the world of work which your students need to develop.

- Identify those which are your responsibility.
- Who should take responsibility for the others?
- Discuss your lists with a careers tutor in your institution.
- Add to or change your lists in the light of this discussion.

How did your perception of your role in relation to employability education compare with his or hers?

Non-teaching Facilities

The Student Charter (NUS, 1993) makes it clear that the quality of students' educational experience is affected by a range of non-teaching facilities and support. Perhaps the most basic of these is accommodation. The quality of students' learning may be affected by substandard accommodation. Many universities have expanded student numbers rapidly over the last few years. The building of student accommodation has not always kept pace with this expansion. Where this is the case, the university interested in the quality of student experience may decide to develop alternative services. The accommodation requirements of non-traditional students may need special consideration. Institutions interested in encouraging applications from mature people may wish to explore ways which they can help them into family accommodation (or provide double rooms for married couples). If the institution is interested in recruiting students from some ethnic-minority groups, they may need to consider providing single-sex accommodation with particular rules and facilities.

Traditionally, Wednesday afternoons and Saturday mornings were free of teaching to enable sporting and other activity to take place. Pressures to use teaching space more intensively is leading some institutions to reconsider this policy. The Student Charter (NUS, 1993) points out that the quality of students' educational experience is affected by the recreational facilities of the institution and whether teaching is arranged to enable students to take part in such activity.

Civil (1991) notes that medical services are relatively uncommon within further education. 25 per cent of larger colleges have medical services and few of these include a doctor. On the other hand, most (75 per cent) offer a health-education programme at institutional or departmental level. Within higher education some kind of medical service is often provided. This service may deal with health problems (for instance, through an on-site doctor's surgery) rather than active health promotion. A higher or further education institution that is concerned with the quality of the whole student experience may wish to consider how it should be involved in matters such as the prevention of drug and alcohol abuse and the promotion of safer sex, good eating habits, fitness and so on.

I have already described the pain that personal growth and transition can cause to students. Many students find that they change their most basic beliefs during their period of study. Some students experience a crisis of faith. Others find religion for the first time. Such students need access to support, perhaps through a chaplaincy (on or off site) or a student-support group, to explore the implications of the changes in their belief system.

Management, Teaching and Student Support

The most important resource for the support of student learning is excellence in teaching. For this reason the Student Charter (NUS, 1993) includes the training of lecturers and the right for students to provide feedback on teaching. The development of support services for students should therefore be located within a total learning environment that takes into account the yearly and programme cycles of education and training. It implies that the staff providing student support have access to the decision-making systems within the institution in order to locate student support within a global learning framework.

The role of the institution in providing student services includes the development of targets for the quality of support offered. It should also publish arrangements and policies for aspects such as student progress, learning support, equal opportunities, information provision and criteria for achievement. It might set minimum standards, so that students know what they can expect, but also what is expected of students (for example, rules, disciplinary procedures and health and safety arrangements). The communication of rights and duties to students may also occur at departmental and course level (for instance, in terms of the assessment, teaching and qualifying arrangements for particular programmes). The institution should also ensure that systems exist to collect and use student feedback on their own performance and that of the institution.

The HEFC and FEFC have set up systems to assess quality of provision within institutions, including arrangements for student support. Such assessment is located within the framework of the institution's own quality control arrangements. This provides the institution with an opportunity to use the information relating to national standards as a springboard for its own definitions of quality and the development of distinctive services which meets the needs of its students.

There will be some students who fail to achieve an appropriate level of performance and therefore fail their course. Such failures may be more common in institutions which take reasonable risks and open opportunities to non-traditional applicants than in those which play very safe. Failure may also be less common where an institution lacks a rigorous system for monitoring standards. For this reason I do not believe that failure or drop-out rates should be a criterion for quality, unless they are excessive. Students who fail the course are unlikely to be pleased about their experience. Some will consider that they have been treated unfairly. An institution that is concerned to ensure that its standards and conditions of assessment are as consistent as possible will wish to develop a standardized system of appeal. The Student Charter (NUS, 1993) suggests that grounds for appeal should include extenuating circumstances, maladministration or sexual or racial discrimination. At present institutions' appeal systems differ widely. It is not always clear what may be the subject of a *complaint* and what may be ground for an *appeal*. Some systems appear to be geared to minimizing administrative effort rather than guaranteeing comparability of standards.

Some institutions refuse any reconsideration of internal academic judgments. This seems to me to be the aspect of assessment that is most likely to vary within and between institutions. It is a particular threat to the reliability of assessment in institutions (such as most universities) where most work contributing to particular qualifications is marked and moderated internally.

Institutions interested in promoting comparability of standards need systems for uncovering and dealing with instances of variation in the standard of academic judgments. For example, a university could allow students to produce strong

---

Enquiry Task

Find out what committees in the institution are responsible for assuring the quality of the total provision of the following aspects of student support:

- guidance and counselling on entry;
- tutoring and assessment systems;
- financial and personal advice;
- careers guidance;
- medical services; and
- assistance with accommodation.

Look through minutes of these committees.

- Where responsibility for aspects are shared between departments or areas (for instance courses and student services may share responsibility for study-skill development), to what extent does the committee system consider the student experience holistically?
- Are there other systems which look at the whole student experience in these areas?
- Identify any areas where the formal quality assurance is carried out systematically.

Identify the criteria for success implied by the way the system is operating.

---

evidence that a particular piece of work may have been graded incorrectly (for instance, if the mark is substantially different from the student's normal performance in that subject) and allow them the right to formally request that their mark be moderated by another internal or external examiner. Of course, such a challenge is only possible where the feedback is available to students about grades for particular pieces of coursework or examination scripts. You may feel that such an opportunity would open floodgates or undermine the authority of the university. In this case, the institution itself may need to develop the facility (perhaps through the use of information technology) to spot where such apparent inconsistency is occurring and check on the accuracy of marking, perhaps through a targeted double-marking system. Such systems are discussed in more detail in Chapter 6.

Summary

Initiatives such as the charters for further and higher education and the Student Charter are leading funding councils and institutions to consider student support as fundamental to quality issues. These issues include:

- guidance and counselling on entry;
- tutoring and assessment systems;
- financial and personal advice;
- careers guidance;
- medical services; and
- assistance with accommodation.

Each of these may be managed by a specialist service, integration into programme support, outside agencies or (most likely) a combination of each of these.

The starting point for quality may be students' need and satisfaction or student rights and responsibilities. For rights to be meaningful, students need access to independent appeal and grievance procedures and to see targets for institutional commitment clearly translated into outcome criteria. Employer and community interests have a place in quality assessment through specific targets for institutional performance related to employer needs or the involvement of organizations such as TECs in planning and delivery.

Pressures on institutional funding and changes in conceptions of teaching and learning are resulting in an increasing role for libraries and learning-resource centres. This involvement needs to be managed and its quality monitored through institutional systems.

A central student-support function may have a role in coordinating:

- the direction of student support;
- guidance and counselling;
- informational services;
- accreditation of prior learning;
- skill enhancement;
- specialist services for particular student groups;
- liaison with other functions and outside agencies; and
- systems for advocacy.

Through:

- the collection of evidence;
- dissemination;
- direct action; and
- evaluation and review.

Students need information about:

- entry requirements;
- the relationship between assessment, course requirements and whole pro-grammes;
- alternative routes to desired outcomes;
- services available to them; and
- their own progress and achievements.

Learner-centred programmes raise particular quality issues. Students may be helped by records of their progress and achievement, especially in relation to:

- negotiated learning and assessment;
- feedback and assessment;
- goal setting; and
- identification of study support needs.

Workplace learning may raise quality and support problems, such as:

- isolation;
- the quality of placements;
- ambiguity over relationships with students;
- equivalence with institutionally-based programmes; and
- access to resources.

In these circumstances, quality criteria which rely purely on the assessment of learning outcomes are clearly inadequate.

Education involves change and transition and therefore pain. Students may need counselling and support with emotional problems which are created by the process of transition and change, in particular:

- changes in self-concept;
- tensions in interpersonal relationships;
- conflicts between home and students' roles and responsibilities; and
- financial problems.

In addition, students may require vocational preparation including the develop-ment of skills for employment and knowledge of career opportunities.

Non-teaching facilities are important in the quality of student experience. These facilities include:

- accommodation services;
- recreational facilities;

- medical facilities; and
- chaplaincy or other spiritual support.

Student support raises a number of management questions:

- the place of student support in the total learning environment;
- the place of student support in the senior-management system;
- its relationship to other policy areas (e.g., equal opportunities, assessment);
- appropriate criteria for assessment of each area;
- the creation of systems for communication of rights and duties;
- the creation of systems for monitoring the operation of rights and duties; and
- the creation of systems for the collection and use of student feedback where duties and responsibilities may be properly exercised across a number of operations and departments.

Entry for the Reflective Diary

What philosophy should underpin the provision of support for students?

What alternative models are available?

What are the costs and benefits of your preferred model from the point of view of the:

- student;
- lecturer;
- support staff; and
- institutional management.

Identify some of the dilemmas inherent in your model.

Are there ways in which these dilemmas can be resolved?

Notes
Annotated List of Suggested Reading

Further Education Unit (1994) *Quality in Guidance for Adults*, London, FEU.
Although this pack relates particularly to adults, the issues it raises are of concern to all students. Section 2 includes a useful summary of some approaches to quality. Section 3 deals with the main aspects which must be taken into account in setting standards for guidance and counselling and establishing a monitoring system. Section 4 tabulates key principles within a quality framework. Section 5 explores training issues and Section 6 describes 6 case studies.

Department for Education (1993) *Further Choice and Quality: National Charter for Further Education*, London, DFE.
Department for Education (1993) *Higher Choice and Quality: The Charter for Higher Education*, London, DFE.
These describe principles by which provision within the sector will be judged. They are essential reading for all lecturers and should influence policy at all levels.

References

ASHCROFT, K. and PEACOCK, E. (1993) 'An evaluation of the progress, experience and employability of mature students at Westminster College, Oxford', *Assessment and Evaluation in Higher Education*, 18, 1, pp. 57–70.
CIVIL, J. (1991) 'Managing student services', *Coombe Lodge Report*, 22, 8, pp. 639–87.
COUNCIL FOR NATIONAL ACADEMIC AWARDS (1992) *Case Studies in Student-Centred Learning: CNAA Project Report 36*, May, London, CNAA.
DEPARTMENT FOR EDUCATION (1993a) *Further Choice and Quality: National Charter for Further Education*, London, DFE.
DEPARTMENT FOR EDUCATION (1993b) *Higher Choice and Quality: The Charter for Higher Education*, London, DFE.
FOLLETT, B. (1993) *Joint Funding Councils' Libraries Review Group: Report*, Bristol, HEFCE, SHEFC, HEFCW and DENI.
FURTHER EDUCATION FUNDING COUNCIL (1992) *Funding Learning*, Coventry, FEFC.
FURTHER EDUCATION FUNDING COUNCIL (1993) *Council Report. No. 11*, 23 December, Coventry, FEFC.
FURTHER EDUCATION FUNDING COUNCIL (1994a) *Council News. No 15*, 20 June, Coventry, FEFC.
FURTHER EDUCATION FUNDING COUNCIL (1994b) *Press Release*, 4 May, FEFC.
FURTHER EDUCATION FUNDING COUNCIL (1994c) *Disability, Learning Difficulties and Further Education*, Coventry, FEFC.
FURTHER EDUCATION FUNDING COUNCIL (1994d) *Council News. No. 13*, 11 April, Coventry, FEFC.
FURTHER EDUCATION FUNDING COUNCIL (1994e) *Guidance on Recurrent Funding Methodology 1994–5*, February, Coventry, FEFC.
FURTHER EDUCATION UNIT (1982) *Tutoring: The Guidance and Counselling Role of the Tutor in Vocational Preparation*, London, NICEC and FEU.
FURTHER EDUCATION UNIT (1990) *Individuality in Learning: A Summary Bulletin*, London, FEU.
FURTHER EDUCATION UNIT (1993) *Managing Learning: The Role of the Recording of Achievement*, London, FEU.
FURTHER EDUCATION QUALITY COUNCIL (1994a) *Guidance and Counselling in Higher Education*, London, HEQC.
HIGHER EDUCATION QUALITY COUNCIL (1994b) *Higher Education Projects Digest, 1*, Summer.
KLEEMAN, A. (1991) 'Student issues and concerns', *Coombe Lodge Report*, 22, 8, pp. 695–702.
NATIONAL UNION OF STUDENTS (1993) *NUS Student Charter*, London, NUS.
SHACKLETON, J. (1991) 'A strategic view', *Coombe Lodge Report*, 22, 8, pp. 691–4.

Chapter 5

Staffing and Staff Development

In this chapter, I discuss staff development in the context of the recognition of people as a valuable and valued resource by institutions and funding councils. I explore the implications of national standards for the accreditation of staff training at a time of rapid change. Systems of appointment, induction and promotion are considered as quality issues. Models of appraisal and their application in the promotion of institutional quality are analysed. I discuss models for the organization of the staff development function within the institution and the ways that individual staff development effort and the support of the team and organization may interrelate to enable individuals and the institution to function efficiently and effectively.

The Context for Staff Development

The most expensive resource in colleges and universities is people. The Further Education Unit (FEU, 1993a) suggests that staffing represents 80 per cent of college budgets. Teaching and learning tend to be complex human processes that depend upon the quality of the interaction between the teacher and learner. This in turn depends on well-prepared and well-trained lecturers. The involvement of staff in planning and staff development can feed into the quality of the institution's work and the maintenance of standards.

The funding councils are interested in linking funding to the quality of provision. For example, the Further Education Funding Council (FEFC) has set up a Quality Assessment Committee that will assess institutions and departments against a 5 point scale. Where an institution receives a low rating (4 or 5) on inspection, it will find its future viability a cause for concern. The Higher Education Funding Council has a similar system which it operates across subject groups. Central to both quality assessment systems are the support of teaching and learning, and the competence and scholarship of lecturing staff (see for example, FEFC, 1993).

The funding councils take a keen interest in how the money they provide is spent, focusing especially on quality and efficiency. The Conservative Government of the 1990s aimed to achieve increased efficiency and effectiveness through an element of competition between providers, for instance, through new responsibilities for training given to the Training and Enterprise Councils (TECs). They have also been keen to stimulate consumer demand for a quality service (for instance, through the publication of GCSE and 'A' Level league tables). These developments require colleges and universities to search for ways of increasing (or at least maintaining) quality, while reducing unit resources. Targeted staff development is likely to be a key component of this strategy.

The FEU suggests that incorporation is encouraging colleges to develop more sophisticated approaches to the management of its staff to ensure that they have the skills needed to implement the strategic plan. Since colleges and universities are responsible for managing their own funds, and since these funds are becoming tighter and tighter, staff development policies must become more focused on the needs of the institution and the 'customer', rather than on the needs of the lecturer. Senior managers may decide that the best way of ensuring that staff can further the college's plans and mission is to involve them in formulating these plans. This depends upon organizational structures that encourage involvement and a staff-development strategy that will make such involvement productive.

In Chapter 2, I suggested that colleges and universities may approach the business of human development through the establishment of a culture of continuous change directed at improvement, perhaps in combination with other models, such as investment in people or total quality management. This sort of approach has been developed in response to the need to deliver a new kind of service to new groups of students. The emphasis is therefore on flexibility to meet an uncertain future. The FEU points out that the knowledge and skills to operate this kind of flexibility must permeate the workforce. It can no longer reside exclusively in managers.

National Standards in Staff Development

Staff development in colleges and universities is moving away from being an *ad hoc*, individually oriented affair. It is increasingly seen as part of the quality control process and as a method of enhancing academic standards. Quality audit has made it a more public process and this has led to a sharing of practice. The FEU (1993b and 1993c) suggests that the quality and extent of what is offered by individual institutions is variable and that there is a need for rigour and consistency in standards of various aspects, such as initial teacher training and management.

This has led to an interest in the development of national standards for various aspects of staff development. Within further education, these have tended to focus on National Vocational Qualifications (NVQ), (these are described in more detail in the next chapter) under the Training and Development Lead Body (TDLB) and the Management Charter Initiative (MCI). As yet, there is not a lead body specifically for education, but one seems likely to be developed before long. Interest has been growing in National Standards for Effective Investment in People as an alternative system for accreditation against a national standard. These awards are made after an assessment by a TEC that an institution's staff development system is worthy of public recognition under the Employment Department 'Investors in People Initiative'. (This is described in more detail in Chapter 2). Within higher education national standards are emerging based on the development of programmes of study accredited by the Staff and Educational Development Association (SEDA). SEDA has set up a system for accreditation that involves an examination of course aims, content and assessment to ensure the inclusion of key issues and competences. The further education sector has been fortunate in having the Further Education Staff College (FESC) and the Further Education Unit to disseminate good practice. These are now to be merged into a new body (FEFC, 1994) which is charged with supporting the performance of individual institutions, providing staff development opportunities for governors, lecturers, managers and support staff, researching and disseminating good practice and undertaking curriculum research and development projects.

These professional organizations could do much to ensure that institutional staff development does not become too inward-looking and to provide some sort of national standard of good practice in staff development. Since the new further education organization is also charged with developing and implementing aspects of government policy, such as the National Charter for Further Education (DFE, 1993), it may be tempted to define quality in terms of its financial masters. The way that the Government has set up its funding makes this particularly likely: for instance, the block grant it receives from the FEFC will reduce from 60 per cent

---

Enquiry Task

List the skills and knowledge that you already possess under the following headings:

- doing your present job;
- extending this role in a way that appeals to you; and
- doing a different job within the organization that appeals to you.

What evidence would you be able to present that would convince an outside observer that you have these skills and knowledge?

List evidence you might collect to create a personal development portfolio that might be used in an assessment of competence under the following headings:

	Evidence
• Existing competences	e.g., Qualifications obtained . . .
• Existing performance	e.g., Summary of appraisal interview . . .
• Development opportunities	e.g., Existence of a personal development plan . . .

List any staff development needs that have been revealed by this process using some of the headings below:

- work-based learning or mentoring;
- work shadowing;
- accreditation of existing learning and experience;
- short course or conference;
- long course;
- independent learning programme; and
- other.

Which of these should be your priority?

---

of its income to 20 per cent over three years, and the proportion tied to specific government initiatives will increase from 30 per cent to 50 per cent over the same period.

The advantages of having national standards for staff development is becoming obvious. They provide a common language for describing the human-resource implications of a development plan. They provide a means of defining levels of competence and so a way of describing and assessing competent performance that can be the basis of self-assessment and the analysis of staff development needs. In addition, at a time of increasing quality assessment and quality audit, national standards provide recognizable benchmarks for assessing the adequacy of staff development programmes. Of course, they cannot provide the whole answer to quality questions. Institutions and individuals will continue to have particular staff development needs that may not be answered by reference to national standards.

Management and Teaching Effectiveness

The new focus on quality assessment and the need to promote academic standards has led to a more systematic and professional management structure within institutions. Recent developments, such as the Management Charter Initiative (MCI), indicate a growing awareness that management is an area that requires particular skills and knowledge (FEU, 1993b). The tradition within higher and further education of more or less 'amateur' managers, with little or no formal training or assessment in management (as opposed to a subject) may be coming to an end.

The training of managers has taken various forms in the past. These have included the development of diploma courses in educational management in the post-compulsory education sector, traditional MBA courses, short courses and in-house training initiatives. These are increasingly coming together under the MCI, linked with the NVQ systems, with a variety of competence-based assessments that are suitable for managers at various stages of their career. Some of these are linked to courses and qualifications at a variety of levels from certificate to master's degree. The training that managers require covers a variety of aspects of the job, including operations management, finance, information systems and managing people. It is increasingly expected that managers will be familiar with relevant theories and have clear ideas about how they fit with the needs of their institution. They will be aware of a range of management techniques that might be planned within a given situation (such as SWOT analysis — strengths, weaknesses, opportunities, threats — within strategic planning).

The knowledge of possible and actual systems and procedures that a manager needs is extensive. He or she will need to understand figures and their applications. Numbers will need to be understood as another kind of adjective as well as definers of some sort of truth. Finally, managers need an awareness of the ways that politics and economics affect future possibilities and challenges. The focus on a range of expert knowledge and skill has implications at all levels of the institution. Lecturers who do not acquaint themselves with this context are failing to protect the educational environment of their students. You need this kind of knowledge to argue for resources. You also need it to argue for your educational values. The increase in the technical competence required in management must not disguise it as a value-neutral activity. It is part of your role as a lecturer to demand educationally defensible solutions to practical problems. You also have a responsibility for the sound management of your institution. Research in schools and colleges (e.g., Rutter *et al.*, 1980; Richardson, 1967) repeatedly indicates that successful institutions are those in which staff support each other, involve themselves in planning, are willing to expose and discuss problems and have high expectations of themselves and their students.

Enquiry Task

- List the ways that lecturers can contribute to the management of the institution.
- Discuss your list with an experienced colleague and add to it if necessary.
- Compare your actual contribution to possibilities suggested by the list.
- List management decisions that affect your students to which you have contributed.

Do you contribute sufficiently to the quality of your institution?

The Appointment of Staff

The quality of staff is not just the product of a staff development process, but also involves the management of staffing issues at all levels and at all stages. One of the most crucial stages is that of appointment. A system that does not enable the appointment of the most appropriate person for each particular post represents a serious threat to quality.

The starting point for determining an appointment is likely to be the identification of a particular staffing need. Institutions should have systems of determining need that are not based entirely on the historical staffing complement. Every vacancy that occurs provides the opportunity to review whether a direct replacement is appropriate or whether the opportunity should be taken to change the post or to redirect its cost for other purposes. It is important that the system is both thorough and speedy. Systems that do not include timeliness as a criterion for effectiveness may lead to advertisements being placed at a suboptimum time of the academic year.

A system for determining the need for a particular appointment that is sufficiently discriminating is likely to go a long way to achieving a clear definition of the responsibilities and performance expected from a successful candidate (the job description), and a clear definition of the qualities, experience and qualification that are prerequisite for that performance (the person specification). In drawing these up, care should be taken to include only those aspects that are strictly applicable for the role and to avoid criteria that may be directly or indirectly discriminatory. For example, an upper-age barrier may effectively discriminate against women, since women take a career break to bring up children more often than men, and therefore may have less time to achieve defined experience and qualifications.

The process of application should be clear. Whether the post is to be filled by an internal or external appointment, it should be advertised in a way that will reach the maximum number of the target population. In order to determine what types and placements of advertisement are most productive, recording systems are needed with the facility for fine discrimination. If this evidence is lacking, advertisements for staff in particular subjects or at particular levels may be placed in the wrong journal or at the wrong time.

The selection process should be viewed from the point of view of the candidate as well as from the institution. For instance, an institution that demands several copies of the application material may suggest to potential applicants that it is both mean and highly bureaucratic. In my experience, many institutional application forms are very off-putting and usually seem to have more to do with administrative convenience than with the pursuit of the best candidate for a particular post. Some categories on standard application forms may be irrelevant or intrusive (for instance, questions about marital status — I have often been tempted to reply 'variable'). They seldom fit an individual's curriculum vitae and may discourage talented and busy individuals from applying at all. It may be better to signify in the application details the headings that must be included in an application and accept that they will come in non-standard (but often very revealing) ways. The process of selection should be examined carefully to ensure that it is as fair as possible and likely to reveal the best applicant for the post. Shortlisting may involve a variety of staff. I have observed a short-listing system whereby a range of interested staff are invited to rate (according to an agreed scale) and comment upon applications. This process often reveals problems with particular applications and strengths in others that have been missed by the departmental manager. The process of selecting from a long or short list should not be so elaborate that it intimidates potential candidates, but should be thorough enough to reveal the qualities required. Thus, the selection process for a teaching post may well require the inclusion of a teaching exercise. On the other hand, account should be taken of the difficulty a candidate will find in presenting to a group of 'unknowns' while being assessed at the same time. In my experience, the problems can be minimized by leaving the choice of subject matter to the candidate and by providing clear guidelines as to the length of the session, whether questions will be additional to that time, the number of students within the audience, their level of experience and the audio and visual equipment that will be available in the room.

Interviewers should be clear about their role. Some training or guidance may be needed to ensure fairness and equity. I have found that interviews provide more comparable evidence if each candidate is asked the same questions, these questions are decided upon before the first candidate is interviewed, discussion is left until all candidates have been interviewed and all candidates are invited both to ask questions and to add any additional information that might help their case at the end of the interview. The interview day should be viewed from the point of view of the candidates. It might include an opportunity to discuss each of the courses with the course leader, an introduction to research activity and a tour of the site. This enables the candidates to put the interview questions in a context, and may result in candidates, whether successful or unsuccessful feeling that the institution is a welcoming and high-quality establishment. You may have experienced an interview for a post at an institution that made no effort to make the candidates' day a pleasant and informative one. If so, this experience probably gave you an understanding of some of the ways in which the interview day may enhance or damage the college or university's reputation.

Promoted posts should be treated in the same way as any other. Staff within the institution should have access to clear job and person descriptions and equal opportunities should apply. Senior managers sometimes 'know' who they are going to appoint. This can lead to the temptation to cut corners in the selection process or to write the job and person descriptions so that only that person will apply. Such temptation should be resisted. The process of formulating promotion posts in terms of institutional needs rather than the qualities of a individual staff member is important to quality. The provision of equal opportunities through an open selection process can reveal talents, experience and qualities in a staff member that, even if that person is not yet ready for promotion, may be developed for the future. It is my experience, that women in particular, but also some men, undertake work of great value, but out of the limelight. A closed selection process may yield a senior-management team that consists of people interested in public systems (since this kind of work is documented in committees attended by other senior managers), at the expense of the 'hearts and minds' part of the management role.

The Induction of Staff

A central part of a staff development strategy directed at quality is the induction of new staff. This process should embrace support as well as teaching staff. These groups have interests in common and, perhaps, should experience some aspects of the staff induction programme in common. This common experience could be the start of a process of team building that includes all staff. If the induction process is to start to weld the teaching and support staff into a team, with shared meaning and values, the staff-induction programme should not consist of a series of lecturettes. Some staff-induction programmes feature some of the worst and most boring examples of teaching found in the whole institution.

MacDonald (1992) surveyed fifty-one institutions of higher education to find out about their induction programmes. Few institutions had no induction programme for teaching staff but only twenty-one included all support staff within their induction programme. Fourteen appeared to have no central provision for support staff at all.

The induction process should be designed as carefully as any other programme and subject to the same approval process. This implies that the starting point should be clearly articulated aims and objectives. These should inform the content and timing. Since induction is essentially a process designed to facilitate learning, teaching methods should be explored with the same rigour as with any other programme. Finally, evaluation should be incorporated at the stage of programme design.

The outline above begs the question of whose interests the induction programme is to serve. Some of the interests of the senior management and new staff may be in common: for instance, lecturers and managers will be interested in developing an understanding of teaching, learning and assessment arrangements. Others may not. For instance, teaching staff may not be very interested in the committee system in the first weeks of their appointment (but this may be one of the first things presented to them). Some institutions may be giving unintended messages through their induction programme. For instance, the overt message may be that it is a caring institution, but if the only concerns that are addressed

Enquiry Task

Consider the following list of essential information and knowledge about an institution:

- the names and duties of key staff;
- the management structure of the department and institution;
- the structure, content and assessment of particular programmes;
- the committee system of the institution;
- the institutional mission statement;
- the aims and objectives for particular programmes and departments;
- the institution's and departmental strategic plans;
- action plans for particular programmes;
- the availability of learning and library resources;
- the theoretical model underpinning particular programmes;
- routes for dealing with problems with:
    - teaching hours;
    - student progress or attendance;
    - teaching resources;
- routes for dealing with suggestions for change
    - to the curriculum;
    - to other aspects of policy;
- policies on the following:
    - staff development;
    - appraisal and the probationary period;
    - appointments and promotions;
    - equal opportunities;
    - assessment and marking;
- arrangements for each of the following:
    - car parking;
    - stationery;
    - claiming for travel, materials etc.;
    - how teaching hours are calculated;
    - room booking;
    - catering and staff breaks;
    - phoning;
    - contractual entitlements;
    - lecturer absence; and
    - obtaining financial support.

In discussion with a colleague new to the institution add to this list. Put the list in order of importance to a new member of staff.

Does the order that new staff actually receive information reflect their priorities?

in the programme are institutional ones, with a focus on administrative systems, this is unlikely to be believed.

Everyone's interests will be served by a programme that is carefully timed. A quick 'blast' before term starts is unlikely to make any real contribution to the quality of the institution's work. Staff need particular information before classes start. Perhaps the initial programme should start with that material only. Other elements could then be fed into a programme that might occur across the first year and include taught sessions, discussion groups, open forums for questions or difficulties, mentoring systems, printed materials and finish up with some sort of assessment and evaluation at the end of the first year. Arrangements would need to be made to accommodate teaching and support staff starting at various times during the year. MacDonald found that institutions with well-established staff development units are able to provide a more coherent and elaborate programme than those that rely on lone individuals or departments.

Each of us can have an input to the form of the induction process. It is important to explore current practice and decide whether it is run in the interests of new staff or the institution and whether it addresses the immediate interests and concerns of new staff.

Enquiry Task

Consider the list of essential information and knowledge about an institution that you created in the last enquiry task.

What method of presentation would be most appropriate for each type of information.

Information	*Method of presentation*
e.g.,	
• Names and duties of key staff.	Written in a handbook
• Aims and objectives for	Presented in a lecturette.
a particular programme.	
• Departmental strategic plan etc . . .	Group discussion.

Are the present methods of presentation to new members of staff appropriate?

List suggestions for improvements to the induction programme.
Discuss them with new members of staff.

Find out what is the best route to communicate these to senior managers.

The Purposes of Appraisal

The person and job descriptions that underpin a quality appointment process can act as a starting point for staff appraisal. They will provide the essential blueprint against which self-assessment or other judgments become meaningful. National standards may also be of assistance in specifying job descriptions and identifying skill gaps. They can provide a means by which staff can articulate the skills that they possess and their staff development needs. Such specification and articulation is a necessary prerequisite for each of the models of appraisal described below.

Appraisal can be a central process in the development of staff, depending upon its underlying purpose. The purposes of appraisal can be various. For instance, Evans and Tomlinson (1989) point out that purposes may be related to accountability and control: that is, appraisal may be used as the source of data for making comparisons between people. Where this is the case, the kind of data that will be collected will be the sort that can be easily tabulated and compared: in particular, numerical data. The value of such data for managerial functions stems from its spurious objectivity that makes it is less easy to challenge than narrative types of data. This can be particularly important where the data is used to determine a person's pay. In addition, it provides a basis for decisions that avoid the need to grasp any complexities and is therefore time efficient for a manager dealing with a range of issues and decisions affecting many individuals.

Unfortunately, appraisal based on accountability may work against the development of the individual. This is because the individual has to work within a real and complex world that is not captured by bureaucratic data. For instance, individuals are seldom totally in control of their teaching environment. They rely on colleagues and institutional systems to support them. 'Objective' data on their performance that showed them to be doing relatively well, might be a reflection on their position in the power structure and their ability to command resources to help them meet the objectives set by the institution or the help and support that they received from colleagues. This may go some way to explain the impression that it is easier to gain performance-related pay if you are higher in the institutional management structure.

The issue of appraisal has been linked by the funding councils to that of quality. The Higher Education Funding Council for England (HEFCE) withheld a proportion of its funds to individual institutions until they had in place a system for the allocation of performance-related pay and its award on an individual basis. It seems impossible to allocate performance-related pay without some system of staff appraisal. Since the withholding of performance-related pay from individuals will inevitably be seen as punitive, the linking of it to appraisal suggests a model based on control and top–down judgment. This model of appraisal assumes that variables in education can be controlled: that one 'A' Level group is much like another; that one subject is as easy to teach as another; that all teams are equally cooperative; that the external marketing potential for programmes in different subjects is much the same. Reality is much more complex and varied.

Turner *et al.* (1986) define this kind of appraisal as enabling summative assessments on which basis judgments about tenure and relative levels of individual performance may be made. Such summative judgments may be made on the basis of levels of student performance, observation of teaching, the assessments of teacher knowledge and research expertise as well as more personal aspects such as the perceived attitude of the person and whether they undertake high-profile activities. This kind of appraisal is not only inherently unfair, but also rests on the assumption that people will be motivated by external threats and inducements. It fails to take account of people's emotional needs and perceptions and can thus do much damage to morale. For instance, it seems that most lecturers in further and higher education believe that they are doing well. In reality the vast majority of staff *are* doing a more than satisfactory job: for instance, HMI (1991) found that 90 per cent of teaching across eighteen further education colleges and 90 per cent of higher education teaching was satisfactory or better. Most staff would reckon that a person who was labelled as 'below average' is not doing a good job. By their very nature, rating systems will place half of staff members as 'below average'. Within post-compulsory education, most of these 'below average' lecturers would in fact be perfectly satisfactory. A label of 'below average' will be likely to be extremely demotivating for most them.

In summative systems, it is assumed that staff get better at their job only by their own efforts. The system is designed to produce simple, easily analysed data. The needs of lecturers tend to be complex. Their development needs may be a cocktail that includes emotional support; changes in institutional systems; skill development; reinforcement of team membership and so on. Each staff member's cocktail will be individual and will not be satisfied by a standard appraisal event.

Appraisal may also be introduced to meet political purposes. The political purposes of appraisal relate to the control of behaviour and are more often compatible with accountability than individual professional development. Appraisal can be used to control staff behaviour and to satisfy particular interest groups. The way that this is managed is usually to manipulate the criteria for 'success'. Thus, in an entrepreneurial climate, one criterion for success may be the amount of external funding an individual brought into an institution. Externally imposed performance indicators are central to the use of appraisal for control purposes.

Summative appraisal often rests on the assumption that appraisal is about rooting out incompetence and that lecturers need to be 'found out'. This justifies the imposition of externally determined criteria. Incompetence must certainly be dealt with, but I would maintain that the appraisal process is an inappropriate forum for this. Summative appraisal looks backwards, because the principal function is assessment of performance. The assumption is that lecturers are controllable by managers and that success is the result of individual effort.

The guidelines produced by the Higher Education Quality Council (HEQC, 1994) suggest that all institutions should have an appraisal system. However, far from recommending a system based on judgment and control, it seems to be recommending that the system should be focused on staff development and career progression and be confidential and supportive. It recommends an openness on procedures and outcomes and a culture of support developing from appropriate training for appraisers and appraisees. This approach to quality, based on agreement and supported development, seems at odds with one based around the award or withholding of performance-related pay.

Within a developmental model, staff members themselves, in conversation with their appraisers, identify realistic and appropriate performance indicators, towards which they can work. It thus becomes apparent that professional development models of appraisal are incompatible in a number of respects with purposes of appraisal related to accountability and control. In particular the emphasis is on self-assessment and professionalism rather than external accountability. It relies on an assumption that the purpose of appraisal is to identify and build on competence. Its basis is a trust in the individual and willingness to disclose problems.

The outline of the problems inherent in certain models of appraisal above is not intended to lead you to view appraisal in a negative light. On the contrary, appraisal can be an invaluable aid to lecturer development. It can enable the lecturer to gain enhanced job satisfaction and benefit the institution by targeting development.

It is my contention that developmental appraisal which looks forward, because it is focused on the professionalism of the lecturer within the institutional context, is a highly appropriate staff development tool. It recognizes the complexity and variety of the lecturer's working context and the role of cooperation rather than competition, where the role of team working is often central to real development and change. Developmental appraisal rests on an assumption of individual professionalism that makes an ownership of personal goals an appropriate model.

Enquiry Task

Do you know:

- what criteria are used in the appraisal process in your institution;
- whether appraisees were involved in determining the criteria, structure and purpose of the appraisal system;
- how appraisers are chosen in your institution;
- whether you can influence the choice of your appraiser;
- whether you can influence the agenda;
- whether you can bring your own evidence to the appraisal;
- who has access to the information collected; and
- what happens to the information collected?

Find the answers to any questions where you are not sure.

Systems for Successful Appraisal

Appraisal should be the keystone of staff involvement in institutional quality. It can be a means of developing the quality of student experience or satisfying outside bodies that a system exists for such a purpose. These two ideas can, but need not necessarily, be complementary. In this section, I will discuss the preparation that is needed to ensure that both these requirements are met. My analysis is built on a belief that a developmental model of appraisal is most appropriate for an institution that is genuinely interested in achieving and assuring quality and academic standards.

One of the criticisms of a developmental process of appraisal is that it does not necessarily meet institutional needs. Unless work is undertaken to ensure the staff members' understanding of the institutional context, particularly the institutional resource and strategic context, unrealistic expectations may be raised. People may be disappointed when all the help they identified as necessary does not materialize because of resource constraints or because of other institutional priorities.

The preparation of staff for an appraisal system might start with the relationship between the individual staff member and the mission of the institution. External auditors will expect that the institutional mission permeates the whole process and that it is discussed alongside the aims individual staff identify for their teaching activity. You need to be involved in the institutional and departmental as well as the personal focus of appraisal if you are to get the best out of it. You may find that you do this best if *you* are the one to identify major areas of strengths and weaknesses. Appraisal that is built into the collaborative development of institutional and departmental policy and strategic planning is less likely to become overly focused on the individual needs.

There seem to be certain conditions that facilitate successful appraisal. In particular, communication and clarity of purpose seem to be important. This implies that staff 'ownership' from the start of the design of the appraisal process will aid its effectiveness, but also that there will need to be a system for drawing new staff into that shared understanding in subsequent years. Staff involvement is therefore crucial at all stages, from design to implementation to maturity and review and evaluation, to prevent systems from becoming static and unresponsive to changing needs and staff membership.

A second issue in appraisal is the control of data. Data should be collected only for agreed and defined purposes. Those who will have access to that data should be agreed. You should be sure that any further disclosure of the data collected will occur only with your explicit permission. It is tempting for the manager to take the leading role in determining these guidelines but it may be wise to resist this temptation. If staff do not feel secure in the arrangements of control and confidentiality, they are unlikely to be open about their needs and difficulties and the developmental purpose of the appraisal system may be undermined. It is my experience that staff, if given a voice in these decisions, will often come to the same conclusions as a reasonable manager. I have also found that where the need for disclosure of information to a third party is identified, permission is seldom withheld by the individual. Where the appraisal system is in some way 'owned' by the staff, they have a vested interest in making it work.

It is important that you are clear about what is being appraised. This might centre around your defined role and the aims of the institution or department. This presupposes that the demands of your job are clear and are not subject to unnegotiated 'drift'. This model of appraisal suggests that it is not an 'event', but rather a process that involves you in the preparation of the agenda, preparation of evidence, the interview, recording of the results, agreement of the record and outcomes and finally some follow-up. The process outlined above implies a departmental or institutional culture of evaluation. If you have no evaluative data, you cannot undertake effective self-appraisal. Without evaluation, there is no way of knowing that objectives identified are appropriate or whether they have been achieved.

Appraisal systems may be set up well but fail at any stage because the 'ground rules' have not been kept to by individuals. For instance, vigilance is needed to ensure that there is no cutting of corners in preparation and that rules as to confidentiality or the use of data are not broached. The appraisal itself involves preparation and training for *all* involved and that this preparation and training needs to be built into a continuous system.

Appraisal of Teaching

Appraisal of teaching may link to the purposes of the institution and to the context. The question of what is to be observed is easier to answer if teaching is seen as a performance activity, that may or may not be linked with learning. If it is linked with learning, you need to ask who is best placed to assess the influence of teaching on student learning and how this data might be captured. Since learning is an internal process, you may consider that observation of teaching by a senior manager or colleague is less likely to 'get at' this than the students' own assessment. This does not mean that nothing can be learned from observing teaching. Indeed there seems to be a link between teaching quality and learning outcomes (Entwistle, 1992). The point I am trying to make is that observing teaching can only be indicative, and so it should not be used to make summative judgments on a lecturer's effectiveness. As a developmental tool, it is fine.

Criteria for teaching need to be developed. These may include agreed indicators of good practice in areas such as preparation, communication and organization of teaching events and follow-up and assessment. The value of these indicators may arise as much from the process of discussion by which they are determined as from their use in practice.

Enquiry Task

Think about the evidence about your teaching that you might collect in preparation for an appraisal interview. Decide on what sort of indicators might signify progress or positive action on your part:

Criteria   *Indication of positive action*

e.g., Planning   e.g., 1. Objectives are clearly stated.
                                2. Activities are planned as part of a progressive sequence of learning . . .

List the evidence you might collect in preparation for your next appraisal interview.

Can you relate your performance to the institution's mission and/or development plan?

New teachers are sometimes employed on fixed contracts. They have often been excellent practitioners in their particular academic or work-related sphere and are having to develop new skills. They can find these skills take time to develop. This can make them feel deskilled and very insecure. Those responsible for the observation should recognize that there are many forms of good teaching, lecturers usually believe in what they are doing, all of us find criticism hard to take and all may learn more from praise. Rawnsley (1993) points out that the teaching observed may be affected by factors outside of the lecturer's control; for instance, the nature and location of learning resources and teaching materials available, access to good reprographic facilities and class size.

Given the difficulty, sensitivity and limitations of observation of teaching, it seems humane and sensible to make certain matters subject to discussion with the teaching staff. These include what will be observed, the timing of the observation, the methods to be used, who will undertake the observation, criteria for success and to what uses judgments will be put. In any case, I believe that lecturers should be invited to provide their interpretation of the context and the events occurring during an observation, before verbal or written statements are made about their performance.

Observation of teaching can provide only a fraction of the evidence relating to the quality of teaching provided by an individual. It cannot be the only, or even perhaps the main, yardstick for judgments of the teaching quality of an institution. Nevertheless it cannot and should not be entirely separated from such judgments. It seems to me that institutions that take teaching quality seriously are likely to wish to introduce negotiated and carefully contextualized observation of teaching into their quality control systems.

None of this is likely to have a real effect on the quality of educational provision unless the institution is clear about the purposes of the observation. Perhaps ideally, these purposes might include the identification of shortcomings in the institutional learning and teaching environment and the targeting of support for educational development. If judgments of individuals' performance are to be made, (as opposed to informal feedback to promote self-knowledge of individuals or judgments of institutional arrangements), the institution will need to invest in training for the observers, moderation of standards of judgments and research into what represents good practice in the various contexts to be subject to judgment. This training should be at least as rigorous and well thought-out as that provided by the Office for Standards in Education (OFSTED) for its inspectors.

Enquiry Task

Arrange to video your teaching during one session.
(You could use a fixed camera, or if this is too obtrusive, and you have the right type of camera, ask a colleague or a student to place the camera on his or her knee with the eyepiece facing upward.)

Comment on the following:

- the clarity of your instructions;
- the extent to which students are clear about the purpose, process and intended outcomes of the session;
- the suitability and flexibility of the groupings you use;
- your non-verbal behaviour; and
- the nature of your questioning.

Who talked the most? You? Male students? Female students? Who did not talk at all?

Professional Updating, Quality and Standards

A developmental model of appraisal can only be part of the answer to the problem of professional updating as it relates to quality and standards. The process is too *ad hoc* to amount to a strategy on its own.

The direction of staff development can be a matter for committees, but ultimately it has to be organized and delivered by named individuals. In some institutions, this responsibility rests with heads of department by default, since no body of expertise in staff development and updating in the professional business of the lecturer (course development, teaching, learning, assessment and so on), has been built up and maintained in a systematic way. This seems to me to pose a threat to quality, since significant decisions affecting student experience and the core work of colleges and universities will be made without the benefit of an accumulated expertise within the institution and in the research literature within the field of professional development in post-compulsory education. I am therefore suggesting that staff development is not merely an administrative function, but also an expert professional function, that needs the input of experts employed for that purpose. This does not mean that these experts should not have a dual function, and also contribute to other teaching areas. Indeed, the quality of their work is likely to be enhanced if they experience at first-hand the practical difficulties of coping with a changing context of education in real-life classrooms.

Staff development that embraces quality is not a matter for teaching staff alone. Support staff contribute materially to the students' experience and to the quality of work within the institution. As Taylor (1992) points out, quality affects everyone. Support staff have a strong influence on the effectiveness of time management, budgets and interpersonal relationships within the institution. Unfortunately, Taylor finds that teaching staff are sometimes resistant to the creation of teams that include support staff and with some common staff development. You may wish to consider whether you would wish to promote this kind of development in the interests of the quality of institutional work.

Time Management

The institution has a responsibility to provide an adequate environment, sufficient information and a set of structures and policies in which to work. Within that framework, each of us has a responsibility to manage ourselves effectively and efficiently. Because we are professionals, this management will include the way we use our time.

Stress seems to be a major factor in many lecturers' working lives. In my experience, this is sometimes because the demands of the job have increased, the role is defined more broadly (for instance, to include entrepreneurial activity), and regular gains in productivity are expected (for instance, through increases in group size). The effect is to require lecturers to undertake more work. If they are not to sacrifice their home and leisure life, they have to find more time-efficient ways of operating. It seems likely that lecturers are most effective when they have time for direct teaching, to provide some individual support for students who need it, to give feedback to students, to prepare classes, to evaluate and reflect upon experience and to enjoy themselves.

Time management has two main foci: the management of students' time and the management of the lecturer's time. Lecturers have a special responsibility to help students develop good study habits, including time management. Support for the development of study skills is dealt with in Chapter 4. In addition, you will need to explore the ways that you use teaching time with your students. This time is a scarce and valuable resource and should be used as intensively as possible. Students in classes and tutorials should work hard and fast. You may need to consider how you can encourage them to prepare for taught sessions and to follow up the teaching with independent study and reflection (if only at the level of looking at their notes immediately after a session).

Enquiry Task

Plan a lesson carefully and videotape it (see previous enquiry task for methods).

Answer the following questions:

- How long did each task take?
- Did you ensure that each student experienced changes in pace during the session?
- Were there opportunities for students to help or advise each other?
- Was there any differentiation to take account of the abilities or experiences of students?
- Did you help students structure their time (for instance, did you give them a time limit for a practical exercise)?
- How much time was wasted in routines such as waiting for the class to start, clearing up and so on?
- Did you link the lesson to previous ones?
- How much time did you spend interacting with individuals and groups?
- Was this time focused on particular individuals or groups (for instance, male or female students)?
- If you included practical activity, what arrangements did you make for students who finished before others?

Looking back on your answers to these questions, what aspects of your management of students' time do you need to improve?
List actions you might take.

You may find that managing your own time is a more difficult business. There are a variety of steps that you may consider. In my experience, it is worthwhile to start by defining your main objectives for your life. Some of these may relate to your work and others to other aspects of your life. These are the objectives for your time management (rather than, for example, to work even harder), and like all objectives they should be reviewed regularly. Perhaps the most important qualities in time management are the ability to plan and prioritize and self-discipline. Planning involves deciding in advance how you are going to use your time, and including planned times to deal with the unexpected. This means that you may need to keep long- and short-term 'to do' lists.

It is my experience that tasks take less time if they are done as soon after they arrive as possible. The longer you wait, the more likely it is that some essential element will be missing or that you will have forgotten part of the instructions. This implies that you should not aim to achieve tasks just before deadlines, but rather that they should be done well in advance. If you aim for deadlines, something unexpected may happen and you may end up finishing the task late. The beauty of immediate action, especially for unattractive tasks, is that you waste no energy feeling guilty or in displacement activities. In addition, you will gain lots of 'brownie points' from colleagues and managers for your efficiency.

The ability to undertake most tasks as they arrive depends upon a certain ruthlessness. In my experience it is better to be honest about low-priority tasks. There are some tasks (in my case, reading numerous HEFCE documents about capital funding) that will never be achieved. It is probably better to be honest with yourself and throw them away. There are other occasions when you will need to be assertive and refuse extra work. It may be better to maintain your reputation as a good time manager than to agree to extra tasks and allow the quality of your work to suffer.

Paperwork can eat up lecturers' time and detract from their core work of teaching. I always take a diary and pen to staff pigeon holes. A surprising number of memos can be replied to with a simple 'OK' and your initials scribbled on the original note, rather than creating a carefully scripted reply and a file for the original query. Careful records are important, but much filing may be unnecessary. File things that you may need later to cover your back, documents that do not exist elsewhere in the institution or that you really will need. Otherwise, consider throwing paper away. Unnecessary filing is not only time consuming, it also makes essential documents harder to find. Keeping paper in order while you are dealing with it is an important aspect of time management. I have a date-ordered pile on my desk, including papers for committees coming up and so on. This ensures that no unnecessary filing is undertaken, but that papers being processed are easily found. One way you can contribute to the quality of the institution's work is to avoid writing unnecessary memos yourself. Memos create work for others, so perhaps you should avoid writing memos unless you are wishing to create a record, to remind or to inform. Any matter that requires discussion or that is controversial is likely to be dealt with in a more time-efficient way by discussion, either face to face or on the phone.

Work tends to be achieved more efficiently if you are not interrupted. For this reason you may need to restrict your availability to students and others to particular times. An open-door policy may be 'nice', but it is a thief of time. You may also need strategies for dealing with talkative colleagues. It may be better to talk to them on the phone or in their room. It is easier to end a phone call or leave someone else's study than to eject them from your own room.

The final skill in time management is that of delegation. The extent to which you delegate tasks to others depends upon your position in the hierarchy, but also on your ability to trust others. You might look for tasks that could be delegated to students. Many routine tasks could be undertaken in this way. You might also think about delegating some higher-order tasks. For example, I have found that the 'expert' student gains as much from tutoring a peer who is experiencing difficulty with a particular concept as the student with the learning need. I have also explored issues such as peer-marking of work (perhaps, spot-moderated by the lecturer). Assessment is often very expensive in lecturer's time. For any one assignment, you might consider what students could learn from making it a group assignment, from providing an abstract or summary of the main issues, from doing a short presentation or from peer-marking. Each of these alternative forms tends to be more time-efficient than the traditional individual essay marked by the lecturer and, in some circumstances, contributes more to the quality of student learning. Time-efficient assessment methods are discussed in more detail in Chapter 6.

Enquiry Task

List the things that interfere with your management of time. List the ways you cope with them.

What are the costs and benefits of each of these methods?

Methods of coping	*Benefits*	*Costs*
e.g., Overworking	Admiration of others.	Continual tiredness.
	Maintains self-image	Neglect of family.
	as competent worker.	Lack of outside interests.

Keep a log of the way that you use your time for a week.
What have you learned about your time management from this *log*?

Are there things you might do that would transform the situation?

Management of Self and Others

Poor time management leads to stress but stress may have a number of other causes. It may be produced by feelings of frustration, for instance, where a head of department restricts developments you feel are necessary. The effects of stress may be various. You may find yourself obsessed with thoughts of work, perhaps to the extent that you cannot sleep. You may find yourself experiencing curious emotions, perhaps panic attacks. On the other hand, you might develop physical symptoms of stress, perhaps migraines, stomach upsets or continuous infections. The important thing is to recognize the symptoms of stress and to deal with them. Levels of stress that affect your physical and mental wellbeing should not be accepted in the long-term. The ultimate symptoms of stress are breakdown in relationships and in mental and physical health. No job is worth this level of suffering. Even at a purely instrumental level, stress is dysfunctional and leads to lower quality work. The solution to stressful situations is not always obvious, but a starting point may be to identify and then analyse the causes of the stress.

Lawrence (1988) states that an important factor in people's level of achievement is how they feel. Feelings of low self-esteem can be a cause of stress and lead to a vicious circle of low self-esteem and a lack of achievement. One way out of this problem is to explore the sources of your self-esteem. Lawrence found that high self-esteem may be related to the development of skills in common with counselling skills: for example, skills of communication, listening skills, the ability to empathize with others and the ability to recognize and focus on our own strengths.

Enquiry Task

List:

- things that you like about yourself;
- things your students like about you;
- times when you work best in the classroom;
- your professional ambitions; and
- the skills you have.

From these lists, define your best qualities. How are you going to value and advertise these from now on?

You will be fortunate if your interaction with others is never a source of stress. Most of us find that other people are major stress factors. One of the ways of coping is to analyse the nature of the transaction you are having with these people, and to decide whether you need to change the way these transactions are framed or react to them differently. Ways of analysing transactions and of dealing with problems through assertion are described in Ashcroft and Foreman-Peck (1994).

The quality of your work is likely to be affected very directly by your interactions with certain individuals. In some cases, this influence will be entirely beneficial. In this case you need to value it and find ways of preserving the relationship. In others, things have gone wrong for one reason or another. Where this has happened, you may need to take action in your own interests and in the interests of the institution.

One model of understanding and managing your interactions with others is provided by transactional analysis. Berne (1964) and Harris (1967) provide useful guides to this process. Transactional analysis is based on the idea that each of us learns to interact with others through the kind of attention we receive as a child. Some of us received positive 'strokes' (or units of attention) in the form of unconditional regard. For others, positive attention was conditional on approved behaviour. The need for strokes, and strokes of a particular kind, persists into adulthood. You may find that your interactions with others do not provide you with the kind of positive strokes you need. If this is the case, you will need to be assertive and seek them out. Alternatively, you may not be providing others with the positive regard they need. If this is the case, you may find that your relationships with them improves dramatically if you find opportunities for communicating positive regard.

Some people may lack experience of positive strokes of any kind. They may have grown up with a preponderance of negative strokes. This produces a double-bind for these people involving a very negative self-image, and a tendency to reject or discount any positive feedback they receive. If you often deflect praise or look for ulterior motives in those who express a good opinion of you, you may need to consider the effects of this behaviour on others, and to learn to accept positive strokes.

Another set of ideas contained within transactional analysis is the notion of a life 'script' that determines how you define the world and how you behave. Each of us may be restricted or liberated by a particular set of messages we learned about ourselves when we were young. We may learn that it is either acceptable or not acceptable to exist, be healthy, succeed, feel emotion and so on. Some 'useful' messages can become too extreme: for instance, we may learn to have high standards, or that we must be perfect; that we should be helpful or that we should always please others rather than ourselves. One way to improve our interactions with others is to understand and take account of their life scripts. Another is to find out about our own and decide to change them if necessary.

The theory underpinning transactional analysis describes each of us as having the capacity to act as a 'parent', 'adult' and 'child'. The parent in us is drawn upon when we care for others or wish to criticize or control them. The adult is drawn upon when we are analysing or questioning. The child is the emotional part of ourselves, drawn upon when we cry, laugh, have fun, sulk and so on. Problems in interactions can occur when people habitually interact with us using a mode with which we feel uncomfortable. For instance, there are some managers who feel most comfortable in the parent mode. You may find that the relationship with them works well when you need comfort or help, but when you want to be taken seriously, you may find yourself feeling frustrated without knowing why.

Your transactions with others may be parallel, where both parties are using the same mode (for example, child–child, or adult–adult). Alternatively, transactions may be complementary, where people are operating in different modes, but that sustain each other (for example, child–parent). Parallel and complementary transactions tend to be self-sustaining and last for some time. On the other hand, transactions may be referred to as crossed. Crossed transactions occur when people are in different, non-complementary modes (for example, child–adult, or adult–parent). Crossed transactions often break down in confusion or anger.

You may find it useful to analyse transactions occurring in relationships that are not going well to see if you are being pulled into a complementary transaction you do not want (in the instance above, parent–child) or into crossed transactions (for instance where you approach someone with an 'adult' query — 'How can we solve this problem?', and receive an inappropriate response, such as 'The problem is your fault.' — a 'parent' response).

Where, for one reason or another, your interactions with others are not going well and you wish to change them, you may find it helpful to employ assertiveness techniques. Assertiveness should be distinguished from aggression. It does not imply threats or intimidation, but rather open, honest and direct communication that recognizes your own rights and boundaries and those of other people. Assertiveness is not about always getting your own way, but rather making your wishes and opinions clear so that they are taken into account.

Most assertive statements use the word 'I'. They involve saying what you need to say and nothing else, recognizing other people's position but nevertheless

---

Enquiry Task

Analyse your institution in terms of:

Strokes	Is it stroke starved? What kinds of stroke are given?
Messages	What positive messages are given to employees? What negative ones are also given?
Managers	In interaction with you, do they have a favourite mode (child, adult or parent)?

---

stating your own and the ability to give and to receive criticisms and praise without a defensive reaction. Assertiveness does not come easily to many people. If this is the case with you, you may need to ask for time before you respond to a request or statement in order to formulate an unambiguous reply that states your position without any get-out clauses.

Most change in education is not as beneficial as its supporters hope nor as extreme as its detractors fear. This is because of powerful disincentives to people to really change their practice. Implementing change is a stressful business that usually requires careful preparation and training. All change involves both loss and risk. Familiarity with the ways of doing things has benefits. Change involves a loss of these benefits. In addition, most practice, even bad practice, has some rewards built into it, that are likely to disappear with change. There is always a risk with change. Unexpected difficulties may arise, planning assumptions may be wrong or the situation may change. In any case, performance may deteriorate in the early stages of change, until people become practised and skilful in the new situation.

Given the real difficulties of change in human situations, effective management will involve the development of a number of skills and processes. The most important skill is the ability to enable others to feel some ownership of the developments envisaged. The importance of real and extensive consultation cannot easily be overemphasized. Consultation is a skilful business, if it is to be seen to make a difference to institutional or departmental planning, but it will help to establish ownership and ensure that the proposed change is as free from unexpected snags as is possible. Effective consultation depends on a climate of free information. All concerned must understand the reasons for change and the constraints under which the planning must take place.

Effective development also depends on well-developed interpersonal skills. People need to have a clear view of their roles and responsibilities. They need to feel that they are valued and that the work done in the past is not dismissed. It is essential to understand the human consequences of development and the threat that it imposes of stress and loss of status. If you are involved in change you may need to identify the support you need. Part of the skill of managing change is the assessment and effective use of the skills available within the staff team and the development of those lacking through staff development. Change involves growth. All staff will not possess the ideal qualities to manage aspects of the planned change, but given training, support and opportunity, many will develop them.

People's feelings are part of reality. It is therefore not rational to ignore emotion in the management of change. It is essential that individuals are encouraged to share the aims of institutional development and to contribute to the planning process. Imposed change may seem to be quicker on the surface, but in the longer run it will lead to cynicism. The opportunities for sabotage or passive non-compliance are too great in education to enable change to be forced. If people are to identify with the need for particular developments, their rationale must be kept constantly in sight. The change agent must be prepared to go back to first principles as often as is necessary.

Effective development therefore takes time and this must be accepted. Good consultation processes help to identify the support available that can then be built upon. Inflexible institutional systems will frustrate this process. It is essential to think about and plan for the 'ripple' effect of change in one area of an institution on other systems and to ensure that aspects that are working well are not destabilized. This implies that the long-term consequences of action are taken into account and that there is a strategic view of the development.

Summary

People are an institution's most valuable resource and therefore their management is a central quality issue at a time of reducing unit funding.

National standards for staff development programmes, based on NVQ and SEDA accreditation are emerging.

Management at a time of rapid change has become a more skilful business, requiring training and knowledge at all levels of the institution.

Systems of appointment and promotion are important quality issues that need careful planning. Both should be non-discriminatory, open and based on person and job descriptions. The process of selection should be tailored to the requirements of the post and should provide a good image for the institution.

The induction of staff should be part of a policy for quality that embraces teaching and support staff. The content of any induction programme should be carefully planned to meet the interests of the institution and of the new member of staff.

Appraisal is an important tool in the development of staffing quality and the identification of staff development priorities. The purposes of appraisal may include accountability and control. Models based on these purposes tend to:

- look backward, because their principal function is assessment of performance;
- depend on easily measured and simple data;
- assume that lecturers are mainly motivated extrinsically and are controllable by managers;

- assume that success is the result of individual effort; and
- assume that goals should be set externally.

On the other hand, developmental appraisal:

- looks forward, because it is focused on professional development;
- reflects the complexity and variety of the lecturer's working context;
- is cooperative and recognizes the role of team working;
- builds on the complexity of internal and external motivation that underpins the effectiveness of most lecturers;
- assumes an individual professionalism; and
- encourages the ownership of personal goals.

Entry for your Reflective Diary

Decide on how you would like your career to develop over the next five years. This might be in terms of the development of particular skills to enhance your work as a teacher, the initiation of particular developments within the institution, a promotion you might want or change of job. Write about what it is about the desired change that appeals to you.

Draw up a fish-tail analysis of the development steps you will need to take:

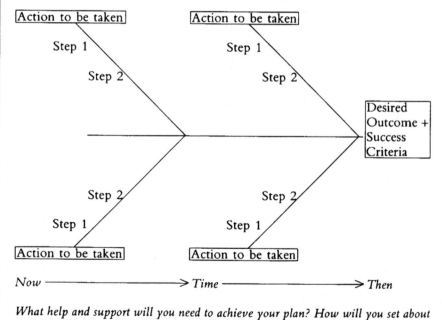

What help and support will you need to achieve your plan? How will you set about securing it?

The appraisal of teaching raises important issues. It is a useful tool in the personal improvement of professional practice, but a more public use of the observation of teaching raises problems of criteria and reliability of judgments.

Individual professional development cannot solve all staff development problems. Institutions are increasingly employing staff development experts and creating coordinated policies and programmes for teaching and support staff, linked to strategic planning.

Each of us has a responsibility to manage ourselves effectively and efficiently. Because we are professionals, this management will include the way we use our time. Lecturers can help students structure their time and take steps to use teaching time as intensively as possible. The lecturer's own time management should embrace planning, prioritization, self-discipline, managing paperwork and delegation. Time management can be a source of stress but stress may also have other causes including low self-esteem and patterns of interaction with others. An analysis of these causes can make the situation easier to cope with and sometimes suggest solutions to it.

Teamwork is essential for effective change. It relies on a number of skills and processes including:

- access to information;
- consultation;
- interpersonal skills;
- empathy; and
- time.

Notes
Annotated List of Suggested Reading

The New Academic, Birmingham, Staff Development and Educational Development Association.
This termly journal was relaunched in 1994. It publishes a range of short accessible papers, including case-study material, covering staff and educational development issues within higher education. Much of the material is closely related to teaching, learning and assessment practice and could be applied equally well within the further-education context. It is also very inexpensive and so probably makes the best candidate for individual subscription were you to subscribe to one journal only. (More details available from: Jill Brookes, SEDA Administrator, Gala House, 3, Raglan House, Edgbaston, Birmingham, B5 7RA.)

References

ASHCROFT, K. and FOREMAN-PECK, L. (1994) *Managing Teaching and Learning in Further and Higher Education*, London, Falmer Press.
BERNE, E. (1964) *Games People Play*, Harmondsworth, Penguin.
BROWN, S., JONES G. and RAWNSLEY, S. (Eds) (1993) *SCED Paper 79: Observing Teaching*, Birmingham, SCED.
DFE (1993) *Further Choice and Quality: The Charter for Further Education*, London, DFE.
ENTWISTLE, N. (1992) *The Impact of Teaching on Learning Outcomes in Higher Education, A Literature Review*, CVCP.

EVANS, A. and TOMLINSON, J. (1989) 'Teacher appraisal: An overview', *Teacher Appraisal: A Nationwide Approach*, London, Jessica Kingsley Pubs.

FURTHER EDUCATION FUNDING COUNCIL (1993) *Circular 93/28. Assessing Achievement*, Coventry, FEFC.

FURTHER EDUCATION FUNDING COUNCIL (1994) *Council News. No. 15*, 20 June, FEFC.

FURTHER EDUCATION UNIT (1993a) *Standards in Education: Using National Standards for Human Resource Management and Development in Further Education. 1 Laying the Foundations*, London, FEU.

FURTHER EDUCATION UNIT (1993b) *Standards in Education: Using National Standards for Human Resource Management and Development in Further Education. 4 Standards-Based Management Development*, London, FEU.

FURTHER EDUCATION UNIT (1993c) *Standards in Education: Using National Standards for Human Resource Management and Development in Further Education. 5 Standards-Based Initial Teacher Training*, London, FEU.

HARRIS, T. (1967) *I'm OK — You're OK*, London, Pan.

HIGHER EDUCATION QUALITY COUNCIL (1994) *Guidelines on Quality Assurance*, London, HEQC.

HMI (1991) *Standards in Education 1989–1990: The Annual Report of HM Senior Chief Inspector of Schools*, London, HMI/DES.

LAWRENCE, D. (1988) *Enhancing Self-Esteem in the Classroom*, London, Paul Chapman.

MACDONALD, L. (1992) 'Induction events for academic staff: Provision and timing', *SHRE Staff Development Group Newsletter*, December, 29, pp. 7–10.

RAWNSLEY, S. (1993) 'Observing teaching', *Observing Teaching: Standing Conference on Educational Development. Occasional Paper 70*, Birmingham, SCED, October.

RICHARDSON, E. (1967) *The Environment of Learning: Conflict and Understanding in the Secondary School*, London, Nelson.

RUTTER, M., MAUGHAN, B., MORTIMORE, P. and OUSTON, J. (1980) 'Fifteen Thousand Hours', in BUSH, T., GLATTER, R., GOODEY, J. and RICHES, C. *Approaches to School Management*, London, Harper and Row.

TAYLOR, J. (1992) 'Staff development at University College London', *SHRE Staff Development Group Newsletter*, December, 29, pp. 6–7.

TURNER, G., NUTTALL, D. and CLIFT, P. (1986) 'Staff appraisal', in HOYLE, E. and MCMAHON, A. (Eds) *The Management of Schools*, London, Kogan Page.

Chapter 6

Assessment and Evaluation

In this chapter, I discuss the influence of the political and funding context upon assessment in colleges and universities[1]. I identify some of the principles of assessment which you may wish to retain in any specification of the curriculum or organizational structure. These principles indicate what is meant by quality assessment. I explore forms of assessment and evaluation and what might constitute good practice from the point of view of the student, lecturer, institution and outside accrediting body.

Background

There has been a plethora of qualifications available within further education for some time. These have included General Certificate in Education (GCE) at Ordinary Level ('O' Level) and at Advanced level ('A' Level), as well as a number of vocational qualifications available at a variety of levels, such as those accredited by the Business and Technical Educational Council (BTEC), the City and Guilds and the Royal Society of Arts (RSA).

In the UK, during the 1980s and 1990s there was a move away from traditional academic qualifications, towards more competence-based approaches. Thus, at the end of compulsory schooling, GCE 'O' Level has given way to the General Certificate in Secondary Education (GCSE), with a more practical, less academic approach. At the same time, sub-GCSE, GCSE and 'A' Level equivalent National Vocational Qualifications (NVQ Level 1, 2 and 3) are becoming more popular. There is continuing controversy over the relatively narrow and academic GCE 'A' Level, the traditional university entrance examination. Students are increasingly attracted to the vocationally oriented General National Vocational Qualification (GNVQ), that, at level 3, is the equivalent of 'A' Level.

While GCSE and 'A' Level have remained examination- and content-focused, the newer qualifications are centred around the assessment of competence. In the case of NVQ, this competence is occupational competence, usually in workplace or simulated workplace settings. The GNVQ also includes academic competence. The point of these qualifications is to assess skills (especially employment-related skills), rather than to develop knowledge for its own value or interest.

The number of students in the UK entering higher education to take degrees or other qualifications is increasing. They are coming with a wider variety of background and experience. Since there are no resources to extend courses and establish a common foundation, lecturers in higher education have started to adapt their expectations and the programmes they offer.

Universities and colleges are increasingly seeing employers, the Government and students as their customers. Since the vast majority of their funding come through these three sources, they are interested in meeting their needs. The Government is increasingly interested in higher and further education as an engine for growth in the economy. Employers are interested in making links with universities as graduate employers and collaborators in research. Students are concerned about their career prospects in a static or shrinking job market.

At the same time, the binary divide between the polytechnics (often focused on applied subject study) and the older universities (more often associated with 'pure' study of disciplines) has disappeared. Applied, work-related programmes at higher education level are therefore primarily located within the university sector. As a result, their appropriateness as a focus for higher education is no longer in question. It is therefore unsurprising that many universities are taking employability and the notion of transferable skill development seriously in their programmes.

The move to competence-based qualifications and the associated shift in students' entry profiles must have an effect, not only on the content of the curriculum in higher education, but also on the way it is assessed. It seems likely that there will be continuing pressure on higher education to strike a balance between meeting the needs of employers and providing a general education.

At further and higher education levels there have also been a number of curriculum initiatives (such as work-based learning, active learning sets, supported independent learning using computers, records of achievement, syndicate work and peer tutoring), that have entailed new forms of assessment and a broadening of the range of assessment methods that a student typically encounters. There is a trend to promote student autonomy in learning and assessment, partly because of increased student numbers, but also in response to student diversity and research into learning.

Implications of the New Context for Assessment

Lecturers in higher and further education are being required to reconsider their assessment practices. I have already introduced some of the policies that are driving change within the UK. The recent White Paper 'Competitiveness: Helping Business to Win' (Department for Education, 1994), summarizes the progress made so far. There are now 500 NVQs available covering 150 occupations. In these, assessment is based on observable competences. It appears that employers are recognizing the benefits of NVQs.

The White Paper sets out the goal of proper recognition of NVQs by universities. It states that credit should be given for vocational qualifications when people wish to pursue academic studies, and vice versa. The other area of rapid expansion has been the GNVQs. These differ from NVQs in that core skills of literacy and numeracy and aspects of knowledge and understanding are included in the assessment. In May 1994, there were 80,000 students on courses leading to GNVQs. The Government's aim is that by 1997, four out of five young people reach level 2, and that by 2000, 50 per cent should reach NVQ level 3.

These developments have implications for teaching methods and assessment strategies. The structure of GNVQ, assessment methods and the learning required differ radically from traditional 'A' Level courses. GNVQs are activity-, rather than knowledge-focused. They require the development of core skills through experiential and collaborative learning. Knowledge has to be actively sought rather than passively given. Assessment is through the validation of evidence against set criteria. This evidence is built up through a portfolio from which the summary statements of the National Record of Achievement are derived. Lecturers are trained to be assessors and validators.

In pursuit of parity of esteem between academic and vocational qualifications, the Government is encouraging universities to assess the implications of vocational qualifications for admissions policy and the content and foci of their courses. There are now incentives for universities to accredit undergraduate and postgraduate qualifications through the NVQ systems (at levels 4 and 5). For instance, students undertaking postgraduate NVQ programmes can obtain tax relief on their fees.

The move to encourage higher education involvement with the NVQ system is motivated by the desire to establish the outcome of education and training with precision and a 'market' in educational and training provision. New definitions of 'quality' are emerging as a result of the emphasis on vocationally oriented qualifications that are more skill-focused, more oriented to employability and less related to the needs of particular disciplines or the transmission of 'high' culture.

Discussion is under way about a new general diploma for 16-year-olds who gain a mixture of academic and vocational qualifications. This, together with the possibility of the introduction of education or training credits for all 16–18-year-olds and vocational GCSEs for 14–16-year-olds, opens the way to a vocational route starting from the age of 14.

Enquiry Task

An implication of the increased diversity of students' entry profile is that not all will be ready to benefit from their courses in terms of background knowledge or independent study skills. Another implication is that an increasing number of students will be used to active modes of course delivery.

Find out what two contrasting departments in your institution do to ensure that students on entry have achieved the minimum level of the following skills and knowledge that they will need to benefit from the programmes on offer to them:

- study skills;
- literacy skills;
- numeracy skills;
- knowledge base;
- collaborative learning skills; and
- information technology skills.

Are any of these areas neglected in the entry criteria?

If so, find out:

- if they are dealt with in a systematic way within the programmes; and
- how the learning experience the students are offered takes account of students' differing levels of experience and ability.

Principles of Assessment

As with aspects of higher and further education, what we understand by quality in assessment is governed by values: our own and those espoused by the institution and those involved in quality assessment. These determine what is assessed, why it is assessed, for whose purpose assessment is carried out and the conduct of assessments.

Assessment should be related to the value statements of the programme: its aims and objectives. As a general principle, the purpose of assessment is to enable students to demonstrate that they have fulfilled the objectives of a particular programme of study and that they have achieved the standard required for the award they seek. Thus, how far the assessments are congruent with the course content and processes (how valid they are) is an important criterion in assessing the quality of an assessment scheme.

It has been recognized by Marton and Saljo (1984) and Ramsden (1992) that assessment schemes have an important effect on the way in which students approach their studies. Some areas of assessment encouraged by the new vocational framework for education, such as higher-order communication skills, are appropriate to higher education and have implications for the social organization of courses. In a scheme of high quality one would expect to see a reflection of the kind of learning required of the student on the course. In higher education, and in much of further education, this would undoubtedly involve the use of higher cognitive processes, rather than simple recall.

Another criterion by which we may judge the quality of an assessment scheme is its coherence across the department or lecturing team. Innovations in assessment may be driven by the learning needs of a more varied student body or by moves encouraged by outside agencies (such as the integration of the NVQ framework). However, as with most innovative work, there is a need for departmental commitment. The energy and commitment of individuals is important in the success of innovation, but it is seldom sufficient. Otter (1992) suggests that innovations by individual lecturers are likely to have limited impact or to fail altogether.

Ideally, assessment should enhance learning. This criterion may be particularly pertinent within changing course structures. Modularization may be taken as an example. This (like semesterization, open learning and mixed-mode forms of course delivery) is usually motivated by the ideal of increased student choice in their pattern of study. However, without careful consideration of the relationship between teaching, learning and assessment, the quality of learning may be sacrificed to greater flexibility. Summative and formative assessment points may be more frequent on modular schemes, presenting a danger that students may be over-assessed or may not have time to reflect on, and consolidate, their learning before it is assessed and they move on to the next module. Some disciplines and the development of certain personal qualities may be best approached through linear progression; through a series of concepts which are carefully ordered and assessed sequentially. The extra pressure put on students in some modular structures and the difficulty in building on students' prior learning (since each student follows his or her individual programme), may encourage surface rather than deep learning (see Chapter 3). As with many problems, careful planning and minor modifications to the structure can minimize the difficulties if they are recognized at the course design stage.

A quality assessment scheme should be clear to the students. It is important that students have access to formal regulations, which set out what is expected of students in (for example) the submission of work to deadlines. Where assessments take unfamiliar forms (such as a reflective diary or syndicate working), you will need to take particular care to set out their rationale. This may seem obvious but students are sometimes confused about what they have to do, when they have to do it and its relevance to their learning.

Purposes of Assessment

The purposes of assessment are closely related to those of education. Atkins *et al.* (1993) define the first purpose of education as the provision of an educational experience of intrinsic value in its own right: for example, the development of a trained mind and attitudes conducive to lifelong learning. They explore the extent that these can be assessed within various course structures.

The second purpose they identify is the preparation for knowledge creation in a defined field (learning the 'discipline'). Atkins *et al.*, recognize that the value of this purpose for all students is now being questioned. This leads to a debate about the appropriateness of various traditional assessment methods for many students, and in particular, the essay and examination.

Vocational preparation is the other main purpose of education. This purpose requires a debate about the appropriate weighting for assessment of competence versus professional understanding. The overarching purpose of assessment is to measure a student's achievement relative to that of others at that level, in order to provide information for a variety of purposes. This relates to the student by enriching learning, signposting progression or enabling entry to higher-level qualification or appropriate employment. It also relates to the bureaucratic functions of institutions. These include awarding qualifications with confidence in their standards, signalling 'good' and 'not so good' performance in departments and communicating the relative standards achieved in the institution to the outside world and funding bodies (for instance, through the publication of league tables of 'A' Level results).

Students need to know the purposes of particular forms of assessment that are used. Most will be familiar with the summative kind where a judgment about the students' achievement is made and counts towards a qualification or in some other way (such as an entry requirement to the second year of a programme). Summative assessments usually come at the end of a course or unit of study. They are not necessarily intended to be a part of the students' learning.

Forms of assessment which provide information primarily for the student as an aid to the students' development and progression in learning are called formative (or diagnostic) assessment. These assessments are often in the form of course assignments. The marking of these provide feedback to students that they can utilize to work on weaknesses and build on strengths. Formative assessment is part of good course design. Formative assessments are not always given weight by students because they are not seen to 'count'. It may help if they relate clearly to the students' objectives: for instance, to summative assessment or employability.

Quality schemes are likely to include a range of different types of assessment. One form of assessment is unlikely to capture the extent of a student's relevant

The Lecturer's Guide to Quality and Standards in Colleges and Universities

---

Enquiry Task

The following categories of abilities and attitudes of individual students are taken from Atkins *et al.* (1993).

Think about a programme you teach.
Which of the abilities and attitudes below are of relevance to the course?
Which are actually assessed?

Cognitive Learning

- Verbal skills: (e.g., listening, reading, writing);
- Quantitative skills (e.g., statistical data or information technology);
- Substantive knowledge (e.g., cultural heritage or subject knowledge);
- Rationality (e.g., logical thinking, analysis and synthesis);
- Intellectual perspective (e.g., appreciation of cultural diversity);
- Aesthetic sensibility (e.g., knowledge or responsiveness to the arts);
- Creativity (e.g., imagination and originality in formulating hypotheses, ideas or works of art);
- Intellectual integrity (e.g., truthfulness, conscientiousness and accuracy in enquiry); and
- Lifelong learning (e.g., awareness of value of education, ability to learn independently, ability to locate information).

Emotional and Moral Development

- Self-awareness (e.g., knowledge of strengths and weaknesses);
- Psychological well-being (e.g., sensitivity and ability to cope with deep feeling, self-confidence, ability to deal with life's difficulties);
- Human understanding (e.g., capacity for empathy, compassion and respect to others, ability to cooperate);
- Values and morals (e.g., awareness of moral issues and traditions, personal set of moral principles); and
- Religion (e.g., awareness and respect for varieties of religious thought).

Practical Competence

- Traits of value in practical affairs generally (e.g., ability to apply knowledge and negotiate, motivation, initiative, resourcefulness);
- Leadership (e.g., capacity to assume authority and to seek advice);
- Citizenship (e.g., commitment to democracy; knowledge of major systems of government; awareness of social issues);
- Work and careers (e.g., awareness of needs of workplaces; knowledge and ability to make sound career decisions, employability skills);
- Family life (e.g., personal qualities relevant to family life);
- Leisure (e.g., appropriate balance between work and leisure); and
- Health (e.g., understanding basic principles of physical and mental health, participation in physical recreation).

Are any aspects under- or over-assessed?

Which abilities and attitudes are prerequisite for reflective practice?

---

knowledge, skills, understanding and competences or all the aims of a programme. This implies that a variety of criteria should be published. These can send important messages to students and staff about the learning intentions of the course.

Clear specification of objectives or learning outcomes opens the possibility that students may be given a choice over forms of assessment. This allows students more supported autonomy and responsibility for their learning provided they meet certain performance criteria. Students can structure their learning according to their interests and preferred way of working. Alternatively, the student may be given control over the timing of assessment, as in the NVQ scheme, where candidates cannot choose the form of the assessment, but they can decide to take assessments when they are ready and keep taking them until they have achieved the requisite standard. However, choosing different forms or times of assessment raises questions about the reliability of assessments. Standardization of markers responses is easier if assessment occurs in standard situations, at a standard time and with a standard task. Judgment about the quality of assessment schemes are bound to be more controversial where the student, rather than the assessor, is given control over one or more of these aspects.

Assessment Schemes can help students to pace their study. In reality, students often complain that assessments 'bunch'. Where the assessment requirements on course components are not well spaced, formative assessment work is likely to be the first aspect to suffer. Students should not have to cope with deadlines that have been set without consultation between lecturers teaching on the same scheme or regard to the teaching programme. The timing and clustering of assessments is clearly an important factor in allowing students the intellectual space to engage in deep learning.

Forms of Assessment and Quality Criteria

I have outlined criteria above that you might use in judging the quality of assessment arrangements and their relationship to the purposes of assessment. Each criterion can be used to evaluate the worth of assessment arrangements and different forms of assessment. I have implied that a major principle by which assessment arrangements and methods should be judged is its contribution to the quality of student learning. This may be considered from the point of view of process and outcome. I have argued elsewhere that the kind of learning we should be aspiring to is based on the Reflective Practitioner Model (Ashcroft and Foreman-Peck, 1994). In other words, assessment should encourage the development of an open-minded, committed and responsible approach to study.

This ideal is related to a developing understanding of the problematic nature of knowledge, the necessity to look at the long-term consequences of actions, to consider actions and ideas in terms of their underpinning values (and not merely their immediate utility), and to be committed to open-mindedness and responsibility as two guiding principles. These qualities go beyond 'deep learning', but I would argue that they underpin quality in learning at further or higher education level. The teaching methods implied by this model are based on enquiry, research and debate. This suggests that assessment methods should reflect these processes.

There seems to be a consensus of opinion at the moment that some professions and levels of study require an extensive knowledge-base and the ability to

Enquiry Task

Construct an interview schedule to find out about aspects of the experience of students within your institution related to:

The pattern of assessment
    e.g., Are the students given a termly or yearly schedule of all the assignments dates for their programme?
    Are the students told on entry or during induction about the various forms of assessment within their programme of study?
    etc . . .

The rationale for assessments
    e.g., Do the students know how each assignment relates to particular course objectives?
    Do the students know what skills were being looked for in the last assignment they completed?
    etc . . .

Regulations covering late submission, resubmission, plagiarism and cheating
    e.g., Do the students know what they should do if they are too ill to complete an assignment?
    What actions are defined as plagiarism?
    etc . . .

Marking scheme, criteria for assessment, weighting of marks
    e.g., Do the students have access to published criteria for marking assignments?
    Do the students know how much individual assignments count towards their final qualification?
    etc . . .

Use the schedule to interview two or three students.

Use what you have learned from this exercise to create a checklist of good practice in the construction of assessment schemes that would be relevant to your department.

Discuss your checklist with your head of department or course leader.

perform in non-routine circumstances using judgment. These situations are in some sense unspecifiable. At the moment there seems to be little agreement about how to translate these characteristics into a competence framework. Below I look at a selection of assessment methods and discuss them in terms of some of the criteria for quality outlined above:

Objective Tests

Objective tests have pre-specified answers. They may be marked by computer. They seem to be most useful where a large amount of information has to be assimilated. The disadvantage of such tests is that they generally require recall, rather than the exercise of judgment or analysis. Their use in some disciplines can offer a distorted idea of the nature of the discipline. For instance, an objective test for philosophy might consist of quotes from various philosophers that the student has to identify. Such a test implies a very limited view of 'studying' philosophy.

The value of such tests depends on the context in which the test takes place and the weight it is given. There is a great deal of difference between an objective test used as a summative assessment and one which is offered as an optional form of self-assessment (perhaps to enable the student to check if he or she is on the right lines). Even so, you may consider that objective tests are suitable only for certain forms of knowledge. For instance, they may be appropriate as a check on factual knowledge and unsuitable for testing skills or analysis.

Essay Papers and Examinations

Framing essay questions which elicit the desired response, while allowing the student scope to demonstrate abilities, requires explicitness and a lack of ambiguity. Essays can allow for personal response, judgment, synthesis, analysis and evaluation, but in examination conditions the student may not demonstrate these skills. Students may be inhibited by the situation or by their inability to remember background information relevant to the analysis. Where questions are disclosed beforehand, students will have more time to demonstrate higher-order abilities. Open-book examinations allow students to refer to the information they need and may reduce the temptation to memorize material. Essays can test knowledge and analysis. They are not generally useful for testing skills. Other forms of examination, such as practical and oral examinations (sometimes called 'vivas' in higher education) can test particular skills and qualities.

Coursework

Coursework can take a variety of forms, including essays, projects, contributions to seminars, laboratory work, and work-based experience. Coursework offers scope for choice, the development of skills such as research skills, presentation skills, the demonstration of initiative and enterprise and collaboration. These may be hard to assess in other ways.

With the advent of competence models and the increasing emphasis given to employability skills, group assessment becomes more appropriate. Such assessments include group presentations, the creation of artifacts for a particular audience (such as a display, a video or a handbook) and group projects (including research projects and reports). Group projects may be a particularly valid way of assessing students' progress towards particular objectives (such as the development of communication skills) but suffer other problems. The products may be ephemeral (for instance, a group presentation), presenting problems of moderation. In addition, the relative contribution of members of the group may not be clear. Mechanisms for getting round these problems have been discussed elsewhere (see Ashcroft and Foreman-Peck, 1994), and include, the establishment of clear criteria and ground rules for dealing with differential achievement among the group. One method I have used is to assume that marks should be distributed equally, unless the majority in any group agrees upon a different formula and notifies the marker of the formula before the assessment point.

Quality Feedback on Students' Work

Feedback on formative and summative assessments should be informative. I have found that comments are more useful to students where they are concrete, specific and timely. General statements such as 'You need to improve your presentation' are unlikely to be helpful. More specific statements such as 'I would have found it helpful if you had signalled in your introduction what was to come later in the assignment' are more likely to help the student to present better work in the future.

Your comments should help the student to know how to achieve well on subsequent summative assessments. The student is unlikely to benefit from comments that contain too many areas to work on, that are vague and non-specific, or that are purely focused on the particular assignment (rather than oriented to skills or knowledge that the student can utilize in the future). It may be better to focus on one or two aspects of an assignment and discuss them thoroughly, than to provide an extended list of strengths and weaknesses.

Some coursework assessment can be both formative and summative. While this signals to the student that the assessment 'counts', the formative intention might be lost or diluted if students focus on the summative grade rather than on how to improve. This implies that there must be a high degree of explicitness about the purposes of assessment and that lecturers should be prepared to recommend action rather than focus purely on judging achievement.

As with end-of-course assessments, what is being aimed at needs to be carefully worked out, and communicated to students. Biggs and Coullis (1982) have developed a taxonomy, called the 'Structure of the Observed Learning Outcome' (SOLO) that you may find helpful in judging the structural complexity of students' responses to assessments. The categories can apply to any kind of subject matter. They specify students' response to assessment at different levels, starting with the '*prestructural response*', where the student includes irrelevant information, or can make no meaningful response. In the next level of response, the '*unistructural response*', the student's answer focuses on one relevant aspect only. Some students are capable of a '*multistructural response*'. This is characterized by an answer that focuses on several relevant features, but which is not fully coordinated. As the

---

Enquiry Task

Analyse the written comments you have made on three recent assessments in terms of the following headings:

- Comments related to that particular assignment (e.g., statements of accuracy, such as 'Robert Maxwell did not own the *Times* newspaper').
- Comments that offer general advice (e.g., 'You need to read more').
- Comments that offer specific advice (e.g., 'You need to read more up-to-date literature. Look particularly at "X" journal: research is often published there before it appears in books').
- Questions that are designed to take the student's thinking further (e.g., 'What implications might "X" theory have for the practitioner?').
- Comments that identify strengths.
- Comments that identify weaknesses.
- Other categories of comment.

Talk to the students who received the comments.

Find out:

- How many of your comments demanded student action?
- How many of these resulted in action?
- Which comments did the student find useful?
- Which comments did the student find confusing?

What have you learned from this exercise?

Identify how you could improve the written feedback you provide to students?

---

student develops, he or she may become capable of a '*relational response*', where the several parts are integrated into a coherent whole, details are linked to conclusions and meaning is understood. At the highest level, the student can make an '*extended abstract response*'. In this type of response, the student generalizes the structure beyond the information given and uses higher-order principles to bring in a new and broader set of issues. The taxonomy above has implications for the establishment of standards. For instance, the higher-order responses involve evidence of understanding and the integration and structuring of subject matter, and so could be used as measures of higher 'standards'.

It has been found that approaches to learning are strongly associated with SOLO outcomes. Van Rossum and Schenk (1984) found that twenty-seven out of thirty-four students who used a deep approach to study achieved an outcome demonstrating a relational or an extended abstract response, but none of the thirty-five students using a surface approach did. Biggs and Coulis (1982) found that when students felt over-assessed, they see their task as the reproduction of information.

In these circumstances, students' planning, composing and reviewing are not complex. When they see the writing task as a structured learning experience, they tend to give attention to audience, style and discourse structure.

Part of the value of assessment lies in the information it can give lecturers about the development of their students' understanding. This in turn should influence teaching strategies. It is important therefore that the assessment regime is conducive to a deep-learning approach.

The SOLO approach is limited inasmuch as it is focused mainly on written forms of assessment. The assessment of performance and personal qualities, as well as understanding, is of particular importance in professional development. SOLO may also be an inappropriate taxonomy for looking at competences, since these are focused on performances, where levels of analysis can be inferred but not demonstrated.

Enquiry Task

- Examine two or three pieces of assessed work from a course that you teach.
- How would you categorize them according to the SOLO taxonomy?
- What evidence have you used to come to this conclusion?

	SOLO Level	*Evidence*
• Student 1		
• Student 2		

What are the implications of this analysis for your teaching and for the feedback you would give to the students concerned?

Do the forms of the assessment you are offering these students need reconsideration?

Resource Issues in Assessment

The change in the unit of resource in higher education creates real problems as far as assessment and the provision of quality feedback are concerned. The signs are that a similar increase in lecturer 'productivity' will be expected in further education, resulting in larger classes in this sector also. As lecturers teach more students, some are finding the marking load crippling. The time taken in marking the work of larger classes represents a real opportunity cost and has implications for the quality of other lecturer activity. It is likely that less attention can be given to feedback. While lecturers are marking, they cannot prepare classes, undertake scholarship or keep up to date with their administration. It is important to consider whether it is wise (or possible) to continue with traditional marking patterns. The alternative is to find other ways of assessing students, that support their learning and remain valid and reliable.

Some indications of the way forward may be provided by the analysis of the purposes of assessment. The existing forms of assessment and structures for marking can then be explored to see if there are alternative methods of achieving these purposes which offer more economy in terms of lecturer time. Some forms of assessment provide the student with feedback as to their progress. This function does not always have to be carried out by the tutor. The lecturer may be better employed in creating criteria that the students can use to mark and provide written or verbal feedback on work done by their peers. The student marker will learn from this process as much as the student whose work is being marked. The lecturer might choose to sample the students' marked work, in order to draw out general issues about content or standard that need to be communicated to the group. If the purpose of assessment is to support the student's learning, it may be better to turn the assessment into a group activity. A few group presentations, displays, reports or projects are generally shorter and easier to mark than twenty-five individual ones. The students are likely to learn as much from group feedback as they would from individual comments, but in addition, their thinking will have been developed through listening to the interpretation of their peers and the need to articulate their own ideas. If the assessment has dual purposes (for instance, to produce a summary mark and to ensure that the students keep up with their studies), you could decide to mark a summary statement or synthesis supported by a larger piece of work or to mark a sample of a major piece of work. For instance, you may require students to produce seven laboratory reports, but 'spot mark' only one.

You may find that you often write the same comment to several students, especially where the purpose of the assessment is to ensure that students are achieving according to the criteria for the course. If this is the case, you may find that attachment sheets with pre-printed comments and tick boxes are more appropriate than open-comments sheets. More sophisticated sheets might also include pairs of descriptors with a scale that you tick:

e.g., for an essay:
Your use of the literature   – – – – –   Your use of the literature
is critical and analytical.   is insufficiently critical.

or for a display:
Your message comes   – – – – –   Your message is vague
across clearly.   and confused.

Whatever you decide to do, you may need to find ways of giving advice and guidance to the group, rather than relying on individual comments. If you can provide good guidance at the start, targeted group feedback at the end and have comments sheets that contain indicators of students achievement of the assessment criteria, you should be able to save much time in writing extensive individual comments.

You will need also to find ways of shortening the assessment task. This may involve you in finding alternative forms for assessment. For instance, you may decide to look for alternatives to the traditional essay, such as role-play essays with a strict word limit (for instance, a newspaper article on an issue you are discussing), asking students to list or map the main issues or concepts under discussion (perhaps in the form of a diagram or poster) or to do a presentation during a taught session. (This final idea has the added advantage that the marking is done in class time, freeing your non-contact time for other work.)

The lecturer's role in assessment is not limited to marking assignments. It also includes setting work, establishing the criteria and guidelines, and moderating the marking of other team members. Each of these aspects may be devolved to students (perhaps as part of a class activity). Students can be invited to design the essay question or assessment task. This will help them to understand the function of particular words in an essay title (for instance, that a word like 'analyse' demands certain types of response). They may design the schedule of assessment criteria, and thus learn how criteria are related to course aims and how they link to levels of student learning. Students may take part in the moderation for the marking of their own work (or if the work is anonymized, for a parallel group), and so learn how to recognize and articulate what is 'good' and 'not so good' work against identified criteria.

Enquiry Task

List the assessment used in the courses you teach this term.

List the forms of associated activity that you undertake for each assessment (e.g., tutorial advice to students, devising criteria, marking, completing feedback sheets, moderating marks, administration . . .)

Work out the total time you will spend on assessment-related activity this term.

Assessment	Associated task	Time taken
e.g., Essay number 1	• Setting/writing guidance	2 hours
	• Discussing with students	1 hour
	• Marking/writing feedback	6 hours
	• Moderating marks	1 hour
	• Administration	1 hour

Do you spend a disproportionate amount of your time on assessment?

There are often alternative forms to other traditional types of assessment that are more economic of lecturer time, but equally valid and reliable. You might consider marking only a proportion of an examination or test, with the students marking the rest for their peers according to a detailed model provided by you. This will give the students a much clearer idea of what a 'good' answer looks like, and introduce them to alternative ways of approaching questions or problems. It also provides you with a check on student performance and a mark to contribute to summative assessment.

The supervision of individual student projects or dissertations often takes a great deal of time. You may need to consider whether student choice should be structured in some way to enable you to support group, rather than individual, work. One way of doing this is to provide a limited number of foci for such research work. In my own college, we run an elective programme for under-graduate and doctoral dissertation support. One of us supports up to sixteen students who are undertaking research in a fairly closely defined area. We meet regularly as a group to review time-management issues and set deadlines, discuss the literature, help each other define research questions, refine research instruments, discuss findings and alternative ways of interpreting them and look for factors that may threaten the validity of the research. Much of the work which would otherwise have to be undertaken in brief one-to-one tutorials is thus achieved with greater economy as far as my time is concerned and with no loss of educational quality.

A move to pass–fail assessment (rather than grading) for all or part of the student's work will reduce the need for cross-moderation and allow the lecturers to concentrate on the learning outcomes of assessment.

Whatever happens in further and higher education, it is likely that we will be expected to do more with fewer resources. This implies that either we start to crack under the strain, or that we find new assessment methods that have value in their own right.

Enquiry Task

Look at the list of assessments that you prepared for the enquiry task above.

Analyse each assessment on the list, using those of the following list of questions suggested by Moore and Davidson (1994) that are appropriate:

- Is this assessment really necessary?
- Does it assess a course's objectives?
- Do you need to assess it so often?
- Can you assess it in class time?
- Do you need to assess the students individually?
- Can the assessment be more specific (e.g., using an objective test)?
- Does the assessment have to be so accurate (e.g., could you move from a grading to pass–fail)?
- Do *you* have to mark it (e.g., could it be peer-marked or self-assessed if you provide a marking schedule)?
- Do *you* have to set it (e.g., can you use a standardized test or let students set the questions)?
- Can you use convergent assessment (e.g., with a limited range of correct response)?
- Could technology be given a role in the assessment?
- Could the assessment be made more valuable?
- Are there better ways of informing students about their progress (e.g., using prestructured attachment forms for mark comments)?
- Are there other ways to select students who need special help?

Have you been able to identify assessments that might be done differently or not at all?

Assessing Competences and Personal Qualities

When it comes to the assessment of competence, concern over 'rigour' is often stated in terms of reliability and standards, rather than the validity of assessment. There have been worries over standards, especially in the context of GNVQs. Reports by the FEFC (1994) and OFSTED (1994) point out that the rapid uptake by students has been at the expense of the establishment of national standards. The standards of awards at level 2 are particularly variable. The FEFC indicate a need to improve the external verification. It may be that establishing standards in this way is inappropriate, and that the elaboration of quality control systems may divert resources and thus be at the expense of the quality of learning. The FEFC reports that in half the colleges quality control systems are inadequate and the volume of documentation associated with recording procedures is excessive.

The problem of establishing precise outcomes that a student must achieve, where part of that outcome is in terms of thinking, knowing or analysing (and therefore must be inferred from behaviour, rather than directly observed), seems to have been underestimated. The Government wishes the National Council for Vocational Qualifications (NCVQ) to review the assessment and grading system and to clarify the knowledge required. You may wish to consider whether outcome-driven, competence-based assessment are simply inappropriate for assessing higher cognitive processes that are not amenable to direct observation or whether success is a matter of refining definitions and processes.

Competence-based qualifications such as GNVQs often include mandatory units that include elements which specify what must be done. These set the standard of performance that must be met and the significant dimensions which must be covered by candidates and appear in the evidence for the successful completion of each unit. The evidence is generated through work on projects, assignments and tests. Most competence-based qualifications, such as NVQs and GNVQs, are designed to be criterion-referenced. This means that students' performance is marked and graded according to prespecified criteria and standards. The criteria may include statements of minimally acceptable or safe performance or of excellence or mastery. Clear, unambiguous specification is central to the criterion-referenced system. Without this, the reliability of the assessment process is called into question and detracts from the currency value of the assessment in the 'qualifications' market place.

In practice, Woolf (1994) suggests that the attempt to be rigorous in specification may solve problems of reliability but create problems of validity through the process of continuing reduction and consequent narrowing of the performances to be assessed. A consequence of the narrowing process is that the number of assessable elements increases. Evermore atomized specification cannot prevent ambiguities occurring.

The real problem for the validity of such assessment may be the variation in conditions in the workplace. Thus, in one canteen kitchen the oven may be modern and have working thermostats, in another it may be antiquated and 'temperamental'. The level and type of competence required for success is different in each case, yet the criterion against which the students are being tested is the same. In an academic context, different lecturers may also interpret criteria for assessment in different ways. This can result in student confusion; the opposite of what was intended by the specification of criteria in the first place. The problem may be that written criteria may mislead lecturers into believing that their interpretation is shared by others. This implies that, if standards are to be maintained, markers need to discuss their interpretation of criteria and read exemplar assessments, perhaps as a staff team development activity.

The problem of shared meanings is likely to be greater in a national system of accreditation that employs many work-based assessors. For instance, according to Woolf (1994) there is virtually no publicly available, systematic research on how assessments are constructed in NVQs. If this is the case, it is not possible to tell whether trainers and assessors are interpreting criteria, range statements, statements of underpinning knowledge and assessment requirements in a similar way. Black *et al.* (1989) found that, despite the fact that lecturers were experienced and had close links with local industry, some colleges delivering specific modules within the Scottish National Certificate deviated in standards.

Agreement in judgment is more than a matter of sharing a common background or expertise, since judgments are complex and context-bound. The Office for Standards in Education (OFSTED) works with experienced teachers to a framework that includes standards, but only selects those candidates for membership of inspection teams who can demonstrate agreement in judgments. These judgments go beyond the stated criteria to a utilization of knowledge about context. These contextual factors seem to be unamenable to precise specification, but are essential to fair assessment in complex interactive situations, especially those that involve dealing with people. You may wish to consider whether the need for holistic judgment and compensation for contextual factors makes the careful specification of outcomes the most appropriate method for assessing competences in higher-level courses.

In the work of professionals, these issues have to be located within a framework of values and ethics. It is generally accepted that occupational competence involves professionals in complex moral decisions. It is also the case that some occupations require personal qualities and dispositions. The caring professions are a good example. The NVQ Care Sector Consortium (1992) has recognized this. For instance, moral qualities appear in the specification from level 3, including responsibility, autonomy, the guidance of others and the allocation of resources: level 5 adds substantial personal autonomy, significant responsibility for the work of others and the allocation of substantial resources.

Winter (1992) has characterized professional work as being essentially about problem-solving. This entails qualities, such as the ability to empathize with the predicament of others whilst remaining detached, that are difficult to assess reliably. Since professionals have expertise, they also have power. This carries with it the burden of responsibility and accountability. He stresses that professional work involves emotions which have to be understood, effectively managed and are developed through reflection on experience. Each individual's stock of experiences will differ and this will lead to individual ways of perceiving and knowing. Occupational competence may thus involve subjective aspects of learning. If assessments are to be valid (that is, if they are to assess the real competences needed within professions), problems must be tackled. Competence-based schemes that focus solely on prestated and observable behaviours, or more traditional schemes that focus on knowledge acquired, may achieve reliability but are unlikely to be valid.

Mitchell (1993) asserts that some criteria intrinsic to the role of the professional, such as duty to the public at large, can be stated as standards and are useful in informing and evaluating professional action. If some discretion is allowed, the observer can take account of contextual factors. The emotions aroused by professional practice may also be capable of general description. For example, within the NVQ care awards, the comfort and support of the partner, relative and friends of those who have died or suffered loss is seen as important. The performance criterion specifies that the worker's own feelings aroused by a client's loss are managed in a way that is likely to be supportive of himself or herself and minimizes the effect on the care setting. This is supported by the specification of necessary knowledge and understanding of the grieving process in relation to those associated with death or loss. On the other hand, many personal attributes may not be amenable to description and furthermore should not be described in standards. Some personal qualities such as 'innovation' and 'honesty' can only appear obliquely in performance criteria.

Problems in assessment in certain professional areas may result from the nature of the work. For example, professionals often deal with situations where transaction are personal or the interests of a client need protecting. Professional action typically involves a number of possible solutions to problems. Professionals often have to deal with dilemmas in practice, and find a 'least worst' solution to moral and practical issues. A practical example may illustrate this. If you find yourself working in a college with several racist teachers, one of whom has actively discriminated against black students, you would have to consider where your moral duty lies and what course of action you should take. This situation would present a difficult task for an assessor who would have to weigh up alternative solutions. Assessors in real professional situations cannot judge on outcomes of action. It is often the case that a course of action is optimal, given the information available, but, because of circumstances outside of the actor's control, the desired outcome is not achieved.

I argue that assessment-led models, where content is not specified, may be inappropriate for quality professional training. An assessment system conveys to the learner what is expected. It seems implausible to suggest that an assessment system, by itself, can ensure the kind of development of moral sensibility that is required in, say, the caring professions. It seems that some educational process of reasoned debate is a necessary prerequisite to fully professional action.

Assessment and the Development of Reflective Practice

The assessment of professional competence should take into account the particular qualities needed for true professionalism. From my experience of having taught children and students of all ages and abilities, I believe that lecturers can encourage all students to engage in the sort of moral consideration and self-critical problem-solving activity that underpins reflective practice. If this is so, we need to develop assessments that both encourage and capture such reflection.

Reflection is an exploratory process where intellectual and affective activities are refined and developed. Boud, Keogh, and Walkers' (1985) model suggests that there are three stages to reflecting. The first is to return to the experience, the second to attend to the feelings connected with the experience, and the third to re-evaluate the experience through recognizing implications and outcomes. This simple model of reflective activity casts the learner as an active meaning-marker. The student has to relate present learning to past learning and the personal significance it has for him or her.

Boud and Knights (1993) have identified some strategies for assessment which encourage reflective practice. A good example is the reflective diary. This has the purpose of promoting learning from experience and of allowing alternative ways of construing the same event. Many of the enquiry tasks and the reflective diary within this book are designed to help you with your self-assessment and to assist and capture your reflection. They could become the basis of an ongoing reflective diary, focused on quality.

Assessment tasks that promote reflection are likely to differ from evidence collected to demonstrate competence. An exploration of feelings and assumptions are usually excluded from the competence-based assessment. Such an exploration would require qualitative response from the assessor, rather than the straight 'can do' or 'cannot yet do' response that criterion-referenced systems demand. The qualities of reflective practice also imply habitual action. Were reflective qualities to become part of a competence-based scheme, there would be a danger that they might be assumed for the purposes of the assessment: a utilitarian response that is inimical to reflective practice.

In ongoing systems of continuous assessment, reflection may be easier to encourage and capture. In order for this to be meaningful, better and worse reflection has to be identified and characterized: for instance, by the detail of observation, the depth of self-insight, the analysis of assumptions and context, reference to principles such as justice and so on. Evidence of thinking and development might be assembled and discussed as an aid to self-assessment and finally to summative assessments. Someone who has been through such a process may be more likely to respond to occupational and life situations flexibly, openmindedly and with responsibility.

Enquiry Task

Define the purpose of the qualification offered by one of the courses you teach.

Identify elements of the assessment directed at:

- capturing practical competence;
- capturing knowledge; and
- capturing personal development.

Create a list of criteria for evaluating the worth of each type of assessment.

Assuring Quality in Assessment

Quality assurance in assessment requires a variety of activity. These are focused on monitoring standards and accounting for quality. The need to be accountable has been influential in the movement towards the specification of behavioural objectives, learning outcomes and competences at the course design stage. This accountability is often operationalized through the activity of a moderator who assesses the judgments of the assessors and may be monitored through the operation of institutional committees and examination boards.

Staff development is needed to ensure reliability of assessment, but also to ensure that the whole assessment scheme (summative, formative and self-assessment) is continuously subject to critical analysis. Internal assessors and external moderators may have different concerns. The moderator should be primarily interested in the maintenance of standards, rather than in the overall experience of students. The internal assessors and the activity of the committee may be directed at wider issues of quality: for instance the relevance of the assessment to the course aims, the balance of assessment methods, the clarity of assessment criteria as expressed to the students, the development and use of practice-based assessment and so on.

The broader questions of validity and the relationship of the assessment scheme to the overall quality of the students' learning experience may be best answered through the process of periodic course or programme review. Such review allows the teaching, learning and assessment of a programme to be looked at holistically and evidence (including evidence about standards) to be collected from a variety of sources.

The reliability of assessment is an important matter and can be checked in a variety of ways. Moderators and assessors can be trained to interpret some aspects of performance according to standardized criteria. Assessment material may be checked against specified criteria and the results fed back to an accrediting body. Consistency of markers can be checked by comparing the marks for a group of students produced by different markers, against those expected. Investigation might be undertaken where one person seems to be awarding marks that deviate from those that would normally be expected. Institutions may use information technology to explore differences between the mean marks and standard deviation of marks given by different markers or typical of different course components or subjects. These can then be explored to find out if a particular group of students are in some way exceptional, or whether one marker, course team or subject area is working to standards that differ from those expected for courses at that level.

Another way of checking on reliability is to see whether one group of students (for instance, female students, students from ethnic minorities, or mature students) seem to be being awarded a different pattern of marks from those awarded to others. If this is the case, investigation will be needed to find out if the assessment scheme is discriminatory (for instance: because of the examples used, the language and cultural context assumed or the type of skill emphasized). An example of this kind of investigation is the study by McCrum (1994) into the reasons why women students in higher education seemed to be awarded fewer first- and third-class honours degrees than men. He found some bais against women in teaching. It is also sometimes assumed that women are in some way more 'average' than men. The discrepancy in the apparent achievement of men and women might be explained by the marking patterns common within subjects that traditionally attract a preponderance of women or men: for example, physics lecturers regularly use the whole mark range, whereas English lecturers seldom allocate marks close to 0 per cent or 100 per cent.

It is important that this issue is taken seriously. It represents an unfairness to able students within the arts and humanities and students who achieve at the lower end within science and mathematical subjects. In addition, it has a distorting effect on the relative weighting of subjects accorded in joint-honours degrees. Thus, in a degree that includes mathematics and history, a student's performance in mathematics is likely to have more effect on his or her degree classification than his or her performance in history.

If one assumes that, overall, abilities are distributed in much the same way in (say) English as in physics students, and that physics lecturers and English lecturers will, by and large, be similarly capable as teachers, many institutions should take action to moderate difference in standards used in marking across subjects (for example, by abandoning marks as the basis for awarding degree classification and using instead particular percentiles within the standard deviation of marks awarded within the subject over a number of years).

In the UK higher education system, some standardization of marking and degree classification used to be achieved through the activities of the Council for National Academic Awards. With the translation of the polytechnics into universities, the main mechanism for ensuring comparability of standards is the external examiner system. This system is probably inadequate and is certainly under strain. If interuniversity and intersubject comparability of standards is important, there is a need for action: for instance, for universities to get together to create and operate a professional and properly paid system of moderators. Without this, there must be a suspicion that a first-class honours degree from one university (or even from one department within a university) represents a different level of achievement than a 'first' from another. In the meantime, many recommendations from CNAA regarding good practice in examination may still hold true. These include the moderation of internal marking by external examiners and the consideration of external examiners' reports by course teams and committees. It suggests that external examiners should have the experience and ability to compare students' performance with that of their peers on comparable courses and to approve the content of proposed assessments and that they should report any substantial concerns that might jeopardize the award to the chief executive of the institution. At present, there is no system of checking on the consistency of judgments by external examiners within higher education, nor is there sufficient training to encourage the sharing of meanings about role and purposes.

Purposes of Evaluation

There is some confusion over the role of assessment and evaluation. These roles overlap, inasmuch as assessment is a central process in the maintenance of standards and evaluation is about the enhancement of quality (standards being an aspect of quality). However, evaluation has a broader and more central role in the quality assurance systems of the institution.

Reflective Practice involves more than 'thinking about' issues. It also requires the collection of evidence and its careful analysis in order to establish appropriate and principled courses of action. To this extent it is evaluation-led: the evaluation occurring as a precursor of action (in order to inform it) and also as a method of discovering the effects of action (in order to improve it).

Like assessment, evaluation can fulfil formative and summative functions. Depending upon its purpose and audience, the 'best' form of evaluation may be 'quick and dirty' or ordered and systematic. The quality assurance system of the institution generally requires the latter type of evaluation. Funding bodies and the Government also favours systematic evaluation, usually of a quantitative nature, as a means to monitor institutional performance (for instance, through the National Charters for further and higher education — DFE, 1993a and 1993b).

As well as accountability and the collection of data related to performance indicators, the purposes of evaluation may include the enhancement of students' learning opportunities; the professional development of teachers and a means of informing course developments. Some of these purposes overlap, but some are incompatible. For example, the type of data that would be likely to facilitate lecturers in sharing meanings is likely to be different from that which would satisfy the funding council as to the efficient running of the institution.

It should be recognized that there may be unofficial as well as declared purposes underpinning evaluation. For example, evaluation can be a powerful tool within an academic community either to challenge the dominant hegemony or to reinforce the status quo. Where such motives underpin the evaluation process, a distorted picture of reality may result: for example through the choice of focus or through the interpretation of data.

Different interest groups will have different purposes for evaluation. These interest groups include students (who may be concerned, for instance, with improving the quality of their learning experience and environment); lecturers (who may be interested in maximizing resources for teaching); institutional managers (who may be more concerned to demonstrate that they have sufficiently developed evaluation procedures than with the results of evaluation); funding bodies (whose main concern may be efficiency) and the wider community and employers (who may be concerned with how closely the students' skills match the employers' workforce needs). Thus, the focus of evaluation is likely to be influenced by the audience for the evaluation and the purposes of evaluator. The evaluation may focus on students, lecturers, other stakeholders in evaluation or the curriculum. It may explore perceptions, values, needs, interests or performance. It may seek to compare one area or institution with another, seek out strengths or identify weaknesses. Its focus may be on accountability or development.

Evaluation and Quality Issues

Evaluation is a problematic issue that is affected by a variety of contextual issues. For instance, an aspect of worthwhile evaluation is timeliness. Some ideas and issues (such as independence in learning) may be introduced early in a course so that they can be developed over a long period. The students may find the early stages difficult. Evaluation occurring too early in the programme could lead to a misleadingly negative result. Conversely, many innovations are introduced by enthusiasts. Evaluation of their performance may give an overly positive impression. The innovation may be better evaluated once it has been implemented by normally committed staff.

Other contextual issues may make a difference to the evaluation results. This is particularly problematic in the evaluation of teaching performance and makes it a very imprecise business. Lecturers are likely to find it easier to achieve a 'good' rating for their teaching in an institution or department that is well resourced and supportive of their approach. Factors such as the size of the group or whether a course component is optional or compulsory may also make a difference to whether the teaching is perceived by students as 'good'. As in the consideration of quality in assessment, quality in evaluation depends in part upon issues of validity and reliability. Many of these issues relate to those outlined in the description of factors that may jeopardize the validity and reliability of research contained in Chapter 10. For example, the results of a small sample of student opinion may not be as significant as those of a larger sample.

The solutions to these problems have much in common with those for research methodology problems. These include the careful construction of the research instrument, ensuring that it is appropriate for its purpose and ensuring the appropriateness of the focus for the evaluation (perhaps by allowing the participants to determine the focus — see Ashcroft and Foreman-Peck (1994) for techniques for student-centred evaluation). Issues of confidentiality are important. Students need to be able to give their comments in confidence, or there is a danger that data will be contaminated by perceptions of social acceptability or power differentials. The final issue is that of the reliability of qualitative data. 'Soft' data is often the most useful for developmental purposes, but may need to be checked by a process of triangulation (for instance, through the use of a variety of techniques, seeking data from different groups of stakeholders in the educational process being evaluated, or subjecting the same data to interpretation by impartial assessors).

Gibbs *et al.* (1988) describes a variety of evaluation techniques. Among the methods that I have found appropriate are open, closed and limited-choice questionnaires; student-constructed evaluation instruments; semantic differential techniques; direct observation of teaching (for instance with a colleague using a structured schedule, or using a video or audio-tape recordings that can be analysed later); interview (face-to-face or telephone); statistical analysis (for example, of students' employment results or drop-out rates); document analysis (for instance, analysing written reports of lecturers on students, against stated criteria); or the analysis of teaching or learning logs.

In assessing the results of evaluation, it is important that the limitation of the data is recognized. Thus, performance can be inferred, but not accurately assessed, through questionnaire or interview data. The evaluation of performance may be best achieved through observation. Questionnaires can tell you about attitudes and feelings, observation cannot. Statistics can be used to explore, but will not explain, trends. Qualitative data can tell you quite a bit about a small sample or limited situation. Quantitative data can describe highly limited aspects (but a larger number of instances) of reality. Qualitative data are useful for developmental purposes, but have limited application for bureaucratic functions. Quantitative data are essential for bureaucratic and administrative functions, but have limited validity as measures of quality.

The important thing is that the technique used should be appropriate for its purpose and that the results should be ordered and carefully interpreted. It is part of the role of the quality assurance system to ensure that appropriate evaluation occurs and resulting action is monitored.

Enquiry Task

Find out:

- the departmental policy on evaluation;
- the range of evaluation instruments used in your department;
- what data is collected from students, staff, employers, managers, the statistical centre of the institution; and
- what happens to the data collected.

Draft your own 'Guide to Good Practice in Evaluation'

Discuss it and refine it with a colleague.

Find out what action you would have to take to influence departmental policy on evaluation.

Summary

Qualifications at further education level have developed from a content-based model to competence-based assessment. This is influencing higher education in terms of student intake, course design and assessment. The Government is encouraging universities and colleges to accredit their programmes through the NVQ system. New definitions of quality that focus on employability and skills, rather than the needs of a discipline and the transmission of culture, are emerging as a result.

Definitions of quality in assessment are related to:

- the aims and objectives of a programme;
- the level of student progress appropriate to the qualification sought;
- course processes and content; and
- the forms and depth of learning required.

The purposes of assessment include:

- measuring student achievement against that of others;
- signposting progression;
- enriching student learning;
- the award of qualifications with confidence in their standards; and
- signalling the level of performance.

Assessment may be summative (counting towards a qualification) or formative (to provide students with feedback on their learning and performance).

Forms of assessment include:

- objective tests;
- essay and examinations; and
- coursework.

Assessment may be group or individual. Each form has advantages and disadvantages.

Indicators of good practice in assessment include:

- marking policies worked out at departmental level;
- clarity about form and purpose of assessment;
- variety of forms of assessments;
- clear specification of criteria;
- careful timing as a support to the students in pacing their work.

Biggs' taxonomy can help you judge the complexity of student response, assess their level of achievement and construct appropriate feedback.

The reduction in the unit of resource in colleges and universities implies that traditional forms of assessment and feedback to students may not remain viable.

New methods may be needed including:

- peer-marking and feedback;
- group assessment and feedback;
- sample marking;
- marking syntheses (e.g., precis, poster, map, diagram);
- use of preprinted attachment sheets for student feedback with pre-specified comment categories;
- role-play essays with word limits;
- practical assessment in class time;
- student-set work;
- student-generated criteria;
- group supervision of project work and research; and
- pass–fail, rather than graded, assessment.

Concern has been expressed about the validity and reliability of competence-based assessment. This may result from:

- difficulties in implying competence in cognitive activity from observable behaviour;
- difficulties in specifying higher-order behaviour;
- difficulties in interpreting criteria in non-standard situations;
- complexity of judgments about professional behaviour; and
- difficulties in defining 'right' answers in the professional context.

The Reflective Practitioner model of student learning implies that criteria for assessment should encompass:

- 'better' and 'worse' reflection;
- feelings and assumptions;
- critical analysis; and
- student response over a period of time.

Quality assurance in assessment requires:

- a system of accountability;
- a system of internal and external moderation;
- a system of course review; and
- checks against performance criteria.

Performance checks might include comparisons of the mean marks and standard deviation in marks awarded by:

- different markers;
- markers in different subjects;
- markers in different institutions;
  or awarded to different student groups.

Evaluative purposes may be summative or formative. Methods should be chosen on the basis of their fitness for purpose.

The validity of evaluation is affected by:

- contextual factors;
- timeliness;
- construction of the evaluation instruments;
- fitness for purpose of the evaluation instruments;
- appropriateness of the foci for evaluation;
- confidentiality of student response; and
- extent of triangulation.

The purposes of evaluation include:

- accountability;
- the enhancement of students' learning opportunities;
- the professional development of teachers;
- informing course development; and
- a micro-political tool for change or the maintenance of the status quo.

The following interest groups have a stake in education. Their perspectives should be captured by the evaluation system:

- students;
- lecturers;
- managers;
- funding bodies; and
- employers and the community.

Each of these groups have their own agenda.

Evaluation methods include:

- questionnaires (open, closed and limited response);
- student-constructed evaluation instruments;

- semantic differential techniques;
- direct observation of teaching;
- interviews;
- statistical analysis of available data; and
- document analysis.

Each of these techniques has advantages and disadvantages.

Entry for the Reflective Diary

- List the six main points that you have learned from reading this chapter and from the enquiry tasks.
- Identify the ways that you intend to change your assessment and/or evaluation practice.
- How has your view of assessment and/or evaluation changed?

Notes

1. This chapter includes contributions by Lorraine Foreman-Peck.
2. **Annotated List of Suggested Reading**

Further Education Unit (1994) *Examining Assessment*, London, FEU.

A good 'technical' guide to quality-assurance issues in assessment that also includes a description of the assessment requirements of the newer qualifications available in the post-compulsory education sector.

Gibbs, G., Habeshaw, S. and Habeshaw, T. (1984) *53 Interesting Ways to Assess your Students*, Bristol, TES.

Gibbs, G., Habeshaw, S. and Habeshaw, T. (1988) *53 Interesting Ways to Appraise your Teaching*, Bristol, TES.
These provide simple, but relatively uncritical, listings of ways of assessing and evaluating students and teaching.

Journal of Assessment and Evaluation in Higher Education.
This journal includes items from every discipline and various countries. This means that there should be some papers of interest to you, whatever your discipline. The style of the papers vary, but some are fairly accessible. It is worth exploring if you are interested in looking at assessment or evaluation issues in any depth.

References

ASHCROFT, K. and FOREMAN-PECK, L. (1994) *Managing Teacjhing and Learning in Higher Education*, London, Falmer Press.
ATKINS, M.J., BEATIE and DOCKERELL, W.B. (1993) *Assessment Issues in Higher Education*, London, Employment Department Development Group.

BIGGS, J.B. and COULIS, K.F. (1982) *Evaluating the Quality of Learning: The SOLO Taxonomy*, New York, Academic Press.

BLACK, J.H., HALL, J., MARTIN, S. and YATES, J. (1989) *The Quality of Assessments: Case Studies in the National Certificate*, Edinburgh, Scottish Council for Research in Education.

BOUD, D. and KNIGHTS, S. (1993) 'Designing courses to promote reflective practice', in *Annual Conference of the Higher Education Research and Development Society of Australasia*, University of New South Wales.

BOUD, D., KEOGH, R. and WALKER, D. (Eds) (1985) *Reflection: Turning Experience into Learning*, London, Kogan Page.

CARE SECTOR CONSORTIUM (1992) *National Occupational Standards for Care*, London, HMSO.

DEPARTMENT FOR EDUCATION (1993a) *Further Choice and Quality: National Charter for Further Education*, London, DFE.

DEPARTMENT FOR EDUCATION (1993b) *Higher Choice and Quality: The Charter for Higher Education*, London, DFE.

DEPARTMENT FOR EDUCATION (1994) *Helping Business to Win*, London, HMSO.

FURTHER EDUCATION FUNDING COUNCIL (1994) *General Vocational Qualifications in the Further Education Sector in England*, Coventry, FEFC.

GIBBS, G., HABESHAW, S. and HABESHAW, T. (1988) *53 Interesting Ways to Appraise Your Teaching*, Bristol, TES.

McCRUM, N.G. (1994) 'The academic gender difference at Oxford and Cambridge', *Oxford Review of Education*, 20, 1, pp. 3–26.

MARTON, F. and SALJO, R. (1984) 'Approaches to learning, in Marton, F. Hounsell, D.J. and Entwistle, N. (Eds) *The Experience of Learning*, Edinburgh, Scottish Academic Press.

MITCHELL, L. (1993) 'NVQs/SVQs at higher levels: A discussion paper to the higher levels seminar', in *Competence and Assessment*, Briefing Series Number 8.

MOORE, I. and DAVIDSON, J. (1994) 'Assessing students more effectively in less time', *Assessment for Learning in Higher Education: Responding to and Initiating Change*, Telford, Staff and Educational Development Association Conference, May 16–18.

NATIONAL COUNCIL FOR VOCATIONAL QUALIFICATIONS (1991) *A Guide to National Vocational Qualifications*, London, NVQC.

OFFICE FOR STANDARDS IN EDUCATION (1994) *GNVQs in Schools, 1993/4*, London, HMSO.

OTTER, S. (1992) *Learning Outcomes in Higher Education: A Development Project Report*, London, UDACE.

RAMSDEN, P. (1992) *Learning to Teach in Higher Education*, London and New York, Routledge.

VAN ROSSUM, E.J. and SCHENK, S.M. (1984) 'The relationship between learning conception, study strategy and learning outcome', *British Journal of Educational Psychology*, 54, pp. 73–83.

WINTER, R. (1992) *A General Theory of Professional Competences in the Asset Programme*, Anglia Polytechnic and Essex County Council.

WOOLF, A. (1994) 'Assessing the broad skills within occupational competence', *Assessment and Competence*, 25, pp. 3–7.

Chapter 7

Course Design

In this chapter, I discuss the political context for course design and ways that course design can take account of the need for flexibility as experienced by the student within the constraints imposed by resource considerations. I look at the role of team planning in assessing the modes and structures that may meet student needs and interests. Aims and objectives as planning tools are considered and their effects on the management, teaching and learning processes that are eventually adopted.

The Political and Resource Context of Course Design

Further and higher education faces a number of challenges to quality and the maintenance of standards in the design of new courses. Many of these result from the rapidly changing context of education. Changes at school level, such as the development of new forms of assessment, the introduction of the National Curriculum, and the growth in the numbers of mature students with a variety of non-traditional qualifications and experience, mean that students arrive with different expectations and experiences.

The UK Conservative Government of the early 1990s sought to encourage a competence model for training qualifications. For instance, it has sponsored National Vocational Qualifications (NVQ) that enable existing capabilities to be assessed and do away with a requirement for qualifications to be linked with courses of study. In other areas it has also been keen to promote the notion of competence criteria. For instance, the accreditation of initial teacher training courses now depends upon them adopting such a model.

The Government also introduced new methods of funding which provide autonomy and some flexibility, limited by the extent that institutions deliver a reduction in the unit of resource and that overall spending targets for the sector are observed. Colleges and universities are required to both cooperate and compete with other providers of education and training, such as workplace trainers linked with the Training and Enterprise Councils and, in initial teacher training, schools.

Among the challenges to quality and standards in the UK has been the doubling of participation in higher education since the start of the 1980s. The Government announced plans to increase student numbers by a further 60 per cent during the 1990s. Further education is set to experience a similar rate of growth and development. This requires that colleges and universities change restrictive systems that sometimes exclude the interests of certain groups of people. We each have to reconsider what students should learn, how they should learn it and how it can be made cost-effective.

Higher education is adjusting to the threat posed to quality by increasing numbers and a lowering of the unit of resource in a number of ways. Group sizes have already grown so that a seminar group of around thirty is no longer uncommon in some areas of the humanities and twenty-five is not unusual in some practical subjects. Mass lectures to groups of more than a hundred students are considered perfectly normal. One-to-one tutorials are becoming an expensive rarity. The projected increase in further education activity makes similar changes likely for that sector. The need to cater for such group sizes, and to adjust teaching and learning methods so that students are still encouraged to develop deep as opposed to surface levels of learning, should be built into the course planning process.

Gibbs (1992) described a number of problems we may face when we teach more students (unless action is taken to prevent these problems). Lecturer experience seems to indicate that quality becomes harder to maintain as class size increases. Courses with smaller numbers of students can afford to achieve clarity of purpose and aims through informal contact with the lecturers. With increasing numbers, it becomes more important to ensure that students understand course aims and what counts as acceptable outcomes of learning. With larger groups, it is more difficult to provide students with feedback about their progress. They may remain unaware of critical flaws in their understanding. In addition, advice as to how to improve may be harder to provide. Advice given to large groups tend to be general in nature, so individual support may be lacking.

Larger groups can create pressure on library and other resources. Accepted definitions of quality support for students may need to change. Careful planning is needed to prevent situations where a large number of students are required to read round a particular topic at the same time. Without guidance, some of your students may not find the right texts and may not read widely or appropriately. Independent study, projects and dissertation support tend to be more expensive in resources, especially lecturer time than is often thought.

Perhaps the most worrying set of problems for course design that Gibbs indicates are the difficulties encountered in 'firing' student imagination and interest while teaching larger groups. Students seem to deepen their learning and develop their interests through discussion of complex ideas with small groups of students and with a lecturer. You may miss the opportunity to get to know students very well and so to cater more fully for their needs. Gibbs suggests that course designers can choose to solve these problems through a tight control of the learning situation or by building in activity and expectations that foster students' independence.

Until recently the areas and rate of expansion in higher education were determined largely by student demand and the willingness of universities to meet this demand by a mixture of new resources and increased productivity. Those of us in universities who wholeheartedly followed government policy and met student demand in this way found that we were severely disadvantaged. The quality of provision was jeopardized when government policy for determining the mix and volume of higher-education activity changed to a mixture of crude workforce planning (for instance, in penalizing humanities and arts-based subjects in order to encourage students to study sciences) and overall resource allocation. The system is likely to change still further as the balance between public and private funding of further and higher education changes, leading to new problems and opportunities.

Commitment in Course Design

Course planning for quality provision involves both formal and informal processes. The planning of new courses or the major revision of existing ones will not be a purely rational affair. Indeed it is irrational to exclude feelings and intuition from the process. The 'best' course planning probably involves an intelligent mixture of informed intuition, strong preferences for the direction proposed and objective data. These are more effectively utilized where there is a course planning team who share and argue over their perspectives and interpretations of the data. Commitment and enthusiasm are probably essential to get a development off the ground and to sustain it. This implies that, in the end, the course planning team will need to reach a broad agreement as to the course aims and principles.

Similarly, students may be more easily attracted by courses which meet their needs and requirements, but also have elements which they perceive as attractive, rigorous and enabling. Quality provision must, in part at least, be defined by existing and potential students. The creation of such courses may involve you in market research and careful analysis of need. This may not be enough. You may also need a degree of creative imagination, a willingness to take risks and a willingness to venture into uncharted territory.

I find Reeves' (1988) contrast of education for use with education for delight to be a useful idea. This notion is related to the debate about fitness for purpose (see Chapter 2). She criticizes education for neglecting the love of truth and pursuit of knowledge and understanding as a useful and good thing for its own sake.

Enquiry Task

For the purposes of the enquiry tasks in this chapter you should have a course design idea that you would like to develop.

- To what extent does your course design idea appeal to you because it reflects the kind of activity you enjoy?
- What skills might it develop in students?
- What elements of it might students find enjoyable?

Discuss your idea with other staff:

- Which members of the teaching staff share your enthusiasm?
- What is it about the idea that generates their enthusiasm?
- What aspects of the idea do some staff have reservations about?

Discuss your ideas with some students or potential students from the target group:

- What aspects of the idea do the students respond to positively?
- Which aspects do they respond to negatively?
- Which responses are:
  a)   affective (e.g., anticipation of enjoyment or boredom); or
  b)   utilitarian (e.g., the development of useful work related skills?)

Course planning teams may need to explore the tensions between education for understanding and skill development. It is likely that courses should include a variety of skill development, but if the focus does not also include critical analysis and knowledge, long-term goals may be neglected. Even in its own terms such education will not be truly effective. In the long-term, economic relevance is not necessarily synonymous with a narrow technical and vocational focus.

Assessment of Needs

Good course development is almost inevitably based on formal and informal assessments of student needs and requirements and those of others (for instance, the Government, professional bodies or employers) and the ability of the institution to meet those needs.

There may be a need to research the external and internal context for change. This process should include the evaluation of what is presently offered by your college or university and by other institutions, the resources available and the enthusiasms and expertise of colleagues. It is important that the analysis of the context for a course design idea does not stop at this stage. An important factor in course design is the availability and level of finance and an analysis of the needs, interests and requirements of potential students. These matters are dealt with in more detail in later chapters.

Mode and Structure in Course Development

Your analysis of student needs may indicate that traditional structures and modes of delivery may not be appropriate to their needs. Increasingly colleges and universities interested in students' definitions of quality are developing alternative structures to the linear full-time course with one syllabus, taken in a particular order and one entry and exit point. For instance, flexibility is part of the definition of quality for some learners. For others it is a precondition for any sort of involvement. To this end, some institutions have developed modular programmes, which may be taken full-time, part-time or via accelerated routes, or any combination of these to suit the individual student's circumstances. Modules may be designed to be common to two or more courses or mixed in various combinations to create particular qualifications. Many courses are now designed with a variety of stepping off and stepping on routes. Mechanisms have been set up for the accreditation of students' prior learning, so that some may gain admission with advanced standing to courses leading to a variety of qualifications.

Of course, there is the danger that these ideas become seen to be a 'good thing' in themselves, and other aspects of quality come to be ignored. For instance, modular courses can have problems of coherence and fail to provide for an appropriate level of intellectual development. At the extreme, they may degenerate into a pot-pourri approach, with no mechanism to ensure depth and breadth of study. Students may not receive the support they need with their developing orientation to study. They may emerge from a course without the experience of being taught by anyone who is able to take their needs and interest into account. In extreme cases, each term the student has to face three new modules, each with an unknown teacher and an unknown and unsupportive population of students. Where the social and emotional preconditions for learning are lacking, quality must suffer.

Some students may need the security of a linear course pattern. On the other hand, some may find traditional study patterns difficult to fit into their working or family life. Institutions may need to consider methods of course delivery, including open and distance learning to cater for these students. I describe factors in the design of open and distance learning programmes in more detail elsewhere (Ashcroft and Foreman-Peck, 1994).

Open learning may have a variety of definitions. The openness may relate to the entry qualification, the possibility of differing rates of progress or entry and exit points, the degree of negotiation possible over timing, content and assessment and the legitimization of non-traditional places and times for learning. This last category of openness often requires the creation of learning resources for the programme so that much of the learning can take place out of contact with the lecturer. Resource-based learning may take place in the home or in the institution. It may involve book material, communicative technology, independent research, peer support and teaching, visits, work experience and talks by visiting speakers. It may support aspects of the programme, enable an enriched or remedial experience for a minority of students or it may comprise the main method of teaching and learning.

Institutional support for resource-based learning is essential if the lecturer is to have the time to assemble and create the resources needed, arrange back-up material for visits and work experience, organize activities and if the student is to view it as a credible alternative to other forms of learning. This support will involve the recognition that resource-based learning is unlikely to be substantially cheaper than face-to-face teaching. Managers should take into account that resource-based learning may involve more investment in time for the management of the programme: time for the preparation of materials, communicative technology, longer library opening hours, the creation of new library and interlibrary services, the creation of new forms of student record and tracking systems within the registry, and training for lecturers in new forms of tutoring and support than would a traditional programme.

Lecturers involved in course design may need to consider whether economies in resources are possible through the design of the programme. For instance, in subjects where learning is not hierarchical, it may be possible for students to experience parts of the programme in differing orders. This will alleviate the pressure on learning resources caused by many students needing the same resource for a short period each year.

Some of your potential students may have substantial prior learning and experience. You will need to decide in what ways this may be taken into account. More and more colleges and universities are designing courses which give some form of advanced standing, so that a student with substantial experience that overlaps with course content may be permitted to miss the first part of the course, or otherwise experience a shortened course, while still being eligible for the final qualification. Other potential students may experience changes in their situation during a programme of study. Universities and colleges are recognizing this and cooperating in credit accumulation and transfer schemes (CATS). These enable students whose circumstances alter to change institutions mid-course without much, or sometimes any, loss of time. The Open College Network (OCN) provides a national framework for such a scheme. Lecturers in colleges can now prepare OCN courses against the guidelines provided. As more and more colleges and universities are prepared to take students from other institutions, you may suffer a net loss of students unless you have a clear process of recognizing credits obtained elsewhere.

Enquiry Task

Find examples offered by your institution of some of the following course structures. (If one or more are not represented in your institution, you may wish to investigate a neighbouring college or university).
Find out from a lecturer involved in teaching each course the advantages and disadvantages of each course structure:

	Advantages	*Disadvantages*
• Full-time linear course		
• Part-time linear course		
• Course allowing for both full and part-time attendance		
• Modular course		
• Course operating admission with advanced standing		
• Course offering more than one terminal qualification		
• Course starts at more than one time in the academic year		

Aims and Objectives

Aims are usually specified as long-term goals of education or an educational programme. Objectives, on the other hand, are shorter-term and observable. This means that objectives should be measurable by specified outcomes or behaviours on the part of your students. Therefore, your objectives might include a detailed specification of the knowledge, understandings, skills or competences and attitudes to be developed by the programme and evaluated in the assessments.

Quality assurance often focuses on the relationship between course aims and objectives and other aspects of course design, in particular content, teaching methods and assessment. The formulation of course aims should also include an analysis of student needs and requirements. However, course design cannot rest solely on this analysis. The aims of a course should also reflect the level required for the qualification sought (i.e., its academic standards) and be appropriate to the skills and knowledge required by the discipline or area of study.

In formulating aims you may need to consider your values and more general aims of education. The underlying values of the dominant culture within society and an institution are bound to influence course design. It is important you rigorously examine them and assess their appropriateness and the scope they allow for alternative interpretations. For instance, Ball and Eggins (1989) argue that personal fulfilment and national unity in a multicultural society are important aims

---

Enquiry Task

Consider your course development idea. What is the most important thing which you hope students will gain from the course?
Express this idea as an aim.

Consider what subject-specific learning and transferable learning the students will acquire.

	Subject Specific Learning	*Transferable learning*
Skills	e.g., how to cook fish	e.g., communication skills
Attitudes	e.g., appreciation of presentation in cookery	e.g., persistence
Knowledge/ Concepts	e.g., hygiene laws	e.g., basic chemistry

Turn each of these ideas into a set of specific objectives.
Match each objective with at least one indicator of successful action in each of the following categories:

a) an aspect of course content;
b) a piece of student behaviour;
c) a particular teaching–learning method; and
c) an assessment task.

Discuss your list of objectives and indicators of successful action with a group of colleagues and a group of students.

Do they agree that your objectives are:

a) appropriate for the students' level and needs;
b) sufficient;
c) observable; and
d) measurable?

Do they agree that each of your indicators matches its objective?

Refine your list of objectives and indicators of successful action.

---

of education, but that lecturers in higher education tend to give greater loyalty to the requirements of their subject discipline and research. The UK Conservative Government of the 1990s gives a higher priority to work-related competences. If your intended programme is to be educational, the aims should perhaps include some reference to the development of students' intellectual and imaginative abilities; understanding and analysis; independent judgment and self-awareness, as well as intellectual skills such as the ability to communicate and to analyse relationships. Aims and objectives should relate to the shared values of the course development team and the learning needs of students. They should be central to the course development process. They are what will give the programme coherence and the course-delivery team and students a sense of shared purpose.

Course design should involve a careful consideration of the relationship between aims and objectives and the processes of teaching, learning and assessment in the course. For instance, if communication skills are to be developed, your teaching and assessment methods should focus on these and include a range of styles of writing apart from essay writing as well as other modes of communication such as oral, visual, mathematical and diagrammatic modes. If cooperative skills are emphasized, group work should also figure in your assessment and teaching. It should be possible for you to match objectives with each of course content, teaching approaches and assessment.

Gibbs (1992) suggests the use of learning contracts with students. These provide students with individualized objectives or agreed learning outcomes and a clear purpose to independent study. He believes that problem-based learning ensures that the purpose of an activity is clear, even where the learning outcome may be various. You may be able to design problems which require a detailed analysis of the knowledge base.

Course Content

The content often seems the least problematic area of course design. Staff expertise and available resources, together with the traditions of the subject area and requirements of validators, potential students and employers provide the framework for these decisions. However, you should be careful that this framework does not become a straight jacket.

Where a programme is relatively complex and involves a variety of components and lecturers, problems of balance of workload and level will become a problem unless it is carefully specified at the planning stage.

Course Operation and Quality and Standards

Admissions

You will need to make a variety of decisions at the planning stage about the operation of the course. Crucial decisions will need to be made about admissions policies. The overriding criterion that should inform all such policies is the reasonable expectation that those admitted onto the course will benefit from it. This benefit may be expressed in terms of the objectives and standards specified in the course document.

You will have to decide about the processes for the admission and the criteria and regulations for the assessment of students. For instance, you may need to specify the normal entry requirements, the processes and criteria for selection, the processes for accreditation of prior learning and opportunities for entry with advanced standing.

The HEQC (1994) recommends that institutions provide clear and accurate information on all aspects of the course, including the admissions routes, associated requirements for entry and how admissions policies will be monitored. You will need to specify systems for ensuring that students have pre-entry guidance: for instance, about the timescale allowed for completion of the course and details of the programmes for which they are applying. This is dealt with in more detail in Chapters 4 and 9.

Teaching, Learning and Assessment

Course documentation will probably make clear how various teaching strategies bring about intended student learning. In any case, the team will have to have clear ideas about the links between teaching, learning and course objectives. One of the most important feedback loops to be considered at course development stage is that between student and lecturer. It is important that student and lecturer are aware of student progress. You may need to build in specified evaluation points, time built in for facilitating student self-assessment and profiling.

You may need to map the forms, volume and weight of assessment and consider issues such as the extent of student choice in assessment, the proportion that 'counts' towards a qualification and opportunities for resubmission of work that fails to meet minimum standards. None of these issues are value-free. The decisions made will open opportunities for some students and close them for others. Each will encourage a particular view of learning and one model of education at the expense of others. It is important that they are congruent with the aims and objectives of the course.

Accountability and Evaluation

Decisions about the management of the course in planning and operation have to be made early in the planning process. Consideration should include the lines of accountability, the framework for periodic evaluation and review, the nature of such evaluation and its frequency.

Evaluation will need to focus on a range of issues as well as teaching, learning, assessment and content from student and staff viewpoints: for instance, the suitability of the organization and location of the programme and relationships with external bodies. You need to be clear as to what will happen to the results of evaluation and how action will be monitored.

Ongoing evaluation of courses should cause them to be developed and modified over time. It is important that the mechanisms to allow examination of the impact of changes are put in place at the planning stage (for instance, dates for periodic major course review). Without such mechanisms, course development may be piecemeal. I have found that this may lead to 'curriculum inflation' as more and more elements are added and none discarded, or 'curriculum drift' as the revised course moves further and further away from its specified objectives.

Enquiry Task

List the constraints and opportunities operating in the development of your course design idea.

	Opportunities	*Constraints*

- Management issues
- Evaluation issues
- Staff expertise
- Available resources
- Traditions of the subject area
- Requirements of validators
- Requirements of potential students
- Requirements of potential employers
- Other

Discuss and refine your list with some of the following:

a) a senior colleague with responsibility for resources;
b) your departmental head;
c) the course leader of a course validated by the same body as would be for your course idea;
d) a lecturer in your subject area;
e) a small group of potential students; and
f) an employer.

Resources

Resource issues are often basic to the quality of a course and need to be carefully assessed at each stage. These issues include the availability of staff expertise, the likely income from fees and other sources, management, overheads and opportunity costs and running and capital costs. These are dealt with in more detail in Chapter 8.

Student time is a valuable resource that should be fully planned at the course development stage. You may wish to define and structure the way your students will use study time and teaching and learning materials. Private study often occupies more than half of the available learning time. Unless it is planned, and this planning is communicated in some detail to all staff and students, student study time may be an underutilized resource.

Library and other provision can help to ensure students have the opportunity for comparable experiences. This implies that the librarian should be involved at the course planning stage. Reliance on set books or learning packages ensures that all students have access to the same material, but presupposes a particular form of learning and set of interests which will be developed by individual students. It also presupposes that the texts will remain in print. You may find it more useful to incorporate strategies for developing students' own research and study skills so that they can seek out the information they need and follow up particular interests in the institutional library and elsewhere.

Resources may be put under unnecessary strain in large courses if the timing of the syllabus is the same for all students. At the planning stage it is generally possible to identify elements which can be put together in different orders without damage to student learning to enable the more economic use of resources. If you decide on a model of tight control of course content and assessment, there may be more uneven use of resources. Where students are given greater choice (albeit within constraints) in assessment, resources will be likely to be used more economically and evenly.

You will probably need to consider whether to design teaching and learning strategies which can cater for increases in group size without encouraging surface approaches to learning. You may decide to develop students' interpersonal and management skills in a systematic way, so that they become capable of managing group projects and supporting each other's learning and providing motivation and deadlines for each other. Gibbs (1992) suggests that study-skill support may be provided by student-organized learning teams, through peer tuition, shared reading and notes and comments on assessed work. You may wish to identify ways of developing and maintaining such structures at the planning stage.

Peer teaching and group assignments can be taken further. Ashcroft (1987) describes a model where students prepare material and teach parts of the syllabus to each other in the absence of the lecturer. One lecturer can tour between several groups to ensure that no problems are emerging and to deal with particular points or queries which the student leader is unable to deal with. In addition, assessment takes the form of group assignments which are peer and self-assessed. Group assignments fit well into courses which value interpersonal skills and problem-solving skills. They are not problem-free: for instance, there may be problems of ensuring that all students participate equally in the experience and that each has reached the required standards. On the other hand, they usually have the additional advantage of reducing the time you must spend on routine marking, allowing you more time for other teaching tasks such as the provision of detailed feedback. The issue of the effective use of management time should be considered at the planning stage. Students who do not have a clear framework within which to study will require more of your support. For this reason, strong elements of structure may be necessary in larger classes if quality is to be maintained.

The provision of student choice tends to require more management time than a compulsory syllabus. You will need to weigh this against the benefits of flexibility in meeting student interests, encouraging creativity and problem-solving. The transformational resolution of this dilemma may be an important part of the course development team's function. A number of solutions are available to judge against the needs of a particular set of students. The decision you make may depend upon their age, level, ability and gender, as well as the educational values underpinning the course.

Resourcing a course is a political process that requires an exploration of values, negotiation and compromise and, finally, agreement on the priorities identified in your definition of quality. If you value independent learning, you may want to concentrate resources at the start of the course so that the necessary skills can be developed. Alternatively, you may consider that simple ideas can be presented unproblematically at the early stage of a course to larger groups or through reading. If you consider critical analysis to be important, you might want to concentrate work in smaller groups towards the start of the course in order to encourage a deep approach to learning from the start. With some types of courses and for some student groups, you may wish to focus on social integration and the development of interpersonal skills and this will affect the amount invested in human resources.

In most teaching situations you will be faced with a group with varying needs and abilities. Where comparability of standards is not an issue (for instance, in many leisure evening classes), not all teaching has to be achieved at the same level. In other cases, where it is important that everyone achieves a minimum standard, you may be faced with students needing individual help. Lecturer time is very expensive and may be best used for more complex group teaching. It may be possible to employ students or instructors to support basic-skills development. Some types of knowledge or skill development may be achieved through library-based or video material.

There is seldom only one possible answer to resource questions in course design. Eventual decisions should reflect the underlying values which the course planning team have explored and prioritized. Each decision taken has opportunity costs and benefits. These need careful assessment.

The Politics of Course Development

If you are to be successful in course development, you will need to develop an understanding of the formal and informal procedures for course development and the maintenance of academic quality and standards within the institution and those operating within any outside validating or accrediting body. In further education this can be a complex matter, since colleges rarely validate their own programmes and most have a variety of validating relationships. Thus, a further education college introducing a new subject may choose to develop it as an 'A' level, a National Vocational Qualification (NVQ), a Royal Society of Arts qualification (and so on) or to go for a combination of these. In any case, a lecturer is likely to teach on, and be involved in developing programmes validated by a variety of bodies, each with their own distinctive style and priorities.

The portfolio of qualifications within further (and some higher) education institutions assumes a network of agencies involved in the course planning process. Recently this has become more complex: for instance, NVQ funding from Training and Enterprise Councils provides a different perspective as colleges learn how to deal with workplace qualifications and the complex accrediting and validating arrangements in 'cooperation' with organizations that are also their competitors.

If your institution has an open management style, it is especially important that you understand the complexity of the micro-political system in your institution. In an autocratic system, you probably only need to convince the head of the institution of the value of the development proposal. (Although even here you may be wise to consult others to ensure their cooperation as well as to gain access to their knowledge and experience.) In more open systems, you will gain resources through skilful negotiation and compromise. New development will usually be recognized by your colleagues as carrying an opportunity cost. If management time and other resources are devoted to one development, another, perhaps prized by others in the institution, may be delayed. Therefore, you are more likely to succeed if those affected by the development in any way have been consulted and their views taken into account. Those that will be affected will include lecturers in related areas, but also staff responsible for library and learning resources, finance, registry and quality control.

Fortunately, this process is likely to yield a variety of insights and creative ideas which you can include in the process of course development. In my experience, it is important that this consultation starts at the earliest stage and continues during the planning process. You may decide not to pursue a course development if informal consultation indicates that key decision makers, such as the departmental head, have fundamental objections to the proposal. Ideally, you should have resolved objections to the proposal before it is formalized and presented to a committee or validating body.

You may experience great difficulty in taking a course development idea to completion if you do not understand and adhere to the formal decision-making system of the organization. Each institution has its own course-approval system. Typically, a major proposal might start with a formal proposal to set up a course development group to the departmental committee. The decision of this committee might have to be ratified by the academic board. The completed course proposal may take the same route before moving on to external validation or accreditation if necessary.

Documentation for a Course Proposal

Information about the process of course approval should be (but is not always) easily obtainable. You may be wise to ask for institutional guidelines as to what should be included in the documentation at each stage and the correct process for approval. If no guidelines exist, it will probably be sufficient to include the following in an outline proposal: the course title and qualification; its rationale; proposed start date; potential demand for the course and the evidence for this demand; the human and other resources required to plan and operate it; its link to present provision and staff expertise; the length, mode and structure; the validating body; external and internal consultation which has taken place; and the proposed management and membership of the course development team. The most important part of this paper will be the rationale. This should state succinctly why the course would be a good thing, whose needs it would meet and how it would be distinctive.

You are likely to need all the elements above in the final documentation, but also a statement of the institutional and other context of the proposal; admissions policy; aims; objectives; teaching and learning strategies; details of the syllabus for each element of the course, with a clear specification of core and optional elements; information about the teaching and support staff; the capital and running costs, including elements such as the library; the expected level of recruitment; the forms of assessment; the assessment regulations and arrangements for student progression or referral at each stage of the course; provision for alternative stepping on and stepping off points; the course management, committee and evaluation structures within which the course will operate; and their relationship to management and quality control systems at institutional levels.

Many of these matters are highly technical and you will need to work closely with senior colleagues to frame regulations and descriptions of operational control appropriately. The quality and standards of the course will be judged in the light of this documentation and through the operations described within it. Therefore, it is important to get it as right as possible from the start.

Documentation tends to be received better if it takes the needs and requirements of the reader into account. Your informal discussions should have enabled you to address likely concerns within the institution. A thorough understanding of the explicit and implicit criteria employed by any external validating or accrediting body is also very useful. The language you use in proposals and submissions is likely to be important to how it is received. It should suit the style of the validators, be very precise, with terms defined and used consistently, if repetitiously, throughout. Absolute clarity and consistency usually makes validation and course operation smoother. Where several lecturers are contributing components of the course document, you may decide to impose a fairly rigid house style and format.

During the approval process you and your team will probably be required to attend committee meetings and answer questions on the proposal. Any inconsistency amongst the course planning team is likely to lead to problems. In my experience, things tend to go more smoothly if you all know the document intimately and understand the way the underlying values have been operationalized throughout.

You will need to define the standards for your particular level of programme. Frazer (1992) suggests that these may be defined in general terms or as specific statements of knowledge, understandings, skills and attitudes to be demonstrated by successful students. I find it most useful to specify standards in terms of the explicit link between objectives and assessment.

Definitions of quality will also take into account the defined purpose of the course. These purposes may be expressed in terms of the interests of a variety of groups with a stake in education. These include managers, students, those who fund the course and validators. In the course design process, it is important that you develop an awareness of the range of potential definitions and the values underlying them. Frazer (1992) identifies qualities, attitudes and skills which are optimal for effective learning. Some may usefully be applied to course design within further and higher education. Many focus on the characteristics of effective learning within a particular body of knowledge, including love and respect for

---

Enquiry Task

Draw a flow diagram of your understanding of the process (formal and informal) for taking a course development idea to completion.
Discuss and refine this with:

a)   a colleague in a related area
b)   a senior colleague

Draw up a list of people and bodies which should be consulted informally and/or formally on each of the following:

	Informal Consultation	*Formal Consultation*

- Course title/qualification(s)
- Rationale
- Length, mode and structure
- Start date
- Institutional context
- Potential demand for the course
- Level of recruitment
- Human resources
- Capital and running costs
- Links to present provision
- Validation processes
- Management and membership of the development team
- Admissions policy
- Aims; objectives
- Teaching and learning strategies
- Syllabus, core/optional
- Forms of assessment
- Assessment regulations and arrangements
- Accreditation of prior learning/credit accumulation
- Course management
- Evaluation/quality control systems

---

scholarship and the subject studied; a desire to learn more and knowledge about how to learn; and competence within the subject. Other indicators focus on 'transferable' aspects of learning such as an awareness of personal limits of knowledge and skills; a range of study and problem-solving skills; the ability to locate information and use it to construct an argument and analyse critically; the ability to integrate knowledge from different fields; and communication and interpersonal skills. Other indicators of quality identified by Frazer focus on the characteristics of the teachers. These include their professional knowledge; a love of, and ability to communicate the subject; a willingness to use feedback to improve teaching; a willingness to work as part of a team; understanding of how students learn, what motivates them and what difficulties they might face; competence with a wide variety of teaching methods. Real quality must be based on careful planning at the stage of course design and self-evaluation at course and individual level. The criteria for good evaluation may be incorporated at the course planning stage.

Enquiry Task

Discuss with a group of colleagues, an employer, a group of students and a senior manager in your institution how the quality of your course might be defined by:

Indicators of quality
- Government   e.g., low wastage rate
- Potential students   e.g., improved job prospects
- The subject discipline   e.g., well-qualified teachers
- Potential employers   e.g., emphasis on communication skills
- Institutional management   e.g., recruits well
- The validating body   e.g., good system of quality control

Consider which of these are, and which should be, included in your planning related to:

a) the course objectives;
b) the course content;
c) teaching and learning processes;
d) the assessment;
e) the course management system; and
f) human and other resource issues.

Summary

- Course design takes place within a political context. It should anticipate change, and flexibility should be built into the system. This flexibility should accommodate changes in staff–student ratios. Creative solutions at the planning stage is required if quality is to be maintained.
- Course planning should take into account the feelings and enthusiasms of people within the institution as well as the assessment of student needs and requirements.
- A variety of modes and course structures are possible and should be explored if student needs are to be met.
- Aims and objectives specify the values underlying the programme and give it coherence. They should be congruent with all aspects of the course.
- Among the processes which should be considered in course design are admission arrangements and requirements; teaching, learning and assessment methods; and systems for accountability and evaluation.

- Course design takes place within a context of limited resources and is therefore a political process. All parties to the process should be identified and included within it.

Entry for the Reflective Diary

- Write about a course that you found particularly fulfilling as a student and that still affects your life or the way you think and behave.
- Identify the elements of the course and its design which made it particularly effective.
- Which of these elements are reflected in the course design you have been working on in the course of this chapter.

Notes
Annotated List of Suggested Reading

Council for National Academic Awards (1992) *Academic Quality in Higher Education: A Guide to Good Practice in Framing Regulations*, London, CNAA.
Pages 31 to 38 provide a good summary of what might be included in a course submission and identifies the questions which both internal and external validators are likely to wish to address in assessing a proposal.

Gibbs, G. (1992) *Teaching More Students: 1 Problems and Course Design Strategies*, Oxford, PCFC.
A useful guide to some of the strategies for teaching larger groups of students which should be considered at course-design stage. He tends to present his solutions as unproblematic and needs to be read with a critical eye.

HEQC (1994) *A Briefing paper from the Higher Education Quality Council: Checklist for Quality Assurance Systems 1994*, London, HEQC.
A very short (three A4 pages) summary of the kind of quality assurance systems the HEQC are looking for in institutions. Paragraphs 4–22 need consideration at the course-planning stage. These paragraphs deal with issues such as selection policies, programme approval and arrangements for course evaluation.

References

ASHCROFT, K. (1987) 'The history of an innovation', *Assessment and Evaluation in Higher Education*, 12, 1, 37–45.
ASHCROFT, K. and FOREMAN-PECK L. (1994) *Managing Teaching and Learning in Higher Education*, London, Falmer Press.
BALL, C. and EGGINS, H. (Eds) (1989) *Higher Education into the 1990's: New Dimensions*, Milton Keynes, SHRE/Open University Press.
FRAZER, M. (1992) *Quality Assurance in Higher Education*, London, Falmer Press.
GIBBS, G. (1992) *Teaching More Students: 1 Problems and Course Design Strategies*, Oxford, PCFC.
REEVES, M. (1988) *The Crisis in Higher Education: Competency, Delight and the Common Good*, Milton Keynes, SRHE/Open University Press.

Chapter 8

Resource Management

In this chapter, I discuss the political and institutional contexts for resource allocation and their effects on practice. I outline some of the principles underpinning various systems of resource allocation in order to help you to understand business planning. I explore some of the ways that you might operate more effectively as a person bidding for resources internally or externally, in order to use them to achieve quality in your work. I describe the process of bidding as an interpersonal and human one, which requires you to understand formal and informal systems.

The allocation and management of resources is crucial to questions of quality. Lecturers are likely to be responsible for the management of resources and also to be in a position to influence, even if only to a limited extent, their allocation. Those who understand some of the principles of resource management, at the departmental, institutional, local and national level, are likely to have more influence on the quality of educational provision in which they are involved.

Funding and the Macro Systems of Education

The UK Conservative Government of the 1980s and early 1990s increasingly used funding in order to direct policy within further and higher education. It achieved this through selective financial support for projects which fit its ideological framework as expressed through its preferred definition of criteria for quality and standards. For instance, much of the further education sector has been required to include National Vocational Qualifications (NVQs) as part of their portfolio of programmes in order to qualify for funding from the Training and Enterprise Councils (TECs). The Further Education Funding Council (FEFC) explicitly rewards qualifications and growth which 'count' towards government targets, and in particular, part-time and work-based routes to achieving NVQs. It has added to the 'value' of NVQs as a performance indicator: for example, by upping the equivalence for funding purposes of NVQ level 2 from four to five GCSE Grade A to C (FEFC, 1994a). In addition, the proportion of students achieving NVQ and inspectors' assessments of the quality of NVQ programmes are explicitly stated as performance indicators of quality which have relevance to funding decisions (FEFC, 1994a). Students are also encouraged to undertake courses accredited as NVQs because they can obtain tax relief on the fees.

Government also controls student intakes and influences the teaching methods and assessment by the way that it manipulates the various kinds of support that colleges and universities receive and the framework of rules in which they must operate. For instance, the moves towards school-based initial teacher training within the UK has been influenced by government-imposed requirements for the accreditation of courses.

In the main, funds for teaching reach colleges and universities in the form of a block grant via the Further or Higher Education Funding Council (FEFC or HEFC) and tuition fees (usually via the LEA). Major changes have been introduced by Parliament in the past few years. For instance, within higher education, the balance of funding shifted after the 1988 Education Act from a major reliance on the block grant to a greater reliance on tuition fees. The method of allocating the block grant was also changed and a system of competitive bidding was introduced. Colleges and universities could 'bid' for additional students at a lower 'price' than the average produced by dividing the block grant by their student numbers. The bidding was competitive and secret. Students were allocated to the institutions within each programme area which bid at the lowest price. The fees remained fixed for all students within a particular programme area.

The process of competitive bidding became almost compulsory for institutions within the Higher Education Funding Council sector. The basis of bidding was that institutions were allocated a core funding (the block grant) for teaching a core number of students. To begin with, the core was 90 per cent of the previous year's grant in return for teaching 95 per cent of the number of students. (This 'efficiency factor' has been somewhat reduced since.) Thus, unless institutions bid for a substantial increase in students each year, their total funding would decline rapidly. If an institution's bid for additional students was unsuccessful, they were virtually forced to recruit a larger number of 'fees only' students to make up the financial shortfall caused by the reduction in the block grant. Whether institutions bid or not, the unit of resource was put under intense pressure and student numbers rose remorselessly.

'Quality' in teaching was to be recognized in the bidding system, by discounting the bid prices of those courses assessed as high quality. Thus a bid might be treated as if it was a certain percentage lower than it was in actuality. This has encouraged colleges and universities to invest more in staff development related to teaching, and in quality control and audit systems. Universities are beginning to recognize that teaching quality will bring in real money, sometimes more than can be realistically achieved by improved research ratings.

The FEFC has set up a system which has some similarities to HEFC. The funding for 1994/5 consisted of a block allocation of 90 per cent of the previous year's funding in return for a commitment to undertake 90 per cent of the activity. In addition, institutions could request funding for additional 'units' of activity, at a rate per unit set by the FEFC, to top up this allocation. There was also an element of funding set aside for demand-led activity. Since the allowance for inflation was only 1 per cent, and the FEFC level of funding for the additional units was below that of many colleges' existing unit funding, there was a built-in efficiency factor created. Should institutions wish to maintain their total funding, they would have to reduce unit costs.

The Government has pursued funding strategies in the further education sector, to ensure that colleges fulfil its agenda. Amongst these was a holding back of £50m from the FEFC funding allocation until new 'flexible' staffing contracts were introduced. It also allocated £30m to the Training and Enterprise Councils (FEFC, 1994b) to ensure that colleges work cooperatively with industry and make their training needs (rather than, for instance, students' long-term interests) a top priority. The FEFC tied its allocation of 'extra' units of funded activity to the extent that an individual institution had fulfilled government priorities (as expressed through the FEFC). It also took into account the average unit costs, and the previous record in expanding student numbers. Institutions which failed to achieve significant growth in 1993/4 and with above average unit costs were allocated none or part of their applications for funding additional to the core (FEFC, 1994b). In addition, institutions were threatened with a reduction in the following year's funding should they fail to meet targets. These policies are encouraging colleges to overrecruit and to accept a low level of unit funding at the margins, even though these will be incorporated into the core in future years (FEFC, 1994c).

In 1993 the polytechnics were absorbed into the university sector and the Higher Education Funding Council was set up. The new universities and colleges of higher education then became eligible for research funding. A system of research rating was set up, and institutions invited to submit evidence of the extent and quality of their research work. The available funds were distributed according to institutional research ratings. The result was that the old universities tended to receive less money for research in real terms than they had previously and the new universities gained. Most universities are keen to make financial gains by an improvement in their position in the next round of research rating. This is creating pressure on staff to publish regularly, whether or not they have anything to say, at the same time as they are coping with larger classes and increasing administrative loads. The result is that some lecturers are put under considerable stress. They may find it easier to cope if they develop an understanding of what is happening within the system and find ways of managing the various demands on their time.

After a couple of years of encouraging expansion within higher education, the Government found that it had been too successful. It reached its targets well before the planned deadline, and decided to put a break on expansion. This was achieved by reducing the proportion of funding contributed by the fees element by around 25 per cent in one year and 45 per cent in the next year. This meant that courses with a substantial number of 'fees only' students ceased to be viable (including many courses franchised to further education colleges), and where expansion was built into the system, this had to be reversed by a fierce reduction in intakes. On three- and four-year courses, where an expansion was often still working its way through, this caused particular difficulty.

It seems unlikely that the Further Education Funding Council (FECE) will be any less a creature of government policy. I have outlined above how further education is being encouraged to expand rapidly within full-time, part-time, government-funded and self-funded provision. The implications for colleges are profound. These include the need to plan for a decreasing unit of resource, increased efficiency year by year and flexibility of staffing (for instance, through an increase in fee paid and temporary staffing). Perhaps the most important lesson is that government funding is no longer 'safe', and that colleges and universities should consider diversification in order to create a broad portfolio of funded activity, much of which is not subject to sudden changes in government policy. This is likely to involve most lecturers within the further and higher education sector in rapid change and development over the next few years.

In addition, colleges and universities are becoming more hard-nosed about resource allocation and control. Everything must be costed and budgeted. Costs and benefits of various courses of action are more carefully assessed. This implies that you need to develop an understanding of resource allocation and the bidding process in your institution and become aware of ways of exploiting opportunities to bring new funds into your institution. It remains essential to assess this activity against a set of core values. It seems to me that, in the new entrepreneurial climate, it is even more important (but also more difficult) to keep asking the fundamental question about quality: 'How worthwhile is it?'

Resource Allocation and Management Style

Institutions vary in the extent of overt competition for resources and flexibility in the internal system to adjust to new demands. Grey (1984) points out that the system adopted within an institution is often related to its management style. In autocratic systems the institutional or departmental head will retain a direct control over resources. The head may have a personal and private agenda, that may change over time. For instance, in one further education college, the principal was keen for the college to achieve a particular high-status development before he retired. The time frame for this development was determined by his need to 'go with a bang', but was stated in terms of the requirements of the institution. Unfortunately this led to problems for the institution, since secretiveness is rarely compatible with efficiency and effectiveness.

Many institutions still operate incremental systems, where resource allocation is adjusted up or down on a historical basis. Alternatively, needs are determined on an apparently rational basis using logical criteria. Usually this involves a formula that includes student numbers and subject weighting. Both of these systems build in rigidities and tend to look to the past rather than the future.

All of the systems described above restrict participation in resource-management decisions. This is likely to have effects on the quality of provision since those allocating resources will not have access to much of the knowledge and expertise residing within the institution. More flexible systems require the political involvement of staff in a process of negotiation and coalition. Openness is a prerequisite for this to operate effectively. In more open systems, ground rules for resource allocation will be stated, but will also be open to the possibility of change as a result of argument. History will be a starting point, not the basis, for resource allocation. There will be an annual round of negotiations about the basis for, and the actual allocation of resources. Competition will be overt and success in negotiation may require areas to establish alliances with other areas. In addition, management skills are required at all levels, first of all to create the case for a particular pattern of resource allocation and later to manage and account for the resources devolved. Many lecturers may find this uncomfortable: the alternative is a historically based allocation or one that relies entirely on the opinions of senior managers.

Principles of Financial Management

It has been an objective of recent government policy that colleges and universities should manage themselves more efficiently. Quality has therefore been defined in terms of productivity, for instance, the throughput of students and the intensive use of site and buildings. The new universities and higher and further education colleges have been given the full responsibility for the management of the majority of their budgets previously enjoyed by the old universities. The new system includes cash-limited budgets, which require tight control of expenditure and income and the ability to carry forward surpluses and deficits at the end of the financial year.

The freedom and responsibilities which the new system has created has led to an emphasis on accountability, and in particular, the need for clear financial records at all levels of the institution where income or expenditure is authorized. In addition, it has been essential that managers have clear and realistic plans for the future. This means that systems for budgetary planning have been put in place.

Birch (1988) describes how management control ensures certain courses of action are maintained and desired ends achieved. Quality control now often involves identifying which key variable should be monitored (for instance, levels of success of students in public examinations), setting 'target' levels of performance for these and having a clear set of actions that follow any failure to meet targets. This requires that a system of data collection and analysis has been set up, and explains the increasing emphasis on administration in many colleges and universities.

In addition, increasing modularization and courses which cut across departments, combined with more delegation of budgets, are requiring measures and methods for mapping the relative contribution to teaching from different departments, set against income provided by the students. This has led to measures such as FTE (full-time equivalence), which can be defined in a variety of ways. Those who understand the range of possible definitions are in a better position to argue for an institutional definition that favours their area (see Birch, 1988).

If the records are to be accurate and plans realistic, budgetary control must be tight, but at the same time, decisions on expenditure must lead to maximum efficiency. There is some tension between these two ideals. Tight budgetary control might imply a high degree of centralization, but efficiency and effectiveness often require that decisions are taken as close to the point of impact as possible. Many institutions are resolving this apparent dilemma by devolving a substantial proportion of the budget, involving many more of their staff in planning and monitoring budgets, but at the same time setting up clear lines of responsibility and monitoring arrangements. This implies that many more staff must understand the financial system and be willing to accept their particular area of responsibility.

It is possible that you may be involved in the control of a budget at an early stage in your career. You may experience frustrations and difficulties with this if you are not given any authority to exercise your judgment effectively. You may be given responsibility but no authority. Even if you are given 'authority' this may be meaningless if your delegated budget is so small or inadequate that real choice about expenditure becomes impossible. You also need information, skills and knowledge to control your budget. You have a right to ask for clear guidelines describing your responsibilities and the limits of your powers. Grey areas, where nobody accepts responsibility or where responsibilities overlap, may cause you difficulties. An understanding of the basic principles of budgetary control can help you analyse the source of problems, and perhaps enable something to be done to rectify the difficulties. As a budget holder you will be expected to further the institution's objectives. Resource management thus becomes part of the 'quality' process. In order to manage this, you need to know what these objectives are, and you may also need access to the institution's strategic plan.

You are likely to have to provide the sort of information which will enable the institution to monitor your financial decisions. You may need to find out what form this information should take. In any case, you should be prepared to justify any decision that you make. This will almost certainly mean that you will need to develop a record-keeping system. You may also need to ask for clarification as to where your discretion ends. For instance, it is essential that you do not commit the institution to ongoing expense without this being approved by a senior manager.

Enquiry Task

Do you know:

- How the budgetary process relates to institutional objectives?
- What happens to unspent income at the end of a financial year?
- What happens if a budget is overspent?
- How cash purchases are processed?
- How often actual income and expenditure is reported to budget holders?

Which of these 'rules' apply in your institution?

- Heads of department may vire expenditure between cost centres.
- Heads of department are responsible for controlling all expenditure and income in their department.
- Heads of department may delegate financial powers delegated to them.

Find out about any areas where you were uncertain of the answer.

Business Planning, Quality and Standards

As colleges and universities become more business-like in their operations, business planning may be used to an increasing extent as a means of translating strategic plans at all levels into action. Business and strategic planning have become part of the way the institution meets its objectives. They embody criteria by which the institution says it wishes to be judged and therefore they have become quality issues in themselves. This means that, if you wish to be involved in or to instigate change, you may need to understand the principles and practice of business planning in your institutional context.

The need for business planning has been created by a political climate that has defined quality in terms of the development of a competitive 'market-place' in education. This political agenda has imposed a particular kind of financial discipline on educational planning. In any new development it is likely that you will be expected to plan the programme or service and resources as part of an integrated process. In the interests of your own and institutional integrity, it is important that you do not see business planning as a value-neutral process. What you wish to do should not *just* be financially profitable, but also congruent with your values and aims.

Business plans can relate to an institution, a department, a programme area or the specific development of a service or course. In each case the headings may be similar, although the level of detail may vary. A business plan should be located in a values framework and include strategic thinking related to the institutional or departmental mission and development plan. The operational context needs to be analysed and related to issues, such as the way the plan links to the management structure and quality control machinery. The context includes the 'market' and the 'marketing strategy'. A business plan should specify human resources which are presently available or which will be needed, as well as physical and other resources. People have feelings and needs. Business planning that sees them as passive 'units of resource' is not only morally dubious but also, in a human, interactive endeavour such as education, doomed to fail. Passion, commitment and shared notions of worthwhileness are issues within business planning as much as in other aspects of professional practice.

A commitment to quality and standards should underpin business planning in education. It should also be manifest within the organization of management-information systems and records, the way student numbers and teaching hours are determined and the ways these impact on other activities. You may need to develop systems for monitoring and evaluation based on data continuously collected and matched against your objectives. Your ability to reflect constructively upon the match between your objectives in business planning and your practice may depend on how well these have been set up and utilized to collect data. Ideally, this planning should be contained within an overall strategic planning framework for the institution. The development with which you are concerned can then become part of a coherent institutional plan for aspects such as the financial forecast, the curriculum plan, the accommodation plan and a marketing plan. Understanding this may help you to achieve your objectives. Senior managers are there to set the initial constraints (ideally these should not be changed mid process), and to prioritize at the end of the planning process. Business planning is then best done 'bottom up' or 'middle out'. If you work in a context where this is not possible, you may experience powerful disincentives to be 'enterprising'. The process of planning may be as relevant to quality as the plan itself. Business planning is one way of developing coherence and communicating internally and externally (although on the last point, the business plan should not be confused with the more glossy presentation of selected aspects which may be served up to outside audiences).

Your institutional mission statement should be sufficiently precise to guide strategic decisions. It should not be subject to change in the short-term. If a mission statement of an institution is changed more than once in about five years, there may be fundamental problems of a lack of direction, clarity, consultation and evaluation at the highest level. This is likely to present you with a fundamental problem in the maintenance of quality and standards.

You may need to develop an understanding of risk factors related to the nature of new ventures if the quality of existing provision is not to be jeopardized. For instance, Davies and Scribbins (1985) point out it is usually less risky to develop a new programme for your existing students than to try to recruit a different type of student to your present programme. Creating a new programme for a new student group is likely to be riskier still. A sudden move away from the core work of your department is likely to be very risky. In business, there has been a recent move towards 'demergers'. There are good reasons for this, businesses (and programmes) seem more likely to succeed if they are related to areas of strong expertise already existing in the firm (or institution), rather than in a new area. You may decide that there needs to be a powerful quality argument before you take the riskier course. The risks in new ventures should be less if it is possible to 'write off' some aspect of the programme if some of your assumptions in the plan are wrong. For instance, options may be dropped. You should model what would happen if some of your assumptions are wrong. This process is called sensitivity analysis (see Birch, 1988 for more details), and is a useful method for assessing the riskiness of a new development.

Colleges and universities need a low-risk funding portfolio. Some have tried to achieve this through a spread of funding sources. They have tended to diversify, for instance by selling services and obtaining research grants. Some of the areas of diversification have proved to be very risky in themselves and others have been entered into for financial, rather than quality, reasons. An example of this riskiness is the move within further education colleges in the UK towards franchising higher education courses. The recent changes in the fee allocation to such courses may lead some colleges into real financial difficulties.

New ventures often make a loss in the first few years. This creates difficulties for departments which have to act within annual budgets and for other courses within them. The accumulated costs of development and recruitment to a new programme may not be repaid until after a growth period of two to three years. Funding in most colleges and universities is usually done too locally. This can reinforce a lack of development in unsuccessful areas and a general lowering of their quality.

You may be concerned that business planning could lead to you or your institution being driven by economic factors, rather than by educational values.

Enquiry Task

Read your institution's mission statement and any strategic planning documents available within your institution and/or department.

What do these indicate about the areas of new development which would be seen as appropriate?

Do they make the institutional policy on the following clear:

• marketing strategy;
• human resources;
• accommodation planning; and
• curriculum planning?

If not, find another way to investigate institutional policy.

This may be a valid concern. Colleges and universities may become more market-centred, but they should not become market-led. The institution, not the market, should set the goals as part of a moral discourse. The work of colleges and universities is and should be about human development (perhaps in specific subject areas). Our goals and purposes should limit the 'business' we are in. The 'market' may shape the direction of development to some extent, but always within these limits. This implies that the key question about a new venture should not be 'Can we do it?', but rather 'Should we do it?'

Applying for Internal and External Funding

Resource management within colleges and universities typically takes place within clearly defined areas of influence which operate some degree of control and autonomy. Understanding the way that influence operates, both at the formal and informal level, may help you if you are to gain access to resources or to influence their allocation. As a reflective practitioner, this will be for educationally valid purposes, not for its own sake.

If it is to be open and well informed, I believe that resource allocation needs to be part of a political process. However, this process can degenerate into a 'game', where the gaining of a disproportionate amount of resources becomes an objective in its own right. As a reflective practitioner, you will need to consider the long-term consequences of this desire to 'win' for other areas of the institution. If these other areas are playing by different rules, you may find it hard to maintain a responsible stance. There is a need for an appropriate forum for a moral discourse in political decision-making.

In general, the principles of bidding apply equally to internal and external funding. Bidding tends to be more likely to contribute to quality if certain principles are born in mind. In outlining these, I am assuming that you are interested in learning how to bid for a relatively substantial level of funding. If you are bidding internally and for a fairly small sum of money, the level of detail and amount of preparation I describe below may be 'overkill'.

The Context

Firstly, your bid should relate to the institutional plan and to your moral and educational purposes. You may find it useful to think about your institution in terms of quality issues such as its success and track record and establish what unique, special qualities it offers. Generally your bid will be viewed more positively if it does not rely entirely upon your efforts (successful action is often about shared ownership). Funded activity takes place in a context, so it is worth finding out about existing networks/links with suppliers, governors, staff, students and parents. These people tend to know the institution and have a valid interest in it. As a reflective practitioner you would in any case be interested in their perspectives. Coincidentally, this interest makes them more likely to respond to requests for help. If you can define strategic areas for development and identify the support required (not necessarily money) and redefine and repackage these in terms of the particular funder's needs (including the priorities identified by your institution, if you are bidding internally), they are more likely to listen sympathetically to you.

In doing this, it is important that you do not lose sight of what your purposes are and issues of worthwhileness.

Bids may be more successful if they are realistic. For instance, in external bidding the cost element of putting the bid together should be taken into account. This may run into thousands of pounds, even for a smallish bid. If you do not account for this, the quality in other areas may suffer as resources, especially time, are pulled away from them.

Your institution should have set limits as to the kind of activity it will support. You may need to do the same. It is important that both you and your institution retain your principles and refuse funding outside of these limits. Companies and others will often renegotiate within them. If you are seeking external funding you will need to discover the rules within your institution about such negotiation. For instance, in most new universities and further education colleges, you will need to ask your senior managers for the authority to negotiate within defined limits. This implies that delegation is possible within the institutional culture where you work, and that clear roles can be established. Where this is not the case, you may find that you are unnecessarily frustrated. Understanding the nature of your problems may help you to find a way of overcoming or coping with them. For instance, you may decide to ask the financial director of the institution or your head of department to accompany you during negotiations.

Once you have decided the nature of the service you wish to promote to your funder (for instance, a research project or some in-house training), find 'disinterested' people (such as business people) who can honestly say that in their opinion the project is a good idea and you are capable of delivering a quality service. This is easier if you have previously developed links to appropriate organizations such as Chambers of Commerce, the Confederation of British Industry, European networks and so on.

Funding as a Political Process

It has been stated above that the Government uses funding as a political tool for change. This is generally true of all funding. Funders usually want change to be embedded in the institution, curriculum and the service you provide. This is neatly described by Harland (1985). She calls it 'categorical funding' and suggests that it is used to facilitate a policy where the policy-makers have neither the statutory right nor the means to implement desired changes without cooperation of those who must implement them. They may proceed to use the normal processes of allocating resources through contracts to implement their policies.

The political process she describes starts with the development of a policy. Funds, generous enough to attract those who can deliver, are then made available (this is particularly potent, of course, when providers have recently felt themselves starved of resources). Voluntary cooperation is invited in exchange for a share of the resources. This implies that you understand the funder's purposes and that they concur with your own. Bidding is more likely to be successful if your bid indicates how institutional change will be 'embedded' once the project is over. It is important to be aware that acceptance of the resources is equated with the acceptance of policy, as well as with the ability to deliver. A clearly articulated set of values is essential to protect against being seduced into uncritically accepting the funder's agenda.

The Funder's Agenda

The funder's purpose should be researched as closely as possible. Depending on the source of funding, you may examine sources of information such as the Secretary of State's speeches, government reports, company reports, local and national press, and reports from Training and Enterprise Councils (TECs). These can help you to assess whether you wish to be associated with the funder's agenda, and if so, how you can state what you wish to do in a way that will appeal to them. For instance, if you are approaching a company, you might use phrases which identify with their corporate identity as expressed in their mission statement.

Funding is about relationships. Establishing and maintaining the relationship with the funder is centrally important. People who administer charitable and other educational funds tend to have priorities in common. These include being able to allocate and spend all the funds at their disposal (the funder is not usually thanked for making savings) and being able to account for their funding decisions to bosses, the auditors and the external world in general. It is usually in funders' interests to maximize the chances of producing results from the funds.

The chances of the funder successfully allocating and spending all the funds at their disposal are increased if they only accept reliable and realistic bids. This implies that your bid should be well costed, reasonable and have a realistic timescale. Being 'cheap' may be a bad idea, and not only for reasons of quality. The effective management of projects must be costed. This may be as much as 40 to 50 per cent of the total cost. Funders may not be impressed if this is left out of bids. Funders generally prefer to avoid uncertainty. Your bid should not suggest the possibility of failure. If you are to preserve your integrity, this means that you should be confident of your ability to deliver. You may find it difficult to bid successfully at first. This may be because funders tend to minimize risk by looking for people with a good track record and so money often goes to people who have received funds before and delivered what was promised. You may need to find a way of demonstrating some previous success, perhaps through external recommendations. Because not all those who successfully bid are good at finishing on time, there are often funds underspent towards the end of the financial year. In some organizations, these cannot be carried over to the next year. If you have a worthwhile project on the shelf *ready to launch*, and the invoices can come in by the end of the financial year, you may be able to find late funding.

Funders usually want to maximize the chances of producing results from the funds. For this reason they may favour bidders who set intermediate targets (e.g., output, finance, dates by which various appointments will be in place) and who promise to monitor regularly and thoroughly. Funders need to make rational, explicable decisions. In order to be able to account for funding decisions funders may use criteria-based assessment. You may be able to find out what these are by getting to know the funder. Part of the skill you need to develop is that of seeing things from the point of view of a potential funder and make life easier for him or her. You may be more successful if you read the criteria and stick closely to the guidelines. It may be worth trying to make a personal contact to discuss the proposal before submission.

Companies tend to have a particular agenda when they become involved in funding. Sponsorship is generally used to provide promotional opportunities. Companies may be more interested in solving problems related to skills and management, than your funding difficulties. They will probably want you to tell them why they should 'add value'. In particular they may not be attracted to funding things which should be the Government's responsibility. You may be able to exploit the desire of many companies to be involved in their community. In general, companies like to be at the leading edge. They usually want to respond to real problems, which reflect their expertise and emphasize quality. Their main priorities tend to include financial soundness, image, reputation, market orientation and excellence. For this reason you may find it helpful to find out what the company thinks its corporate image is and reflect it back to them.

The Bid

The quality of your written plan is likely to crucially affect the success of your bid. There must be demonstrable management processes and structures in place. For instance it should be clear to whom staff are accountable, who signs the cheques and how funds are kept separate.

It may help your case if you make your submission easy to read, for instance by using everyday language rather than jargon. The use of simple language will often help to clarify your purposes and intentions. Your documentation may include a mission or value statement for the project. This provides you with the opportunity to outline your moral agenda and to explain how this fits with the funder's own values. The first few paragraphs of the presentation tend to be the important ones. They should establish the rationale and reflect the funder's agenda. The rest of the project introduction should establish your credibility. The introduction should establish why the funder should support you (rather than somebody else).

In seeking outside funding, you may have to decide on what your attitude will be if the funder asks you to sign away your moral rights. For instance, it is no longer unusual for funders of research projects to demand the right to suppress publication of findings which do not fit their preferred position. (See Chapter 10 for a discussion of the ethical issues this raises.)

You will need to describe the bid, including benefits to the funder. You could start by outlining the context, the institution and its strategic plan. A *few* clearly stated objectives can help to make clear the key stages in achieving the aim. The maintenance of academic standards requires clarity about the expected outcomes of the project: what will have changed at the end of the project. Your documentation may specify how you will monitor progress towards these. You may wish to make it clear that the funder will be informed of progress at each stage and that thorough evaluation will be carried out. You should be able to specify how the evaluation will link back to objectives.

The costing of the project must be specific and realistic. You will probably need a business plan, perhaps including the marketing plan with a timetable. It will probably help the funder if you lay out the budget in the same financial years as they use. This may be different from the August to July financial year now commonly used in the further and higher education sector.

Dissemination

If you are a naturally modest person, you may find it difficult to publicize your success, but dissemination may be very important in extending the life of a project, creating new networks and helping others to improve their practice and learn from yours. Dissemination can take many forms. For instance, you could ensure a press release from the institution or produce articles for appropriate journals with the college or university name at the end and in the text. Simply telling people inside and outside of the institution that you have been successful can help to build your credibility.

Funders generally like to be linked with reports which say definite lessons have been learnt. However, it is important that you are honest about this. Education must involve a commitment to truth, or it is a worthless activity. If the project will make a difference, your project reports should show how. Reports can be written differently for several market-places. Prestigious journals might be included as part of the dissemination as these confer status on the funder and project.

Resource Management and the Measurement of Performance

Birch (1988) points out that the principal measures of performance in resource management are effectiveness (how well the job is being done) and efficiency (what resources are consumed in doing the job). Effectiveness is the key measure when it comes to quality, although, where resources are limited, efficiency will also affect quality.

In order to measure effectiveness it is necessary to specify objectives in measurable terms. For instance, the number of students enrolling on a course may be a measure of its 'attractiveness'. On the other hand, if many of these students fail to complete, there may be problems with the course, so completion rates (or perhaps rates of *successful* completion) may be a better performance indicator and seem to relate more closely to the notion of quality. On the other hand, it may be possible to achieve a high 'pass' rate, but have a substandard product. Therefore the number of students who 'progress' into suitable employment or further study may be a better indicator.

The problem with any measure is that it may distort the very quality it is seeking to measure. For instance, if completion rates are used, lecturers may be tempted to persuade students to stay on course, who would be better changing track. Where lecturers are involved in assessing their students, measurements of 'success' (for instance, the numbers of students achieving a 'good' degree within a university department) may be misleading. Over-generous marking might not be vigorously discouraged if it is in the interest of the institution to have 'good' results.

One of the most common efficiency indicators is the staff–student ratio (the

Enquiry Task

The following organizations are amongst those which fund education-related projects:

Commonwealth Office
Central Government:
    Department for Education
    Home Office
    Department of Trade and Industry
    Department of the Environment
Government Funded Organizations:
    Nature Conservancy Council
    Arts Council
    Sports Council
    English Heritage
    Foundation for Sports and the Arts
    Training, Education and Enterprise Directorate
Charities e.g.:
    MIND
    Save the Children
    Adult Literacy and Basic Skills Unit
    The Laura Ashley Foundation
    The Rowntree Trust
European Union e.g.:
    European Social Fund
    European Regional Development Fund and subfunds to promote:
        regions where industry is closing;
        technology;
        exchanges for young people;
        assistance to Eastern Europe;
        training for women;
        groups undergoing sudden social change; and
        open and distance learning.

What information on these sources of funds are held in your institution? Are there institutional arrangements to approach some funding agencies (e.g., the European Union) through an outside agency?

Choose two or three of these organizations and look through the information available to discover:

• their motivation;
• what they can offer; and
• what they would expect you to deliver.

SSR). The SSR can be worked out according to a variety of formulae. Understanding these can help in making a department look 'good'. An emphasis on SSRs will generally have the effect of reducing the taught hours within programmes, increasing class sizes and/or requiring lecturers to teach more hours over the teaching year. Each of these approaches, and sometimes all of them, are used within further and higher education institutions. As with all performance indicators, there are costs as well as benefits in this form of 'efficiency'. Unfortunately, the costs (usually to quality) may not be as easy to measure as the benefits (usually financial). An emphasis on SSRs does not necessarily reduce unit costs, if other costs are not controlled. The FEFC emphasizes cost-efficient expansion (FEFC, 1994c). There is an increasing emphasis on efficient space utilization. Again, this can be worked out in various ways, and using a particular formula can add to the apparent 'efficiency' of an institution or department. Both the FEFC and HEFC insist on accurate and consistent data on space usage (see for example, FEFC, 1993).

It is now a government requirement that colleges and universities monitor a variety of the performance indicators. For example, the FEFC (1994d) includes amongst its performance indicators for cost effectiveness: achievement of the strategic plan and FEFC agreements; increases in student enrolments; proportion of students finishing the academic year; the proportion achieving their 'learning goals'; and number of 'qualification aims' achieved. These performance indicators are further broken down into the contribution the institution has made to a variety of national targets for efficiency and effectiveness. Unfortunately, this monitoring requires complex and comprehensive management-information systems and people to work them, which can lead to an increase in administrative costs. The Government is aware of this and may start to look more closely at the proportion of income that is allocated to central overheads. Some colleges and universities are anticipating this and have begun to devolve functions previously performed centrally, so as to appear to have lower central administrative costs. Some even apportion the costs of many central functions to teaching departments, although this creates responsibility within departments for costs over which they may have no control. The effect of this kind of device may be to remove incentives for tight control from those who are responsible for spending, since it is not they who suffer the consequences of any overspending.

Institutions have been required to measure and publish their performance in

---

Enquiry Task

Find out:

- what performance indicators are used in your institution;
- how they influence funding;
- what proportion of institutional expenditure is allocated for teaching;
- what proportion is allocated to central administration;
- how decisions about central administrative resource allocation are taken;
- who can influence the amount of resources allocated centrally and how central resources are spent.

a variety of areas. This has generally led to much tighter control of costs, and probably to less waste, but perhaps we have been too uncritical of this process. Most types of performance indicator can have a mildly corrupting effect if they are used in the wrong way.

Resource Management and People

People are the most valuable and expensive resource within most colleges and universities. Their effective management requires an understanding of emotions and motivation as well as some understanding of the logic of deployment. It seems to me to be irrational to go for a purely rational model of human-resource management!

The human resource that the institution has at its disposal includes teaching and non teaching staff, and also students. This resource can further be divided into the deployment of time and the deployment of energy. These are not necessarily the same thing. It may be possible to order someone to devote a particular amount of time to a particular task (though, perhaps not a good model of management), but it is unlikely to lead to quality work unless the person feels committed to the work and its outcomes. Good quality teaching, perhaps more than any other professional activity, involves relationships between people, the flow of ideas, passion and commitment. None of these are possible without real motivation.

Total Quality Management (TQM) is one model of human-resource management that takes motivation into account. It has been discussed in Chapter 2. TQM is a model of management, derived from industry, that includes five guiding principles (Further Education Unit, 1991): the creation of an appropriate climate; the focus placed on the 'consumer'; management by data; people-based management; and continuous quality improvement.

There are possibilities and problems in applying the model to managing people in the educational context. The needs and interests of those who are paying, for instance the Government or an employer, may be in conflict with those of students. If the students are assumed to be the customers, the extent of their involvement in course design and evaluation remains problematic. For instance, they may not be aware of their own learning needs. Part of the job of education is to open new possibilities. The process of learning and of change can be painful, or even unpleasant, on occasions.

Management by data rests on the assumption that data represent the full facts. In education, which is about processes occurring (at least in part) in people's minds, this cannot be assumed. TQM talks in terms of 'proof' of success or improvement. The 'quality' of student experience that results from course development may be as much the result of informed empathy with the student on the part of the development team as direct application of data as fact. This does not mean that evaluation and surveys should not be conducted and systematically fed into the resource-planning process, but it is important that you are clear about criteria or indicators of success.

The model requires that when success is achieved, it should be publicized internally and externally, so that all those who have contributed can be recognized and further motivated. People-based management implies that the management system is participative and encourages staff at all levels to identify problems and potential solutions. Joint problem-solving and teamwork, involving managers, lecturers and support staff, are central to this process, as is the recognition and acknowledgment of individual contributions.

If the commitment of all staff is to be harnessed to the pursuit of excellence, an open-management system is required, that gives 'ownership' and responsibility for improvements to teaching and non-teaching staff. This ownership is not restricted to the staff member's own area of work, but operates anywhere where cross-functional problems exist. Such systems tend to work better where an institution is not under threat and where change can be carefully considered before implementation. Recently change in education has been imposed externally rather than developed and owned by the staff team. In addition, externally imposed processes, such as the introduction of performance-related pay, may act in direct conflict to the achievement of quality and the maintenance of standards, especially the development of team approaches to these.

Continuous quality improvement seems self evidently a 'good thing'. Unfortunately the current context of education demands response to a constantly changing government agenda. Time to achieve a shared view of quality and a gradual and planned progression towards it are central to the maintenance of continuous quality improvement. Attempts to rush the process have been found to be counter productive (FEU, 1991). This is problematic in systems destabilized by rapid and externally generated change.

Summary

Governments use funding to direct policy and require colleges and universities to introduce changes. Sudden changes in government policy have led some institutions into financial difficulties and may have posed a threat to quality and standards. This has caused a move towards diversification and away from a reliance on government funding, sometimes for financial rather than educational reasons.

Within institutions, resource allocation is related to management style. More open styles of management enable negotiation and therefore tend to be more political. Devolved systems of allocation and control require clarity in management, targets, accountability and recording.

Business planning is an increasing feature of development within colleges and universities. Business plans should be related to the strategic plan and to educational aims. The motivation behind business planning should be the enhancement of the quality of provision. A business plan may include:

- an assessment of the market;
- the marketing strategy;
- the resources available and needed;
- a specification of management systems and accountability; and
- the impact of the plan on other activities.

Business planning should take place within a framework of clearly articulated values.

Institutions like to minimize risk. Different types of development carry different levels of risk. Sensitivity analysis, where you work out what will happen if some of your assumptions are wrong, helps to minimize risk.

If you are applying for internal or external funding, you may be more successful if your bid fits within the institution's strategic plan and involves others. It is important to get close to the funder and to realize that funding is a political activity. It may be worthwhile researching their agenda to discover if it is compatible with your own and that of the institution. Funders usually want to be sure that they can spend all their funds, be able to account for them and avoid uncertainty. They tend to favour people who finish on time and produce results.

A bid for funding should specify:

- what will be achieved;
- the management structure; the rationale;
- objectives;
- how it fits into strategic planning;
- outcomes;
- systems for monitoring and evaluation;
- realistic costing;
- a timetable; and
- your strategy for dissemination.

Various performance indicators are used in further and higher education to measure efficiency and effectiveness. Some of these are imposed by the Government

---

Entry for the Reflective Diary

Write about the link between resource allocation and your students' educational experience in one or more of these areas:

- teaching materials;
- room decor or allocation;
- central library and learning resources; and
- staffing.

List actions you might take to improve your students' access to appropriate resources. e.g.:

- action to influence policy;
- creating a bid (to an internal or external funder) for particular resources; and
- better use of existing resources.

Decide upon a course of action and write a justification that would be explicable to others in terms of identifiable improvements in quality.

---

and influence quality. Each has a variety of possible definitions and each can distort practice if used in the wrong way. The costs of performance indicators are not usually as easy to measure as their benefits.

People are the institution's most valuable resource. Their feelings and motivation may be as important to their effective management as 'rational' deployment. 'Total Quality Management' provides a potentially useful model of human-resource management, although there are some problems in relating it directly to the educational context.

Notes
Annotated List of Suggested Reading

Birch, D. (1988) *Managing Resources in Further Education: A Handbook for College Managers*, Blagdon, The Further Education Staff College.
A comprehensive guide to basic resource management, that includes information on how to work out indicators such as SSR and plan and manage budgets.

Grey, L. (1984) 'Managing resources in schools and colleges', in Goulding, S., Bell, J., Bush, T., Fox, A. and Goody, J. (Eds) (1984) *Case Studies in Education Management*, London, Open University Press.
A short case study that includes a description of the way a typical well-run further education college allocates and manages its resources.

References

BETHEL, D. (1993) 'Linking quality with funding in European higher education', *Newsletter of the International Network for Quality Assurance Agencies in Higher Education*, Hong Kong, HKCAA.
BIRCH, D. (1988) *Managing Resources in Further Education: A Handbook for College Managers*, Blagdon, The Further Education Staff College.
DAVIES, P. and SCRIBBINS, K. (1985) *Marketing Further and Higher Education*, York, Longmans for FEU and FESC.
FURTHER EDUCATION FUNDING COUNCIL (1993) *Council Report. No. 11*, 23 December, FEFC.
FURTHER EDUCATION FUNDING COUNCIL (1994a) *Council News. No. 13*, 11 April, FEFC.
FURTHER EDUCATION FUNDING COUNCIL (1994b) *Council News. No. 15*, 20 June, FEFC.
FURTHER EDUCATION FUNDING COUNCIL (1994c) *Guidance on the Recurrent Funding Methodology 1994–5*, February, Coventry, FEFC.
FURTHER EDUCATION FUNDING COUNCIL (1994d) *Circular 94/12: Measuring Achievement*, Coventry, FEFC.
FURTHER EDUCATION UNIT (1991) *Quality Matters: Business and Industry Models and Further Education*, London, FEU.
GREY L. (1984) 'Managing resources in schools and colleges, in Goulding, S., BELL, J., BUSH, T., FOX, A. and GOODEY, J. (Eds) (1984) *Case Studies in Education Management*, London Open University Press.
HARLAND, J. (1985) *TVEI — A Model for Curriculum Change*, Sheffield British Educational Research Association.

Chapter 9

Marketing and Recruitment

In this chapter, I discuss marketing as an essential aspect both of income generating and quality. I consider elements of an appropriate marketing strategy including the analysis of the marketing mix, the creation of promotional materials and systems for collecting market intelligence and improving communication with actual and potential students. Student interests and needs and admissions processes are identified as key to a marketing policy that has the enhancement of the quality of provision at its heart.

The Context for Marketing and Recruitment

Marketing is becoming a feature of life for more and more lecturers. It is a function of the rapid change many of us are experiencing. As target numbers from the Government are capped and average income from each student drops, institutions are faced with reduced units of resource (and sometimes reductions in total income). This is leading them to seek new sources of income, and in particular, to generate income from outside of government sources. Some of the difficulties faced by colleges and universities have been discussed in earlier chapters on resource management and course design. These difficulties require institutions to discover new markets, to build on their strengths and rectify weaknesses (often within market forecasting, product development, pricing and quality assurance for non-traditional areas of work), in order to meet the needs of new student groups. Income generation and marketing therefore go hand in hand.

Marketing is much more than selling. It is about the public face of your institution. It is a central issue in determining who comes to your college or university and the reception they get. For these reasons, I see marketing as a process that should be centrally concerned with quality. As such, it should involve as many of the employees of an institution as possible. This includes support staff as well as teaching staff and managers. I have also assumed that institutions should be market-centred, but not market-led. This implies that your college or university should have a clear mission that allows you to look at potential developments and ask the question 'Should we do it?', rather than 'Can we do it?' Marketing in education thus becomes part of the moral enterprise of the institution as well as a practical business.

Since the 'customer' is usually the student, I will refer to them as such in the rest of this chapter. Nevertheless, it should be kept in mind that colleges and universities do have clients and customers other than students, and these are likely to increase. The notion of marketing within education as a moral enterprise concerned with the quality of education rests upon a belief that the student is at the centre of the learning process, and that we are there to serve their interests and needs. In the process of serving our students' interests, we may (and perhaps should) also serve the interests and needs of our subject, other interest groups and the wider society, but this may not be the primary aim of our work. You may decide to find out as much as you can about your students' or potential students' needs and interests, in order to devise ways of meeting them at every stage. These stages may include the development of an understanding of what you can offer, the process of application and interviewing, course delivery, and follow-up work on student outcomes.

Effective marketing depends upon the attitude of all members of staff. It builds on an awareness, sensitivity and response to the needs and interests of students and potential students; an understanding of how these relate to the educational process; a willingness to become involved in promoting the institution or department and what it can offer; and a willingness to change and adapt to meet identified needs and educational aims and aspirations.

Definitions of Marketing

Marketing is identifying (or anticipating) and satisfying client requirements within budget. Within education it should be much more than 'promotion' of the institution or its products. I am suggesting that a quality approach to marketing should influence all aspects of institutional life, but particularly its links with outside bodies and the planning process.

Marketing involves the analysis of the marketing mix within an institution or department. This mix includes the services or programmes which are offered, particularly their range and quality, the expertise available and the mechanisms to determine their quality. It also includes the 'price' of these products. The price may include fees, although for many courses it is not the 'customer' who pays the fee. It will certainly involve an assessment by the students of the opportunities lost to them by participating in the programme or service you are offering. This 'opportunity cost' is relative to the value of the particular programme to the potential students and a comparison of that value and cost relative to those offered by institutions elsewhere. Within education, it should also include a consideration of the values underpinning a programme. Should the 'price' of a programme not support these values, the programme becomes unviable in educational terms.

The third element in the marketing mix is the 'place'. This includes the institution's atmosphere and catchment area, although these may be altered to meet the needs of potential students. For instance, if programmes are offered through forms of open learning, the geographical location of the institution need not limit the catchment area. The value dimension of this decision is considered in detail in Ashcroft and Foreman-Peck (1994), but includes the notion that a variety of locations may be valid for learning, and that the student may control the time, place and perhaps the direction of study. It is an essentially empowering process.

The final aspect of the marketing mix is that of promotion. This involves aspects like advertising, the prospectus, publications and marketing events. Within education, this promotion should be within a framework of truth and accuracy. You should not be interested in recruiting as many students as possible by whatever means, but rather, in recruiting those who will benefit from what you have to offer.

Marketing consists of a mixture of these four categories. The marketing skill is in recognizing constraints and, within these, achieving an optimum balance between the elements.

Aims of Marketing

The language of marketing is taken from business and is off-putting to some lecturers. This may be because they are worried (perhaps rightly) that it may encourage a desire to create profit through increasing volume, irrespective of considerations of worthwhileness. The aim of marketing within education should not be primarily to maximize profits, but rather to enable the institution to serve the community through educationally defensible programmes, subject to rigorous quality criteria, while at the same time remaining financially viable. It is pointless unless it is based on student satisfaction and worthwhile learning.

On the other hand, some financial independence from the Government is desirable, if the institution is to retain sufficient freedom from short-term political priorities to pursue an educational agenda that it considers to be worthwhile in its own right. If every area of the institution merely breaks even, it may end up too dependent upon changes in policies of its various funders and may not retain the freedom both to survive and to refuse to participate in particular activities which it considers to be educationally dubious. In addition, some 'profit' is necessary within the institution to finance new developments and activities which are worthwhile but involve an element of risk.

The Further Education Unit (1994) states that one of the major challenges facing further education is to increase participation. They suggest that colleges will need to use market-research techniques to find out what people want and need from the college and to identify gaps in the provision. The definition of the services which a university or college will wish to provide in the light of this data and its mission, might be defined as its vision. Marketing is a key function in achieving that vision.

Marketing enables worthwhile ventures to be launched successfully, but it also provides the language for analysing the 'product life cycle', enabling the department or institution to identify when programmes are becoming educationally inappropriate or unviable and are therefore about to move into decline. The department or institution is then in a position to explore new ventures and markets. Perhaps most importantly, it provides a means by which students' needs and interests are identified and the opportunity to ensure that they are put first. From your students' point of view, this means that courses and administrative systems are designed for the benefit of their learning rather than for the convenience of the institution. This involves each member of staff seeking information about what systems and courses look like from the students' point of view and improving them with that in mind.

Marketing thus embraces researching new and existing students' points of view and educational experiences, as well as finding ways of communicating to new students what you have to offer in terms of corporate image or new programmes.

Therefore, marketing should be a central concern within systems for monitoring quality and standards.

Enquiry Task

Which of the following roles are you involved in?

- Answering telephone enquiries
- Interviews
- Admissions
- Enrolment
- School Liaison
- Employer Liaison
- Setting up/supervising work placements
- Design of course descriptions
- Costing or pricing courses
- Forward planning
- Course evaluation
- Open days/evenings

Do you use these activities as marketing opportunities for existing and new programmes?

How can you use each of them more effectively in the future?

List other activities which you are involved with that could be used as marketing opportunities.

Factors in Successful Marketing

Successful marketing may be facilitated if the institution has a unified marketing system. A senior manager may have marketing within his or her brief, perhaps as the major area of responsibility, in order to develop the various elements of marketing into a successful strategy which promotes quality and appropriate standards. Marketing involves a variety of functions. These include market research related to the educational aims of the institution. For instance, if your institution is committed to access, you may investigate why students come to your college or university, or (more difficult to ascertain) why they fail to come.

The development of a corporate image for the institution or department is an important area of marketing. This includes consideration of values and institutional mission, as well as a wide variety of aspects of the public face of the institution, such as the design of the prospectus, the organization of the reception, the speed of response to mail and telephone enquiries and so on. This is partly, but not wholly, a selling process. If marketing is located within a quality framework it will involve the organization of events and materials with a focus on their educational value as well as more instrumental negotiation.

Every member of the staff of an institution is part of the marketing strategy of the institution for good or for ill. Everyone who meets members of the public is projecting an image of the institution and retailing messages about the attitude of the institution to various groups of people and types of activity. This implies that marketing should be a cooperative activity, with a high degree of information gathering and exchange between areas. Each member of staff may be trained and alerted to marketing and market-intelligence opportunities and to the relationship between these and the institutional and departmental aims and mission. In this way a sound marketing strategy implies good staff relationships and a facilitative management structure.

A key area in a marketing strategy is the assessment of its effectiveness. It may be necessary to set up systems for assessing how cost effective the strategies adopted have been and whether they have operated to the benefit of actual and potential students. For instance, a number of further education colleges are assuming that resource-based learning is an 'answer' to a range of access problems. It is entirely possible that the time put into developing, selling and managing the resource facility may be greater than that required for traditional teaching or that this form of facility fails to meet the needs of particular groups of students who find it hard to access information other than through face-to-face communication.

These elements include what is usually referred to as 'market research', including researching the perspectives and interests of client groups. This process is discussed in more detail below. Market research is only one part of an effective marketing strategy. It also includes the development of systems for deciding upon strategic pricing of the programmes and services offered. Costing is an accounting function that helps to ensure that an activity will not unknowingly make a loss. Pricing is a separate skill, which takes account of costing but is not determined by it. There is no intrinsic reason why the price of an individual programme should equate to its full direct costs plus the normal levy for institutional overheads and the contribution to surplus. Nevertheless, all costs of an institution must ultimately be recovered from some source.

In business, pricing is a marketing function. Within education, it may also reflect educational values and mission. Nevertheless, pricing should result from an analysis of the student's perception of value, what they can afford and what the competition will charge. If a high price reduces recruitment sufficiently, 'marking up' of prices will not necessarily maximize income, contributions to overheads and surplus. The right price may be considerably above, at, or below the full cost of an activity (including a charge for institutional overheads and a contribution to surplus). If the price is below full cost, the institution or department can make a decision that this activity will continue but the price will make an unusually low unit contribution to institutional overheads. This will usually be because the programme is seen to have a particular value in terms of its quality or contribution to community needs. There have to be very good reasons for maintaining something 'unviable' in the long-term.

Within institutions of higher and further education which are short of money, there may be a temptation to trim costs wherever possible. This is not always wise. A higher price may enable added quality to a product and increase its perceived value. More importantly, higher costs may enable the achievement of significant educational goals. Sometimes adding a small amount to the cost of a product can add a great deal more to educational quality (and incidentally to its potential price and the 'percentage' profit it bears). This requires you to have access to someone within your institution who has the skills to link marketing decisions with those for strategic planning and quality assurance.

Marketing is also about selling yourself, your institution and the programmes you offer and making sure that as many people as possible know about your success stories. This is usually achieved through general and specific publicity material and more direct selling techniques. Selling may involve research of potential clients, especially past and present students, to find out what they like about you and what they need in order that you can keep selling to them. Relationships with ex-students therefore become important. They may become future students and they may introduce others to you.

Marketing within a quality framework involves the development of promotional material with a focus on educational values, benefits to students and good design, as well as the development of links with the media and potential sources of sponsorship or funding. However, marketing embraces much more than this. It involves the prioritization of development and the development of systems to maximize desirable learning outcomes and student satisfaction at all stages.

Selling may involve you in a consideration of alternatives. For instance, a marketing perspective encourages you to consider whether you can provide other educationally valuable programmes for existing and past students, or indeed whether you can find new students for the programmes you presently offer. The notion of the lecturer as salesperson may involve you in a distinct shift in professional identity, and one that you do not particularly welcome. In order to manage this you may need to develop particular skills in questioning and listening, but perhaps just as important are those more mundane research skills of storing, ordering and sorting through data.

Lecturers involved in marketing may focus on the features of the programme, and forget to mention the benefits to the potential student and how it meets their needs. You are likely to know more about the programme design than benefits to any particular student. This can make it appear to be a 'safer' area to talk about. Talking about the benefits of what you can offer involves risk. After all, potential students know more about their perception of the benefits than you do and they may feel entitled to raise objections to your interpretation. It may help you to cope with this if you have evaluative data available about student perception of existing courses within the same area. If this kind of data is not available, you may be able to view these objections as important information, which might help you to meet student needs. This allows you to think about objections, rather than feeling insulted. Where they are based on misunderstandings you may be able to be more specific. Where they can be compensated by other advantages, you may be able to point this out.

The most important skill in selling is closing the sale. Professional salespeople aim to get a commitment to 'buy' the product before the customer leaves. They do not go on with their selling once the customer is convinced. They ask for the 'order', and then stop selling immediately. Of course 'selling' in education is not quite like this. In business the objective may be to sell whether the product is right for the customer or not. In education this ought not to happen.

Enquiry Task

List all the resources which are potentially available to you within your department to 'sell' new developments:

Human resources
> Lecturers teaching courses
> Lecturers supervising work placements
> Students
> Secretaries . . .

Facilities
> Telephones
> Data-base mail shots
> Mail shots 'piggy backing' on other developments
> IT Networks . . .

Events
> Conferences
> Open days . . .

Categorize how each of these are presently being used (if at all)

e.g., to provide potential students with information about the features of new programmes;
to provide potential students with information about the benefits to them of new programmes;
to find out about what potential students want and need;
to identify particular groups which could be followed up at a later date. . . .

How might some of them be better or more systematically used?

Researching the Client Perspective

The aim of market research is to find information that will help to determine attractive activities to offer or to measure how effective a promotional programme is, or is likely to be. This requires that you clarify the marketing and educational issues you want to address, the target groups you want to get into contact with, and what is the most cost effective way of making this contact.

The research of the perspectives of potential students may involve primary and desk market research, the coordination of market intelligence, strategic research and perceptual mapping. It may enable the market to be more accurately segmented and more educationally relevant programmes to be designed. Segmenting is the process by which you determine some aspects of the precise nature of your target group, for instance its age, occupation, class, attitudes, and then look for ways of informing them about the ways you can meet their educational needs and interests.

The kind of market research undertaken by many commercial companies is beyond the resources of most colleges and all but the largest universities. We are often forced to place a greater reliance on informed intuition, which can then be checked out in a rough and ready way.

Getting into contact or talking to potential students can be expensive unless they already attend the institution. If potential students can easily be found 'grouped' together in some other institution (such as a school), the group focus interview can be a useful technique. This allows you to talk to a group of around a dozen people to find out about their views, educational needs and interests. Other methods of data collection include telephone surveys and postal questionnaires. Each of these methods can be expensive and require careful planning. They will not guarantee you an accurate picture of student needs: these data need interpretation. They can help you with, but should not determine, decisions about the content, timing and delivery of the programme and its location and fee. These decisions have to be set within a framework of educational philosophy and within the institutional mission.

Desk research may be an answer to the problem of costs. For instance, if the institutional management-information system is appropriately set up, it may be possible to interrogate institutional records to determine trends in the student population. If these indicate that particular groups are using your programmes more often, it may help you to direct your marketing effort. You may not always be able to find out about the interests and needs of particular groups at first hand, but there is a variety of research available that may be applicable to your situation. For instance, if you find more women or mature people are becoming interested in the sort of education programmes your department is offering, you might look at the specialist research in that area, such as that undertaken by Bartos (1989) or Ashcroft and Peacock (1993) to find out about the ways other institutions have adapted their educational and organizational arrangements to meet the particular needs of mature women.

Other sources of useful marketing information include press reports of various statistical surveys. For example, the *Times Higher Educational Supplement* recently undertook a survey of 1,000 16-year-old pupils (Utley, 1994). The results showed further education colleges are associated with low-achieving students and lower-level courses. The survey showed students get their most useful information about the options open to them for training from prospectuses and careers teachers. It also revealed potential students rated aspects such as well-qualified teaching staff, academic standards, the chance to extend knowledge and the choice of subjects above the advice of friends and parents and relevance to employment. It also appears female students are more likely to consider study at a further education college than male students and students coming from middle and lower socio-economic backgrounds are more likely to choose to study at a further education college than students from the highest group. This kind of information can help you to target effort in the short-term (for example, develop a high quality prospectus emphasizing academic/teaching standards and subject choice, get talking to careers teachers) and develop longer-term goals (for example, change the low-achievement image by creating success within higher-level work and publicizing it).

The press can also provide useful information about the impact of technological, economic or social trends. Organizations, such as trade associations or chambers of commerce, are often in touch with particular 'segments' of the market and can be useful sources of information. Another useful source of market intelligence is information about new developments from well-resourced competitors often obtainable through their promotional material. It is important to use these data to inform your decisions, but not to determine them. Whatever action you take should have as its primary focus the student's learning and the enhancement of quality and standards.

Perceptual mapping is the process by which you can investigate the values placed on various elements of the 'package' you might offer and students' or potential students' perception of the quality of each of these elements relative to those on offer elsewhere. This enables you to identify and build on your areas of strength, and take corrective action in areas which are of importance to students but where the programme you offer is perceived as low quality. Areas which are seen as low quality but also as of little significance to your students can be given a lower priority.

This is vital information for your marketing. A concrete example might illustrate this. Some years ago I was asked to investigate what attracted young women to a technology based course in media studies at a further education college, when other courses in technology were recruiting a largely male student group. The course tutor was of the opinion the students had been attracted by the excellent facilities and equipment offered by the college. On investigation I found that although the female students rated the equipment as 'good', this was of little importance to them. They were attracted by the opportunities the course offered for personal expression and its social relevance. It seemed the course recruited young women despite, rather than because of, the aspects emphasized in its marketing!

Admissions and Interviewing

The admissions process begins with the first contact between the prospective student and the institution and ends with the student starting on the programme. All aspects of this are part of an induction process. They also relate to the marketing function. The aim in managing this process should be to make it as easy as possible for prospective students to enquire, apply, enrol and pay. The whole process should be viewed from the student's standpoint.

A quality approach to admissions will embrace aspects of course design and documentation as well as more obviously aspects such as the way applications are received and dealt with. The Further Education Unit (1994) and Higher Education Quality Council (1994) recommend properly thought-out systems are created to provide a speedy response to enquiry and admissions. Such a system might include the provision of accurate course information, clear information about admission requirements and arrangements for accreditation of prior learning, systems for consideration of record of achievement and for calling up references. On a personal level, students may need individual guidance. If interviews are used, they

---

Enquiry Task

Take a course you are involved with and/or you are interested in developing.

Design a student questionnaire with a five-point scale to discover student perception of the quality of various elements of the 'package' and the importance of each of these elements to them, e.g.,

	How good is it?	*How important is it?*
	Poor Good	Low High
	1 2 3 4 5	1 2 3 4 5
Teaching methods		
Topic covered		
Classroom equipment		
Library facilities . . .		

Create a visual representation of your results.
From this, identify those areas where you might:

- find out more;
- change;
- include in your marketing.

---

have a right to expect these are managed by well-trained staff. Once a candidate has been through the admissions procedure, they should receive a clear letter of acceptance (with or without conditions) or rejection. Institutions will also need a clear policy for aspects of confidentiality, for instance, with whom they are prepared to discuss the reasons for rejection and what information they are prepared to divulge.

Recently colleges and universities have worked hard to develop strategies for marketing and for equal opportunities. Because admission and interviewing have been seen as separate from marketing, these initiatives have often remained unconnected, or even perceived as being in conflict. Marketing should be a means to further institutional policies. Central to effective marketing is the notion that every aspect of a service should be thought through to make it 'user friendly' to those it aims to serve. This implies that the needs of particular groups are considered. It also implies a high degree of efficiency and friendliness at every stage of the process which will benefit all potential customers.

The marketing function should facilitate the search for new groups of students who may benefit from what we have to offer. This can often lead to a widening of opportunities for groups who have previously been denied, or had restricted access to, education at a particular level. This may be easier if appropriate budgets for marketing and clear target numbers for recruitment are available and if the institution as a whole and at the highest level is committed to marketing its programmes to a wider audience. In any case, the characteristics of potential applicants to courses are changing, and institutions must adapt to this in order to maintain recruitment. For instance, the Committee of Vice Chancellors and Principals and the Standing Committee on University Entrance (1989) reported an increasing interest in the development of links with further education and an increasing emphasis on vocational education. Smithers (1991) found BTEC students had at least the same chance of being accepted onto courses within the old polytechnic sector as 'A' Level students. Despite a growing acceptance of non-traditional entry qualifications across the further and higher education sectors, there remains opportunity for more differentiation in response to the supply of applicants in particular subject areas. For example, Fulton and Ellwood (1989) found within universities some high-demand subjects such as law and business studies focus heavily on young 'A' Level applicants whereas others, such as English and social work, have a strong tradition of accepting older and non-traditionally qualified applicants. They found a similar pattern with subjects with recruitment problems. Mathematics and electrical engineering generally look for traditional 'A' Levels in a restricted range of subjects but education and computing do not. This evidence appears to indicate that a marketing perspective does not necessarily account for the whole increase in non-traditional entrants to higher education. Traditional or non-traditional recruitment may also result from the effect of the dominant ideology within a particular subject area.

The older universities have fewer recruitment problems and perhaps less of an incentive to meet the needs of a broad range of potential students. Fulton and Ellwood found they are especially likely to use average 'A' Level points as a performance predictor during the selection process. Even though they recognized considerable doubts as to their validity, the language of 'standards' was frequently used to justify this policy. This seeming contradiction is relatively unchallenged because predicted and actual 'A' Level scores are particularly simple and convenient in the preliminary sift of applicants and the topping up of quotas towards the end of the recruitment period. Their seeming objectivity makes it easy to justify decisions to applicants' families and others, but has little to do with quality.

A marketing perspective on access, recruitment and admissions could have far-reaching implications. Once the process has been examined from the point of view of various groups within society, the need for more flexible, accessible and learner centred colleges and universities may be revealed. The Further Education Unit (1992) states such places should be organized to meet the needs of individuals with different learning experiences and qualifications. Many institutions have set up systems for accrediting prior learning. Others have created facilities to bring students with specific areas of weakness 'up to speed' so they can pursue higher-level qualifications than would otherwise be possible. In the future, differentiated learning routes through qualifications, perhaps based on the model created by the National Council for Vocational Qualifications (see Chapter 6 for more information about this model), may become more common. This implies that the admissions tutor's role will change from one of assessing the candidate's ability to one of diagnosing the right entry point, programme of study and the need for enrichment of the standard curriculum.

Fulton and Ellwood (1989) found institutions vary widely in their approach to admissions. Examples of good practice include institution-wide policies, publicly stated, the establishment of access centres to develop and promote good practice and institutional systems for monitoring admissions. Their recommendations include: the ability to complete a course, not the highest possible grade, should be the basic criterion for admission; performance indicators should reward the recruitment and successful progress of non-traditional students; and those involved in admissions should have access to adequate time and resources.

Enquiry Task

Think of a particular course or programme where you are involved in admissions. Do you know the following:

- The proportion of applicants who come from the following groups:
  women;
  men;
  mature people;
  people from ethnic minorities;
  disabled people;
- The proportion of applicants from each of these groups who are successful.
- How this compares with the representation of these groups in the population as a whole;
- How these proportions compare with courses of a similar type elsewhere?

Find out the answers to any questions where you were uncertain.

Examine all aspects of the admissions process, from the initial information materials and their dissemination to the induction of new students onto the course, to see whether it could be made more user-friendly from the point of view of groups of potential students underrepresented in the programme at the moment.

Marketing Perspectives on Quality

Marketing can and should feed into quality assurance mechanisms in various ways. Good practice in marketing should enhance quality in learning. For instance, both depend upon clearly articulated, achievable and measurable objectives. Both depend upon identifying and meeting student needs and interests and can be enhanced by feedback from students. Both depend upon quality targets.

Davies and Scribbins (1985) point to a number of reports which are critical of marketing approaches within colleges and universities. Many of these criticisms relate very directly to some of the quality issues I have discussed in this chapter. For instance some commentators have criticized the narrowness of traditional further education recruitment and the neglect of some groups such as women, ethnic minorities, the unemployed and mature students by some colleges and universities.

Quality in marketing can lead to quality in teaching and learning, as the information gleaned informs and broadens course development. Quality can be enhanced as the public becomes more informed about educational issues and the opportunities available. The consideration of the needs of the market may lead to a clarification, or even a review of the mission of some institutions. Market orientation enables links to be established with employers, community groups, schools and other agencies. This can enrich the curriculum offered within the institution. In the context of professional and vocational education, a move away from the notion that the professional educator always knows best may facilitate quality, since the professional cannot know best if he or she remains wilfully uninformed about the context in which he or she works, and wilfully excludes potential students from that context.

Pricing and Costing New Developments

I have suggested above that pricing is a marketing function and costing is an accounting function. The pricing policy should support institutional objectives, while ensuring (in most cases) cost recovery. An appropriate pricing policy will be flexible enough to take account of student perceptions, but this must not be a cumbersome process, since speed of response is important. Most people warm to organizations which provide speedy response.

In costing an activity such as a course, various types of costs must be included. These include fixed and variable costs. The fixed costs will remain the same whether or not the course fully recruits. These costs may include development time, recruitment costs and so on. Labour is likely to account for most of the variable cost, but it will also include some teaching materials, perhaps room costs and so on.

Both direct and indirect costs should be accounted for. Direct costs include the extra resources which must be paid for in order to provide the programme. These include those elements described as fixed and variable costs above. In addition, each course or programme should make some contribution to institutional overheads. These include the costs of the salaries of the managers in the college or university, finance, registry, reception, buildings, grounds, catering and so on. A flexible pricing policy allows various areas to make different levels of contribution to institutional overheads, depending upon what the market will bear. On the other hand, pricing below the full cost will require other programmes to bear a disproportionate amount of the institution's overheads. This will have the effect of diverting resources away from these existing programmes and may affect their quality. (See Chapter 8 for more detail about the effects of pricing policies on quality.)

The Government has encouraged institutions to take additional students 'at the margins'. The concept of 'marginal costs' rests on the idea that where a facility is already up and running, adding slightly to its use does not add greatly to its costs. Thus, if a course is running for a group of students at full cost to each of them, it may be worth your while to add an additional student at a lower fee. This has proved a seductive argument for some institutions, but it lowers the unit of resource, and perhaps the quality of what is on offer. Perhaps marginal costing should only be contemplated in areas of non-core activity, and then only in the short-term.

The final cost that needs to be considered is that of opportunity costs. I have outlined above how opportunity cost may operate from the student point of view. It also operates for the institution. If you are involved in a particular development, you must reject another. There is a limit to how many developments a department or institution can be involved with at any one time. Pursuing development 'A', means development 'B' is delayed, or perhaps, not even considered. If the institutional managers are concentrating on income generation, they cannot focus to the same extent on cost reduction, and vice versa. The assessment of opportunity costs is difficult, and cannot be precise. Nevertheless, it is probably worth attempting.

Enquiry Task

Take a potential development. Estimate the cost of the elements which must be included and find out the 'normal' institutional rate for each:

Direct Costs:	*Rate per hour*
Teaching time	
Lecturer-time preparation and development	
Support-time preparation and development	
Management time	
Administrative time	
Room costs. . . .	

	Unit Costs
Consumable materials	
Non-consumable materials . . .	

Indirect Costs	*Rate of return*
Institutional overheads	
Departmental overheads	
Contribution to institutional surplus . . .	

Using the Media

A few institutions, especially universities, may feel the only constituency that matters to them is the national one. I believe part of the work of universities and colleges is to inform their local community about what they are doing. The local community is directly affected by the work of the institution. Some of these effects are beneficial, for instance the provision of employment. Others, such as parking problems and increased traffic, are not. In the same way as industry often spends quite a bit of time and trouble to make links with the local community, even when this community is not part of the 'market', universities and colleges, and you as a lecturer within the institution, should also be seeking ways to communicate with the community.

Of course, it is very seldom that colleges and universities have no local students or potential students. Local people may be persuaded to use their local institution of further and higher education if they believe it has a 'good' reputation, or it 'does interesting things', as well as through direct marketing. The only way they can gain these impressions is if someone, usually individual lecturers, have ensured they are informed about successes or interesting events within the college or university. It is easy to get carried away and to end up saying or writing what you believe the audience wants to hear. As educationalists, it is particularly important that we maintain a respect for truth and accuracy. If you succeed in attracting students onto courses which are misdescribed or are unsuitable for their needs, you will have had a very direct and adverse effect on the quality of the institution's work.

Newspapers, radio and television can be expensive to use as a means of advertising, or free, if they are used to transmit carefully constructed stories. These stories are generally best told by the lecturers and students involved. Central marketing departments in colleges and universities can help in approving, structuring and placing stories, but they cannot know what stories are available to be told. This means you are an important part of your institution's public relations and it may be useful for you to develop an understanding of some of the principles which underlie the use of the media. I know of one further education lecturer who is able to get a positive story about the creative arts section of the college where he works into his local paper almost every week. He achieves this by understanding how his local media works and by making publicity a priority. He justifies this use of time and effort in various ways. He sees the celebration of staff and student achievement as encouraging desirable learning outcomes, as a way of informing potential students of the educational opportunities open to them and as a method of encouraging non-traditional applicants.

The first principle in the use of local media (or national media for that matter) is to target your message to the audience for that media, without distorting its truth. This means you have to know who the audience is. For instance, local radio and television stations usually spend a lot of money researching their audience and have a clear 'profile' of the listener or viewer. This profile may be available to you for the asking. You may find it useful to target your message to a typical member of that audience.

The local media often has a particular mission to focus on local issues. If you can give your message a 'parochial' slant, it may increase its relevance and therefore its likelihood of success. This may require more than an emphasis on the fact that the story comes from a local institution. You may also be able to include some reference to the way your 'news' may affect local people. Newspapers and talk-based local radio has a lot of space to fill each week. If you can provide interesting and well-structured editorial material, it may be welcomed. If you are going to use the local media, it will help if you get to know some key people within the media organization. The person referred to above who was particularly successful in using his local press, has built good relationships over the years, which started with a meeting with the deputy editor of the newspaper. He has persuaded the paper to allow him to use the press for a termly student newspaper that is delivered free alongside the normal newspaper deliveries. He now regularly places students for work experience with the paper. He knows the kind of stories the paper needs, how they should be presented and the right tone and language. In addition, he knows the people well, so they trust him, see him as reliable, look on his input in a favourable light, and he can phone them to discuss a story and the best angle to take.

If you wish to use local radio and television, you may be called on to 'perform', usually in the form of an interview. This performance is often live. This means you will need to be very well prepared. You should know your facts and have decided what message you want to get across, no matter what question you are asked. When you arrive, you may be surprised at how little attention or preparation you are given. If you are appearing on local radio, you may find yourself in a separate glass box from your interviewer, and he or she may not speak more than a sentence to you (just to get the voice levels right) before the interview starts. The interviewer may not look at you, or even fiddle with equipment while you speak. You may be cut off if your replies are not fairly short and to the point. This can be unnerving. You may find you come over better, if you can turn your chair so that you face the interviewer and look at him or her directly, if you make a note of the first names of any co-interviewees and refer to them and if you speak as conversationally and with as much enthusiasm as you can. Do not be too afraid of going over the top. If you do, more people will remember you and your educational message.

One of the most important things to remember is to use simple and non-specialist language and to avoid giving lists of information. It may be better not to have extensive notes in front of you. A list of two or three key points may ensure you focus on the main issues. I have found it is easier to communicate if I do not read from notes (written language rarely comes over well in speech) nor shuffle paper noisily. You will be doing well if your audience can remember one or two points from the interview and if you can decide what these should be, and find ways of emphasizing them more than once.

Stories that are not initiated by you may be more problematic. These will tend to be hard news and may have an angle (for instance, a scandal or other bad publicity) that is not obvious to you at first sight, that may be damaging to the college or university. Unless you are experienced and have permission to deal with this kind of issue, it is probably best to tell the interviewer you cannot reply at the moment and then seek the guidance of a senior manager.

There are likely to be occasions when you wish to create an advertisement for the local or national press. Some of the principles outlined above are applicable here. In particular, you should avoid giving too much information. Readers will take in just two or three simple points and an address to find out more. The advertisement should focus on the reader's point of view. You may decide to emphasize the benefits to them rather than listing what you have to offer. The size of print for different parts of the advertisement is important. You may consider giving the aspect that is most attractive to the reader the largest print. This is unlikely to be the name of the university or college. I have found it is useful to ask an experienced colleague to look at your copy with a critical eye when you think it is complete. Are there any redundant words? The fewer words you use the more the essential message is likely to get across. Is the result pleasing to look at, or are there too many different type-faces or insufficient white space around the central message?

Newspaper advertisements tend to be very expensive. If you are dealing directly with the paper you will need to have a clear idea of the budget available, the size of entry you want and so on. You may be offered various deals for repeat advertisements and advertisements in other papers owned by the particular group. You may be pressured to make a quick decision. In my experience these offers often remain open if you insist on time to consider them. It is often worth haggling over the price. The expense of advertisement usually makes it worthwhile to set up proper monitoring systems to record the response to different placements and size of advertisement and also to note how many of the responses actually sign up.

The final point about using the media as an aid to marketing is the need to find out about the resources and systems within your college or university. Many institutions require you to seek permission before you contact or speak to the media. This ensures you receive expert advice and can use the marketing opportunity to best effect. In some colleges and universities there are specialists who can help you build links with the media. Unfortunately, in some others, the message that marketing is an activity that involves the whole staff has not got through and the specialists may be barriers to any direct dealings between lecturers and the media. Such barriers may protect the institution from the remote risk that a well-briefed lecturer might unwittingly provoke unfortunate publicity, but it will quickly stifle initiative. Every lecturer should be a marketer and so marketing expertise must be shared. It if is 'held' centrally, most of the exciting opportunities for communication with the public will be lost.

The use of the media should be located within a clear framework of educational and moral values. It should be about celebrating quality education, achievement and high standards as well as encouraging potential students to take advantage of appropriate educational opportunities. It should not be about the manipulation of truth for marketing advantage or the enhancement of personal reputation for career advantage at the expense of others or of accuracy.

Summary

Income generation and marketing go hand in hand. Considerations of quality should also be included. Marketing enables the needs of clients to be identified and met within budget. It involves:

- the analysis of the marketing mix:
- the range of programmes;
- their price;
- their location;
- and their promotion.

It should also be a moral enterprise. This implies colleges and universities should be market-centred, not market-led.

Marketing involves researching existing and potential students' points of view and changing and communicating what you have to offer in terms of their educational needs and interests. It involves all staff and all systems. All can be involved in researching the student point of view; in looking at existing systems from that point of view and in suggesting ways they could be adapted or initiatives taken to enable students to be served and communicated with better.

Market research can be primary or desk research. It may involve techniques such as:

- perceptual mapping;
- the recognition of research-intelligence opportunities;
- the use of focus groups;

- questionnaires;
- using existing networks set up by other organizations;
- using intelligence collected for other purposes within the institution; and
- using intelligence collected by other organizations, such as the press.

Pricing is an important aspect of marketing. It should take account of costs and value as perceived by the student and as compared with competitors. Achieving the maximum price will involve 'salespersonship'. This means you will have to develop the skills to enable you to sell your successes. Achieving a maximum price may not be justifiable, where this would conflict with educational values.

Admission and interviewing are part of a marketing process focused on quality. They may need to be made more user-friendly. The marketing perspective may enable you to look at the whole process of recruitment from the point of view of various types of user, including those presently underrepresented on your programmes.

Good practice in admissions includes:

- the establishment of systems for the recognition of prior learning and experience;
- the recognition of the value of non-traditional qualifications;
- the establishment of institution-wide policies, publicly stated;
- the establishment of access centres to develop and promote good practice and institutional systems for monitoring admissions;
- the ability to complete a course, not the highest possible grade, being the basic criterion for admission;
- the establishment of performance indicators which reward the recruitment and successful progress of non-traditional students; and
- adequate time and resources for those involved in admissions.

Marketing should feed into and out of the quality control mechanisms. The marketing process should inform development and enable programmes to be more tailored to student needs.

Entry for your Reflective Diary

Think about the things which act as motivators for you in the area of marketing, e.g.,

- meeting the needs of particular student groups;
- the opportunity to know more about your students;
- celebrating achievement. . . .

and those things which sap your motivation, e.g.,

- uncertainty about what is required;
- lack of time . . .

Use your diary to reflect upon the origins of these feelings and whether they may be susceptible to change.

Notes
Annotated List of Suggested Reading

Davies, P. and Scribbins, K. (1985) *Marketing Further and Higher Education*, York, Longman for FEU and FESC.
This is a short, practical book that covers most of what lecturers are likely to need to know about the principles of marketing, market research, implications for institutional structures and promotion.

Salisbury College of Art and Design/BBC Wiltshire Sound. *Saying Yes to Radio — The Video.* Available from Bill Shepley, Salisbury College of Art and Design, Department of Photography, Film and Television.
You may find this video useful if you or your colleagues wish to make links with local radio. It takes you through the necessary preparation for a live interview and into a local radio station to show you how the interview itself is conducted.

The Open College, with SCUE and PCAS (1989) *Successful Admissions: Tactics, Procedures and Responsibilities*, Manchester, The Open College.
This provides a useful and fairly short guide to the complexities of admissions, including processing applications, the annual admission cycle, contacts with the public, the conduct of interviews and open days and sources of information. It also covers aspects of marketing and policy.

References

ASHCROFT, K. and FOREMAN-PECK, L. *Managing Teaching and Learning in Further and Higher Education*, London, Falmer Press.
ASHCROFT, K. and PEACOCK, E. (1993) 'An evaluation of the progress, experience and employability of mature students on the BEd course at Westminster College, Oxford', *Journal of Assessment and Evaluation for Teachers*, 18, 1.
BARTOS, R. (1989) *Marketing to Women: A Global Perspective*, London, Heinemann.
COMMITTEE OF VICE CHANCELLORS AND PRINCIPALS AND STANDING COMMITTEE ON UNIVERSITY ENTRANCE (1989) *Universities' Review of Degree Courses and of Entrance Policies in Response to Secondary Curriculum Changes and Wider Access*, London, CVCP and SCUE.
DAVIES, P. and SCRIBBINS, K. (1985) *Marketing Further and Higher Education*, York, Longman for FEU and FESC.
FULTON, O. and ELLWOOD, S. (1989) *Admissions to Higher Education: Policy and Practice*, Sheffield, Employment Department Group Training Agency.
FURTHER EDUCATION UNIT (1992) *Flexible Colleges: Access to Learning and Qualifications in Further Education: Part 1 — Priorities for Action*, London, FEU.
FURTHER EDUCATION UNIT (1994) *Continuous Improvement and Quality Standards*, London, FEU.
HIGHER EDUCATION QUALITY COUNCIL (1994) *A Briefing Paper from the Higher Education Quality Council: Checklist for Quality Assurance Systems*, London, HEQC.
SMITHERS, A. (1991) *The Vocational Route into Higher Education*, University of Manchester.
UTLEY, A. (1994) 'Pathways and signposts to the future', *The Times Higher Educational Supplement: Synthesis: Marketing Your College*, 18 March, pp. 8-9.

Chapter 10

Research

In this chapter, I discuss research and its relationship to the quality of educational provision within colleges and universities. I look at the funding context for research before focusing on the implications of various definitions of quality in research for the lecturer and, in particular, on the needs of tutors who are new to educational research as a vehicle for developing quality in practice. I also consider some of the issues in writing for publication. In the latter part of the chapter, I explore some management issues in establishing a quality framework for research in higher and further education.

The Context for Research and Scholarship

The important role of research and scholarship within higher education and further education has been emphasized recently, both in terms of their use as a performance indicator for funding purposes, and the emphasis on staff qualification in the assessment of quality (see for example FEFC, 1993). Both may contribute to the quality of teaching within an institution, even if only by ensuring that the lecturer is up to date and well informed. I have found that my teaching often draws directly on my scholarship and research. Conversely, my teaching sometimes raises issues which become a focus for research. I have also found that the process of teaching often clarifies and organizes ideas, that then contribute to my research and scholarship.

Pragmatic considerations cannot be the sole justification for the link between higher and further education teaching and research. After all, an English lecturer who spends four years studying the full stop in the Victorian novel is not likely to apply more than a fraction of his or her knowledge to the curriculum. Research and scholarship must be viewed as important and valuable in their own right. Whether they are 'useful' is not the main point. They are part of the 'job' of further and higher education, and without this function society would stagnate. The creation and dissemination of knowledge is one of the hallmarks of a civilized society. On the other hand, unless such a pursuit of knowledge is underpinned by a secure moral and ethical framework, the result may be anything but civilized (for instance, Nazi experimentation).

Research and scholarship underpin most forms of knowledge. They help to determine priorities and the direction of education. They are about 'knowing' and ways of knowing. Research has some elements of originality, discovery and publication. I argue that activity that is directed at acquiring personal knowledge, or creating new insights, but that is not made public in some way, is not research. I define such private activity as scholarship.

Definitions of Research and Education

Research has been defined in various ways according to the climate of the time and the frameworks provided by particular disciplines. Definitions may be broad and include any type of public activity that creates new insights or responses, or narrow, to include only published activity which conforms to a certain defined methodology and creates knowledge that can be assessed by a particular set of criteria and community of scholars.

The question of definition relates to the status that various kinds of activity are accorded. Thus, in some older universities in the UK, activity conforming to the narrower definition was held to be of particular value. Lecturers within newer universities and colleges may have suspected an elitist purpose in such a narrow definition: in particular, to make research the exclusive province of a particular group of well-funded universities and to downgrade practitioner research and small-scale investigation.

Some well-respected workers within the older university sector and some research associations such as the British Educational Research Association (BERA) question the political purpose of such a narrow definition, especially the way that it disempowers individuals from seeking to push back the barriers to understanding their practice. Traditional definitions of research emphasize a scientific, experimental approach at the expense of more pragmatic, holistic studies which deal with the experience of everyday life and the work of ordinary people and real situations (see for example, Stenhouse, 1975; Elliott, 1991; Schon, 1983).

Recently this debate has become less acrimonious and both types of research have earned respect in many sectors. For instance, the Higher Education Funding Council (HEFC) does not make any such distinction. According to the HEFC (1994), research for the purpose of the rating exercise is understood as original investigation. This seems to be defined fairly broadly and includes the creation of new ideas, artistic creation and design, where these lead to new insights. It also includes the reinterpretation of existing knowledge or ideas which can be related to new products, materials and processes as well as more traditional conceptual papers for publication. It is an essentially public activity. Thus the creation of course material for use within your institution would not count, but a new academic book published nationally would.

The supervision and output of research students are defined as research activity. This means that research students' work 'counts'. The guidelines do not seem to exclude students undertaking masters' degrees with a dissertation element, as well as the more traditional MPhil/MLitt and doctoral students. The successful generation of external funding for research activity counts in its own right as a research activity (see Chapter 8 for more details about external bidding). In addition, institutions will be expected to submit their current research plan as part of the rating exercise.

The research-rating exercise may lead lecturers in higher education to take an instrumental approach. Lecturers in further education will not have the financial pressures on them to produce at all costs. They are less likely to make the mistake of thinking of research as an income-generating activity, rather than important in its own right.

There is a difference between research that is geared to the development of practice and fundamental research. There is also a distinction to be made between research that is undertaken as a worthwhile activity in its own right and that undertaken in order to obtain funding or 'ratings'. In practice these distinctions may become blurred. Income generating, fundamental research may be valued at the expense of research directly related to the quality of institutional practice. In some institutions, lecturers have to be designated an 'active researcher' before they are allowed to bid for research time. In such circumstances it is not always clear whether one is bidding for funds in order to generate income or whether one is doing so in order to be *allowed* to do research.

Research gets to the heart of the educational process. It involves a systematic enquiry into an issue, leading to a public outcome in order to increase our understanding of the world. Research and education are about the pursuit of truth: they are about knowing and discovery. Research and education each involve interpretation and reorganization of ideas. Research differs from education only inasmuch as it must be in some sense original (or confirm or refute other original findings). I would define reinterpretation and reorganization as research activities, if they lead to insights which are in some way 'new'.

Research may offer improvements to existing practice (for instance, many of the enquiry tasks in this book could be used for this purpose), or contribute to a body of knowledge or understanding. It may challenge existing knowledge or practice or explore new ways of doing things. It is likely to contribute to, and be located within, a theoretical framework. The fruits of research or education may or may not be put to some practical and economic use. This is not necessarily the point. If you believe that the pursuit of truth is a moral activity that benefits society, research and educational activities within a clear ethical framework must be worthwhile in their own right. This does not mean that research and education are opposed to utilitarian considerations. Each may have very practical uses and yield economic benefits. Nevertheless, an activity is not research, nor is it education, unless it is about the dissemination or development of ideas.

Enquiry Task

Ask experienced colleagues within your subject area:

- how they would define worthwhile research activity; and
- what activities they would include.

Categorize these activities and definitions under the headings below:

Research as a Process   *Research as a Product*
(e.g., sound methodology)   (e.g., relevance to practice)

Were activities or products which you would call 'research' excluded by the definition above?

Decide on your own definition of worthwhile research.

Decide on the activities which you might actually engage in.

Quality Issues and the Funding for Research within Higher Education

With the creation of the new universities, more higher education institutions have become eligible for HEFC funding for research. The available funds are shared out between institutions on the basis of the 'research rating' for various departments. The ratings are based on the extent of various kinds of research and publication activity. These are arranged into a hierarchy, with some kinds of activity or publication 'counting' for more than others. Thus, writing a book as a sole author 'counts' more than co-editing a book, writing a paper for an international journal counted more than an article in the local press and so on. In order to get a high rating (5) with a coveted 'A' classification, all staff within a subject area within an institution would have to be engaged in published research of the right kind and the department should have achieved substantial non-government funding for research projects.

At a time of decreasing unit resources for teaching across the higher education sector, government funding for research appeared to be one area of expansion. For example, the Higher Education Funding Council for England (HEFCE) announced an increase in funding for research in 1994/5 over that for 1993/4 of 4 per cent. The Government funding for research is fairly substantial: the HEFCE funding for research for 1994/5 was £626 million (HEFCE, 1994a). Nevertheless, institutions would be unwise to rely on this 'protection' of research funding continuing. Research funding is as vulnerable as other areas to changes in government priority.

The use of crude indicators of quality in research had a number of unfortunate consequences. It put tremendous pressure on individuals to publish or face unpleasant consequences. Staff may be encouraged to publish whether they have anything to say or not. Short-term publication goals are sometimes pursued at the expense of longer ones. I am aware of one university department where there was an explicit requirement for all teaching staff to publish a minimum of two research papers a year, without any indication that the papers published should have any value in their own right.

It appears that the HEFCE may share some of the worries about the quality and volume of publication which their performance indicators have generated. It now requires institutions to report on how they distribute money provided for research and on their internal resource-allocation decisions in respect of the research component of the funding (HEFCE, 1994b). At the same time, a new approach is being taken to the research rating exercise (HEFC, 1994). Rating will continue to be on a 1–5 scale for each subject department in a university or college. A 'starred' 5 will indicate a majority of research work of international excellence. Ratings 1–4 may also be starred where a subject department contains research groups with a level of excellence above the overall rating for the areas.

There have been a number of significant changes in the rating process. The new performance indicators will no longer emphasize quantity of publication. Instead, the focus will be on its quality, inasmuch as only the best four publications (or other assessable output) from each individual lecturer over the rating period (1990–6 for the humanities and 1992–6 for other programme areas) will be included in the rating exercise. The categories of activity which will count as research have been broadened. Applied research and publication has been given more status, and output and supervision of postgraduate research students can be included in the submission. The previous criteria seemed to value individual effort over collaboration. Now co-authored work seems to count in the same way as sole authorship. Interuniversity projects count equally for each partner.

One of the more interesting features of the new arrangements is that lecturers will take their contribution to the research rating with them when they move jobs. Thus, you may have undertaken your publication with active support from University A, but if you move to University B before the end of the research rating period, your publications will 'count' for University B. This may increase the importance of past publication records in the selection of new staff, and increase the chances of institutions poaching active researchers from other universities. A good publication record may be crucial to the progress of a career in higher education. Few universities look set to go down the road of becoming teaching-only institutions, and so, if you focus on teaching at the expense of research, you may find that your career progression is blocked within your institution and that your chances of employment elsewhere are reduced. Unfortunately, this may tempt lecturers to more instrumental, rather than principled, action within research.

The rating of research and publication and the value put on them by institutions of higher education have increased the general level of activity and raised the normal expectations of lecturers. This has led to some questioning of the contribution of lecturers in colleges of further education to higher-level teaching. It may go some way to explain the slowing of progress in relation to franchising agreements and other university-validated arrangements with further education, despite government policy to encourage such development.

Lecturers in further education colleges who are interested in promoting higher education course developments may need to develop their qualification and publication profile to that equivalent to a lecturer teaching at the same level in a validating university. Similarly, managers within further education may need to adapt their staff-development policies to take account of the new reality.

Enquiry Task

- Read three contrasting research papers in your subject area.
- Come to a judgment about their relative quality.
- List the criteria you used in coming to that judgment.
- Put these in order of importance to you as a reader.

Which of these would you classify as 'substantive' criteria (e.g., the size of the sample) and which not (e.g., the readability of the report).

What are the difficulties in using subjective criteria to judge the quality of research?

What are the difficulties in dismissing such criteria?

List a set of do's and don't's about writing-up research for a novice researcher in your subject area.

Models of Research

Traditions in research vary between academic disciplines. Thus, in science the quantitative tradition usually prevails, in psychology there are strong qualitative and quantitative traditions and within education (at the present time) the qualitative tradition is in the ascendancy. It is important that you are not restricted in your thinking by the normal ways of viewing research activity within your subject area. For example, a chemist, interested in enquiring into his or her students' learning, may find that descriptive, word-based data provide a more useful basis for reflection. This experience may enable him or her to make the imaginative leap to apply such methods in the subject.

The quantitative and qualitative traditions each cluster around a set of features. Quantitative research tends to rely on the control of variables and the examination of a large number of instances of a phenomena, centred around the notion of disproving a hypothesis. The 'quality' of the research generally focuses on issues of reliability — the extent that the context and results can be replicated. This focus is sometimes at the expense of validity: for instance, whether the right questions were asked or whether the results relate well to the conclusions.

Qualitative research is judged by a different set of criteria. For example, it tends to be problem-centred and pragmatic. It often focuses on complex interactive real-life situations, where variables cannot be isolated without distorting the context in such a way as to make the findings irrelevant. The notion of proof cannot be applied in these circumstances. Hypotheses can be explored, but not tested in any real sense. The situation and changes within them are described and causes or factors suggested more or less convincingly. The 'quality' of the research tends to be ascertained in terms of validity at a pragmatic level (e.g., interjudgmental reliability — whether the reader, respondents and researcher interpret the findings in the same way; whether the problem was solved to the satisfaction of all concerned; whether the right questions were asked) or through an assessment of the extent that certain articulated values are realized by the process of research and its apparent outcomes.

These ideas imply that lecturers have a duty to look critically at their own research and that of others. All research is based on some preconceptions. There are always alternative interpretations or descriptions of research situations and findings. Within the qualitative-research tradition, this notion is up front: for example, in an examination of the plausibility of any claims made. If the conclusions fit with taken-for-granted truths and if error is relatively unlikely given the research methods and the way they are presented, a reader will have some confidence in the findings. Of course, new knowledge and genuine discovery will surprise us. Researchers in the qualitative tradition would want confirmation from further studies located in varying situations, some conducted in different ways, before they would start to have confidence. Those in the quantitative tradition might seek replication of the original context and methods.

Campbell and Stanley (1963) give one of the best outlines of factors which commonly threaten the validity of research. There are some fairly simple questions which we can ask about any piece of research in order to start to assess its quality, the degree of confidence we might place in its findings and the extent to which they might apply in a variety of circumstances. These questions include: how typical is the population/situation; what categories were used; are they the only possible ones; are they relevant to the questions asked; has everything relevant been included; are data rightly assigned to particular categories; are the causes subscribed the only possible ones; are the data sufficient for the claims made for them; what measuring instruments were used; are they appropriate; might their calibration have changed in the course of a study (especially if they include human judgments about classification); has anything happened in the course of the study that might interfere with the results?

The questions above relate to the validity of a piece of research. There are other questions which you might ask which relate to issues of validity only indirectly. For example, you might want to explore the extent of a researcher's expert knowledge. It was probably the lack of classroom-teaching experience on the part of some researchers, leading to fundamental errors in interpretation and focus, that caused the decline in respect for quantitative methods within the teaching profession from the 1970s onwards.

Most researchers will be operating within a theoretical framework and will use established research methods. If these are not made clear to you as a reader, you may find that you cannot have confidence in the findings. You may want to look at the reported data or details of the research design (such as the size of the sample) to see if they are sufficient to substantiate any gain in knowledge claimed. As a reflective lecturer, you should also be concerned with the ethics of the research method.

Of course, the validity and reliability of research is only one measure of its quality. Perhaps the most important question about the quality of a piece of research is whether it suggests to us anything interesting or important. The most significant question may be whether research makes us see reality in new ways. It is for this reason that Freud ranks alongside Einstein in terms of academic importance. He certainly cannot compare on the basis of the ethics, validity or reliability of his research methods!

Practitioner Research and the Development of Quality

Practitioner research is a means of intervening in the functioning of real-life classrooms and institutions and exploring the effects of that intervention. Many of the enquiry tasks within this book might be the starting point for practitioner research. It is a form of enquiry that starts with real problems and issues. It has an essentially moral basis: the point of the activity is to understand and improve practice and the circumstances of practice. In achieving this, a reflective dynamic is created involving the exploration of practice and its congruence with values which supposedly underpin it.

The process of action research (the most usual form of practitioner research in educational settings) has been described in some detail by others (e.g., Stenhouse, 1975; Deakin University, 1982; Carr and Kemmis, 1986; Elliott, 1991). It involves the identification of a problem, exploring its context and creating a plan of action. It is insider research, with the person who faces the problem being the one who acts in the situation and carries out or directs the research. Once a plan of action is identified and is put into practice, the researcher will collect evidence as to what actually happens and how effective the action is. This is followed by evaluation and reflection and the creation of a modified plan of action if necessary. This will then set off another cycle of planning, action, the collection and evaluation of evidence, leading to further planning.

Practitioner research is an essentially empowering process that enables you to undertake systematic enquiry and reflection on your own practice and its context, in order to change both. Practitioner research is grounded in a particular situation. The research is undertaken by the actors in that situation, and so it is self-evaluative. In this sense it is very different from the more traditional forms of 'outsider' research, where the researcher and the 'subject' have different roles and must, by definition, be different people.

One common criticism of practitioner research is that it can be inward-looking and lead to subjectivity and self-deception. The only protection against this tendency is to ensure that other perspectives are brought to bear on the process. For this reason, most workers in the field suggest that good practitioner research is collaborative and that preliminary interpretations of data are shared with others.

As with all research, an important feature of practitioner research is the dissemination of the results. By definition, research is a public activity. One criticism sometimes levelled at practitioner research is that its results can be so particular to one context that they may be of no interest to anyone else. This can be a problem, but most contexts will have at least some features in common with some others. At least in the case of practitioner research, the contextual nature of action and interventions is clear and readers can assess how applicable they might be in their particular situation.

Practitioner research within education has certain benefits. It is more systematic than subjective, impressionistic problem-solving. It can transform seemingly impossible problems by providing new insights into their cause and effects. Sometimes this can lead to solutions which transform the dilemmas lecturers face. It usually equips lecturers with new skills and knowledge and so can be very motivating. The collaboration and sharing of perspectives which practitioner research demands can strengthen relationships. The process of data collection, discussion and reflection can deepen thinking and enable lecturers to gain new insights into their students' needs and new respect for their colleagues.

The outcome of practitioner research is not necessarily the production of new objective knowledge. Instead, as Elliott (1993) states, its value may be in the way it illuminates where our values lie, where we stand in relation to them and ways in which we can improve that relation.

Practitioner research has the added advantage for many lecturers in further and higher education that it is one form of research that adds to, rather than detracts from, the teaching function. It can and should be carried out alongside normal teaching and assessment duties. Time is not diverted from the lecturer's primary role, and the end product is likely to relate directly to that role.

Ways of Getting Started

In this section I am assuming that you are interested in undertaking research, but that you are relatively inexperienced. Getting started on the research process is often difficult for lecturers. During your own education you may have been used to reading large scale and significant studies. You may rightly suspect that you are unlikely to produce work of comparable scale and significance.

Some lecturers will be lucky enough to work in a department that is well funded for research and where there are ready-made and carefully structured research projects which they can join. Most of us have to plough a lonelier furrow and find our own subject, methodology and publishing outlet with little or no outside help. If you are in this position, the first question you might ask is *what* you could research. There are various categories you might consider.

There is a need within all subject areas for fairly small-scale research that illuminates practice. You might use one or more of the enquiry tasks in this book as a starting point for such a project. I started my publishing career with 'stories' about innovative teaching and learning methods and their evaluation (for example, see Ashcroft, 1988). These stories arose out of a programme I was responsible for within the Department of Education at Oxford Polytechnic. The focus was on the development of students' skills in critical analysis and their ability to control their own learning. I found the process of enquiry and my results very interesting and was willing to take the risk that they would interest others also. In fact, this small-scale study created a limited and specialist interest across three continents that I found very encouraging.

Such stories can be developed into a more elaborate enquiry project. In the case above, a project developed that involved several lecturers regularly meeting to talk about definitions and to share data-collection techniques and evidence about their own practice and its effects on students' learning and behaviour. This led to the establishment of the School Experience Research and Development Group and the publication of several papers (for example, Ashcroft and Tann, 1988; Ashcroft and Griffiths, 1989) exploring issues in the development of reflective student teachers.

An alternative approach is to publish conceptual pieces which synthesize and explore existing concepts. For example, when starting the process of writing this book, my colleague and I created a conceptual map of the various ways quality and standards might be defined and approached. It was from this process that a number of alternative definitions emerged, and the political meaning of each became clearer. I was then able to analyse the various approaches to quality and standards advocated by the many parties to the educational process and start to see the logical consequences of each. This conceptual map provided a framework for exploring the issues within this book. The map might easily have formed the basis of a conceptual paper in its own right.

Each of the approaches above can be relatively time efficient. They may be integrated into, and arise from, your day-to-day work. Thus, Ashcroft and Foreman-Peck (1994) incorporated and refined material my colleague and I were using within a staff development programme that we run. The present book has developed from the deeper questions about values which emerged from the writing of the previous book and the daily experience of teaching and managing during a time of rapid change and increased accountability.

I have found the hardest type of research to manage alongside a full teaching load is that based on scientific methods of enquiry. This kind of research is by definition outsider research, since it relies on an objective researcher observing phenomena. The validity of such research usually depends upon painstaking observation and record-keeping, the observation of a large number of instances and repetition of research methods. It is hard to see how such a process could be easily integrated into the lecturer's daily teaching role.

Once you have decided on the focus for your research and the approach you are going to take, it may be useful to think about the final audience for the report. Ideally you will decide on a particular outlet for publication, such as a journal or conference and gear the way you structure your report to their requirements. I must admit to never having taken this advice. Instead, I usually write my research in a way that interests me and suits the material and have then looked for a journal that has papers and guidelines for contributors which match my style and material. (Guidelines are usually found at the back or front of each edition of a journal.)

It is worthwhile taking some trouble to find a suitable journal or other outlet. It is considered unethical to send papers to several outlets at the same time. Since many editors take some time to make a response (most will send papers to outside referees who sometimes take a long time to provide an opinion), you can waste much time by sending a report to an outlet that does not deal with your kind of material.

If you are thinking of writing a book, you will need to choose a suitable publisher. You may find it useful to explore the style of books produced by different publishers, the audiences for whom they cater and whether they are marketing a series into which your proposed publication might fit. Most publishers have very useful guidelines for the submission of book proposals. These usually require you to provide an outline of the book: its length, style and content; the size and characteristics of the target market; details of competitor texts; details of your previous publishing and other experience; and a sample chapter. It is worth taking care over the proposal. An editor may judge your writing skills and style on how clearly you set out what you are going to do. Their main interests and yours may be different. You may be excited about the content of the book and getting a particular message across. An editor is likely to be more interested in whether the book will sell. You may be more successful if you look at your proposal from that point of view.

Another way to get started on research and publication is to attend relevant conferences. These provide a forum for you to get to know key researchers in your field, to talk to them about their ideas and to take part in seminars presented by others to get the 'feel' for what is expected. Conferences provide a vehicle for a range of networking activities. One of these is talking to publishers and the editors of research journals about their expectations and your ideas for publication. You might get to know established authors in your field, and let them know you and what you have to offer. Many lecturers have started their publication career through an invitation to contribute a chapter as part of a book edited by someone they met at a conference.

Conferences can provide a good forum for trying out and refining a paper before submission to a journal. Most learned organizations have annual conferences. Look out for invitations to submit proposals for papers (your library should be able to make sure you receive notification of relevant invitations). Some conferences require papers to be vetted by a referee. You may stand a better chance of acceptance if you get your paper in early. Other organizations such as the British Educational Research Association (BERA) have a policy of accepting all offers to present papers (provided they are received before the stated deadline). Many prominent researchers in further and higher education started their publication career with a paper trialled at BERA.

If you are presenting a paper at a conference, you will need to be disciplined about the time you are allowed. If you are an unknown researcher, this is likely to be short. In my experience, many presenters try to cover too much (for instance, the whole of a research report in less than an hour) which leads to a frustrating and unmemorable experience for the audience. It may be a good idea to apply your normal criteria for good teaching. For instance, I try to make no more than six points and employ a variety of visual aids and teaching techniques. I have used role-play, buzz groups, practical activity as well as plenty of questions and answers. As a consequence, some people have remembered presentations I have made and the main points of the research many years after the event. I bring copies of the full report for members of the audience who want the full picture.

Whatever your target outlet, it is important that you have something interesting to say and that you say it as clearly and simply as possible. As with meeting people, the first impression may be very influential. You may wish to look critically at the way that your paper opens to ensure that your title and first paragraph are as clear, interesting and as closely related to the interests of your readers as possible. Your writing style is important. Papers which are dull or full of jargon are unlikely to be published.

As you progress, you are likely to learn a great deal about the skill of writing

---

Enquiry Task

Identify a problem that you are confronting in the classroom that might be appropriate for practitioner research.

Decide how you might:

- find out about the context of the problem (for instance, when, where, with whom it occurs, what the people involved feel about it . . .);
- draw up a plan of action to improve the problem (for instance, by changing your behaviour, the context of the problem . . .);
- collect evidence as to the effect of your intervention (e.g., by structured observation, fly-on-the-wall observation, interviews, a questionnaire, diary, audio and video-recording . . .).

Decide:

- who should be involved in this research;
- how you will involve them;
- whether they will be involved in the research design;
- what your intentions/criteria for 'success' are;
- who will learn from this research;
- what use you will make of theory in your reflection;
- what assumptions and values you are working with; and
- how you will communicate the results of your research.

Draw up a chronological plan of action.

---

and about your particular weaknesses. Perhaps because I am a teacher, I find it hard not to be didactic. I had to rewrite this section several times in an attempt to prevent it sounding too bossy. I have also had to learn how to break up sentences and avoid the use of too many conditional clauses in a sentence.

You may decide to try to publish something that was created for another purpose, such as a dissertation. In this case it may need a complete rewrite, bearing in mind the needs and interests of the new audience. If you are to publish, you will need to learn to love criticism. I have asked my colleagues to read drafts of this book and to be critical and ruthless in their comments. As a consequence, I have had to take some uncomfortable but valuable criticism. The editor may also have critical comments to make. Chapters have been drafted and redrafted up to twenty times. When the book is eventually published, some reviewers will no doubt dislike aspects of it or disagree with some of my arguments.

You will be very lucky if your first research report is published without alteration. It is more likely that you will be asked to resubmit it with substantial alterations or that it is rejected and you will have to rewrite it before submitting it elsewhere. Some of the comments from editors and referees can be very blunt. It is important that you are not discouraged by this. It is part of the process of learning to be a researcher, a process that may last a working lifetime.

Ethical Issues in Research

Quality in research demands a certain level of ethical behaviour. A mechanism is needed to establish ethical guidelines for research, to ensure that they are communicated to all those engaged in research (including students undertaking a dissertation or enquiry project as part of their studies) and to review their operation.

Guidelines for ethical research practice are available from research associations (e.g., British Educational Research Association, 1992). These usually include the following rights of participants in research: informed consent; anonymity; consultation before filming or other recordings are made; freedom from disadvantage or abuse; and freedom from harm.

The researcher has a clear responsibility to research assistants and students. This includes the responsibility to refrain from engaging in a sexual or romantic relationship with them. I believe that such relationships often result in the abuse of power. A student is particularly vulnerable and powerless in such a relationship. They may fear, rightly or wrongly, that they will be disadvantaged by a lack of support (or even downgrading) if the relationship ends.

Most guidelines will refer to the responsibilities of the researcher to research assistants. All research workers need to be informed of the terms and conditions of their employment and the limits to the tasks expected of them. They should be aware of intellectual property rights with respect to data and their interpretation. Researchers should never represent the work of others as their own and attribution of authorship of any report should accurately reflect the contributions of the main participants in the research and writing process, including students.

The research tradition demands that researchers should not fabricate or knowingly misinterpret data or conclusions. The research findings should be published as widely as possible. Attempts by funders to limit publication are not ethically acceptable, nor is it acceptable to publish findings in a selective way that gives a misleading impression. Researchers should always acknowledge material knowingly gleaned from other sources.

Developing an Institutional Research Culture: Issues of Quality

The establishment of a research culture is at present of particular interest for institutions of higher education. For this reason I focus mainly on higher education within this section. There are further education colleges which are interested in developing or maintaining higher education programmes within particular departments. Managers and lecturers in such departments may also need to consider ways of establishing a research culture, perhaps with limited institutional support.

As with most aspects of management, the establishment of a research culture committed to quality depends in part upon a clarity about responsibilities at various levels. This means that the institution may need a well-articulated strategy relating to the establishment of a research culture and a tactical plan for achieving it within a system of accountability and review. It may need to set up systems for the internal scrutiny of research proposals and reports, feedback mechanisms for linking knowledge gained from one project with others and ways of systematizing knowledge about successful processes (for instance, in bidding for external funding). Without some formal systems, skills and knowledge available in the institution may not be made available to all.

There is a range of questions to be addressed in establishing a research culture. The institution will need to decide whether there should be research managers and whether they wish to promote research as an individual or a team effort. Decisions will have to be made about whether research should be integrated at institutional level (in which case, a cross-institution research centre may be needed) or at departmental level.

It is essential that institutional policy in other areas does not cut across the development of a research culture. For example, if the institution is keen to make research a team effort, it may be unwise to tie individual performance-related pay to research output. If it wishes to promote division of labour as a feature of an efficient research strategy, it may decide to review staff contracts and the use of research assistants for teaching purposes. It may be reasonable to employ staff on temporary contracts for teaching programmes with a limited life, but if this policy is applied to research, it is likely that the institution will lose a mass of expertise at the end of each project. This implies that the institution will need to fund the continuous employment of key research staff in each department.

Similarly, it is important that decisions about research policy should not adversely effect the institution's operations in other areas. For instance, the establishment of teaching-only contracts might look superficially attractive, but such a policy would have knock-on effects on the status accorded to teaching and its quality. Given the integral nature of teaching and research argued in the earlier parts of this chapter, I believe that teaching-only contracts call into question the whole role and purpose of higher education.

It is likely that some decisions will be relegated to departmental level. These may include the extent that academic staff are to be free to pursue their own intellectual interests or whether particular foci for research should be developed. If foci are established, structures will need to be set up to identify areas worthy of support and decide on the formality of any groupings around them (for instance, whether staff should be contractually employed within particular research centres, or connected with areas of research on a looser basis).

Whatever organizational structures are deemed appropriate, some decisions need to be made about what research projects can be supported. The location of such decisions needs careful consideration. There will be costs and benefits in any system. For instance, if the main decisions are made at institutional level, a holistic strategy may be easier to maintain. There may be economies in resources and a sharing of expertise across subject boundaries. Opportunities for interdisciplinary research may be encouraged. On the other hand, departments may be better informed about research priorities relating to their subject and about appropriate production standards.

It is likely that there will be some division of planning, decision-making and activity between the centre and the department, with different levels of monitoring and review. The aim at each level should be to establish shared meanings and definitions, minimize barriers to achievement and maximize opportunities for research. Thus, the establishment of a research culture may be about a shared recognition of the importance of research as a normal part of the teaching role and an agreed sense of direction.

It seems to me that various tasks are better achieved at different levels of the institution. Thus, senior managers and governors may make decisions about the overall funding, including the establishment of research resources. There may need to be committee structures to advise on the funding strategy. Central services may be needed: for instance, lecturers who are routinely expected to undertake research have a right to expect library back up, online research facilities and access to research databases. They should be able to ask for help in the creation of bibliographies and for their institutional library to provide other services such as liaison with other institutional libraries so the lecturer can access their facilities.

On the other hand, the deployment of some resources may be better decided at a level closer to the activity. For instance, the departmental level may be more appropriate for the allocation of personal laptop computers and access to research assistant time. Departmental managers may also be in a better position to know whether remission from teaching is appropriate for a particular staff member and to find creative ways of achieving this.

The institution may need to take a lead in establishing the notion of research as a worthwhile activity, but the departmental managers may be in a better position to stimulate discussion about values and definitions of quality within their subject area.

The department may also be a better place to organize appropriate training in research methods and dissemination of research practice within the department. In some subject departments most lecturers will be trained in the methods of research appropriate to their specialism before appointment and the basic research training provided by the department may focus on the needs of research students. In others, particularly subjects which draw on expertise developed in a vocational context (such as education or accountancy), many newly appointed lecturers will need some research training before they can be expected to be active researchers. In all subject areas, some development in advanced research methods may be needed to take lecturers further. In some, such as science, researchers routinely work in terms and research training becomes part of the way of working. In other subject areas a structured training programme may have to be established. There may need to be a committee system at departmental level to establish principles for the support of new initiatives and make recommendations about pump priming.

The institution has a role in establishing systems of communication so that research activity across the institution is monitored and recorded. It may also be an institutional function to establish broad criteria for the appraisal, appointment and promotion of staff and expectations made of staff related to research. The department is probably better placed to encourage and celebrate achievement in a variety of ways, including the establishment of publishing contracts, mentoring systems for new staff and a programme of research workshops.

The institution and department each have a role in establishing aims and targets for research activity. The institution is probably best placed to encourage practitioner research, perhaps through an educational development or education methods unit. Institutional and departmental aims are likely to be related to the scale and quality of research activity. There is a responsibility at all levels to ensure a balance in research activity and its funding. Over-reliance on single funders can lead to instability. Ranson (1992) points to the need for some stability in funding if the institution is to develop a systematic research programme and avoid purely opportunistic research. Ideally, activity should include individual research, group projects, and a well-supported research student programme.

Success in achieving external funding for research often depends upon fast decision-making. Institutions and departments have to work together to ensure a streamlined process of approval, that does not sacrifice rigour. The quality of an institution's research is likely to depend partly upon mechanisms to look at the values underpinning research proposals to ensure that they are worthwhile in terms of institutional ethos and purposes. This is particularly true in the highly competitive world of external funding.

I am concerned by the notion of a market-led research policy. There may be conflicts between the interests of the funder and the search for truth that is fundamental to worthwhile education and research. Ranson points to concern that research is becoming more reactive and prescriptive and may be undertaken for instrumental purposes. Research that lacks underpinning values and theory tends to be *ad hoc* and descriptive. It may not link to existing knowledge nor be subject to comparable standards. Contracts for this kind of research sometimes include clauses which restrict dissemination. Such restrictions can lead to a pattern of research that gives a misleadingly one-sided picture and fundamentally damages the pursuit of truth. The prevalence of market-led research may be one of the greatest threats to quality and standards in research. The aims and the identity of sponsors of research should always be made clear and academic staff should not agree to conduct research that conflicts with academic freedom. The institution should not compel academic staff to engage in any particular research contract. If academic freedoms are to mean anything, they need to be articulated as explicit criteria for the assessment of quality.

Facilities for Research

Institutions interested in promoting research and scholarship have a responsibility to create the conditions under which research can flourish. This will include establishing an appropriate infrastructure. An important element of this is good

---

Enquiry Task

- If your institution is actively trying to promote a research ethos, list the actions which it has taken which have affected you (in terms of a change in your behaviour or awareness).
- Ask a senior manager for his or her version of the actions which the institution has taken.
- Compare your lists.

What did they have in common?

What aspects were most significant for you and for the senior manager (for example, what actions headed your respective lists)?

---

library and information technology systems. In today's climate, the library or study centre is likely to be as central to the work of lecturers as to that of students. The growth in knowledge, and access to it, requires specialist services within the institution. If staff and students are to pursue their research profitably, these have to be user-friendly. The library or study centre is the place where information about how to access information should be communicated.

You are likely to get more out of the services on offer if you have some idea of the range of opportunities that are open to you, for instance, by the establishment of electronic information networks. All UK universities are linked with JANET (Joint Academic Network), which enables you to access library catalogues and specialist services such as HUMBUL (Humanities Bulletin Board). HUMBUL is geared towards arts and humanities lecturers and has online information about the latest developments in the field. JANET also provides E-Mail and file-transfer facilities. JANET has been extended into 'Super JANET' which is now being implemented in may British universities. This has many additional facilities, such as video conferencing: enabling, for instance, people in London to watch a surgeon perform an eye operation in Edinburgh. JANET is linked to many similar networks by the Internet, a worldwide network of networks. The Internet gives access to a wide range of information, such as international library catalogues, unpublished research papers and conference reports, databases, electronic journals bulletin boards and so on. For example, it is possible to examine the text of the Dead Sea Scrolls held in the Library of Congress in the USA.

Information can be browsed using gophers, or 'subject trees', which work rather like a taxonomy. Many institutions are developing their own interfaces with the Internet services, that offer a more user-friendly approach. An example of this is the Bodleian Library's BARD service (Bodleian Access to Remote Databases). Once you know the service that you wish to access, you can connect to it more quickly by using tools such as Jughead (Jonzy's Universal Gopher Excavation and Display), and Veronica (Very Easy Rodent-Oriented Net-wide Index to Computerised Archives), rather than by working through the subject trees. To fully exploit the information available, you will need access to E-Mail and downloading/file-transfer facilities.

There are both advantages and disadvantages to this explosion of electronic information. It enables far wider and more rapid access to information, especially that held overseas. It also enables researchers to publish directly onto the network and receive comment and information from their peers. However, it is not always easy to verify the quality of the material published. Another problem with allowing access to a mass of unpublished research is that it makes plagiarism much easier to accomplish and harder to detect.

Campus networks are an increasing feature of institutional life. At the simplest level these can enable staff to pass messages without using paper. At a more sophisticated level, they can allow tutors to collaborate on research and write jointly, and gives them access to a range of institutional information (for instance, room availability and library listings) from their study. In these systems, a central computer (the server) generally holds data and programmes such as word-processing, database and spreadsheet packages and allows multiuser access.

Other systems can be accessed via CD Rom (Compact Disc Read-Only Memory). For instance, ERIC (Educational Research Information Centre) on CD Rom enables you to find out what journal articles are published in the field of education. (International ERIC contains the British Australian and Canadian Education indexes.) If you want to survey books available in your subject, you could use TES Bookfind, which includes about 500,000 titles. You can search these databases by author, title, subject heading or keyword. Some databases, such as TES Bookfind and ERIC, include summaries of the contents of the book or paper.

These systems require investment on the part of the institution, firstly in setting them up and establishing access to them and secondly in enabling continuing access. Information technology is continuing to develop and institutions that wish to be at the forefront of research are likely to find that they must continue to find funds to maintain and update their hardware, software and online facilities. It is important that lecturers understand and use the opportunities that this provides for them. The vast quantity of information and variety of ways in which it can be accessed can be bewildering. Library staff are constantly exploring new technologies for information access, and are often committed to working alongside information technology staff to find the most appropriate ways of exploiting such tools. They should be able to communicate with library users about new developments, and so enable them to access such sources for themselves.

Support for Research Students

The Higher Education Quality Council (HEQC, 1994) makes it clear that the level of support for postgraduate students is a crucial issue for judging the quality of research within an institution. This focus may have arisen from government worries about the waste of taxpayers' money and the talents of individuals which is suggested by the low levels of completion of students studying for research degrees.

The HEQC recommends that institutions should have guidelines on the support of postgraduate students and that these are communicated to students and supervisors. It advises that guidelines should include procedures for the appointment of suitably qualified supervisors and the specification of the roles and responsibilities of all concerned. Students should know how much support they are entitled to and how their progress will be monitored. They should have an introduction to the resources and facilities available for research activity. They need information about the procedure for conversion to a higher or lower qualification and grievance and appeal procedures.

It is now a normal expectation that training will be available for supervisors for their role and that students will receive a coherent training in research methods. Indeed, it is increasingly a requirement for funding for MPhil and Phd students from bodies such as the Economic and Social Research Council.

Each of these developments requires a system of policy decision-making and review. They imply that accountability for research activity should be located within the institution's committee and management systems. These systems should be capable of ensuring that each student receives a sound educational experience (including training in research methods) that is planned and monitored as carefully as any other course or programme. This may be more difficult for postgraduate research than traditional programmes, because the programme of research and the training needs of students tend to be more individual. Some arrangements can be in common (for instance, a generalized research-methods course), but others are likely to be particular (for instance, updating in particular subject matter and the approval of the dissertation title).

The individual nature of postgraduate work can make it a fragmented business,

---

Enquiry Task

List the features which a potential postgraduate research student should look for before signing up with a particular institution.

e.g.,   a substantial programme of research training;
      a track record of supervision in a particular subject. . . .

Create a list of student entitlements which might be contained in a research student handbook.

e.g.,   a defined level of tutorial support;
      work returned within a defined time scale. . . .

If you work in an institution that has postgraduate research students:

- discuss your lists with some of them;
- add to your lists in the light of this discussion;
- find out which of these features and entitlements are available and how they are communicated to students and potential students.

If you are interested in undertaking postgraduate research but work in an institution that does not have research students, contact a neighbouring institution and ask them for the programme details for postgraduate research degrees in your subject. Ask if you can be put into contact with some students currently studying with them.

Carry out the investigation above.

---

with more opportunity for slippage in the usual standards of performance and evaluation. For this reason, the language of student rights and entitlements may be particularly appropriate to this area. If students have explicit rights (for instance, as to the speed of return of work, level of supervision and availability of facilities, equipment and training), they can become part of the system for monitoring performance.

The institution may need to consider how it will protect vulnerable students from exploitation or harassment. Because of the individualized nature of their work and its supervision, postgraduate students do not have the protection of the group. They therefore need explicit and carefully thought-out systems for complaint. These systems should protect the student from unreasonable behaviour of any kind, including, inadequate support, breaches in confidentiality and assault or harassment. The institution may need to consider if systems should be available at any level that the student deems appropriate and how they should be publicized, so that issues can be dealt with at an early stage.

Staff Development and Research

Institutions of higher education interested in promoting a research ethos may need to recognize that it is unlikely that all members of staff see research as part of their day-to-day activity. Specific events and processes may need to be introduced to raise the profile of research and to communicate the expectation that all staff should be regularly engaged in research activity. It is not fair to raise the expectations of staff if no strategies are in place to enable those expectations to be fulfilled. Many staff may not feel confident in their ability to undertake research. They may need training in relevant research methods, help in identifying foci for research and help in managing their time.

Some institutions are introducing mentoring systems for new staff in their first year. The mentor may be expected to work through a record of progress and achievement with the new member of staff, collecting evidence of developing competences in defined areas, discussing it and observing practice. I have found that mentoring of more experienced staff requires active structuring if it is to be useful. In addition to training and initiatives such as the establishment of records of progress and achievement, key people in the institution may need to set up structures to make research and publication easier. For example, at Westminster College we have run a symposium at a conference and asked a number of colleagues to contribute; we have obtained a contract for an edited book that will allow several inexperienced colleagues to co-author chapters with more experienced authors; and we are negotiating a contract for a series of books which will also allow several colleagues to publish.

Expectations about teaching and administration must be tailored to the level of expectation the institution has for research. Day-to-day teaching and administrative practices can prevent academic staff from undertaking research. This implies that systems should be examined and streamlined to make them time-efficient as well as thorough.

Time for research may need to be timetabled and protected in the same way as time for teaching. For instance, all meetings and teaching timetables might be confirmed before the beginning of each term. Staff could then be expected to publish an individual research timetable, showing when they will be undertaking research and therefore unavailable for other duties.

Enquiry Task

List the skills, knowledge and attitudes you need to be a successful researcher:

Skills	*Knowledge*	*Attitudes*
e.g., Observation skills	e.g., Resources available	e.g., Perseverance

Discuss your list with some colleagues who are inexperienced in research.

Which of these skills, knowledge or attitudes do they feel they need help to develop?

Order your lists in terms of priorities for training.

How do your priorities compare to the staff training that your institution provides?

What actions might you take to encourage your institution to provide a better focused training?

Summary

Research and scholarship are central to further and higher education and the quality of teaching. Research is a systematic, public activity, that includes originality of findings or interpretation. It may be defined broadly or narrowly. HEFC favours a relatively broad definition that includes:

- the creation of new ideas;
- artistic creation and design, where these lead to new insights;
- reinterpretation of existing knowledge or ideas which can be related to new products, materials and processes;
- conceptual papers for publication;
- supervision and output of research students; and
- external funding for research.

Research may or may not be put to practical use. It is of value in its own right.

HEFC funding for research is based on a rating exercise. Recent changes to this process include:

- inclusion of only four outputs per staff member;
- applied research given more status;
- inclusion of research student activity; and
- individual staff contribution to the rating exercise follows them when they move jobs.

The rating exercise has raised the general level of expectation for research activity for lecturers in higher education and those in further education engaged in higher-level teaching.

Traditions in research vary according to the subject, but should not restrict activity. The quantitative research often includes:

- the control of variables;
- the examination of a large number of instances of a phenomenon;
- the notion of disproving a hypothesis; and
- focus on issues of reliability.

The qualitative research often includes:

- a problem-centred approach;
- focus on complex, interactive real-life situations, where variables cannot be isolated;
- the exploration, rather than testing, of hypotheses; and
- 'quality' of the research ascertained in terms of validity at a pragmatic level.

Questions which may be asked to assess the quality of research include:

- how typical is the population/situation;
- what categories are used;
- are they the only possible ones;
- are they relevant to the questions asked;
- has everything relevant been included;
- are data rightly assigned to particular categories;
- are the causes described the only possible ones;
- are the data sufficient for the claims made for them;
- what measuring instruments are used;
- are they appropriate;
- might their calibration have changed in the course of a study;
- has anything happened in the course of the study that might interfere with the results;
- what do you know about the researcher's expert knowledge; and
- was the entire research process ethical?

Practitioner research is a means of developing practice. It starts from real problems and may involve a cyclical process: reconnaissance; planning; action; data collection; evaluation; reflection; reformulating plans; and so into another cycle. It is a form of insider research, grounded in its context, that can empower the practitioner-researcher. It has an emphasis on congruence between values and practice. Because it can be inward-looking and subjective, external and alternative perspectives should be sought in interpreting data.

Lecturers wishing to get started on research and publication might find it helpful to:

- consider time-efficient foci and methods;
- develop a sense of audience;

- investigate the requirements and style of various publishing outlets;
- follow publishers' guidelines for papers or book proposals;
- attend conferences to find out what is expected and to make contacts;
- learn the skill of writing; and
- learn to love criticism.

Research should be located in an ethical framework that might include the following rights of participants in research:

- informed consent;
- anonymity;
- consultation before filming or other recordings are made;
- freedom from disadvantage or abuse; and
- freedom from harm;

The establishment of a research culture within an institution is likely to involve:

- strategic and tactical planning;
- systems for policy-making, scrutiny and report;
- consideration of key posts;
- decisions about the level of integration;
- consideration of relationships between research and other policies;
- decisions about the formality of research groupings;
- provision of resources and facilities; and
- consideration of the ethical framework.

The rights of research students and assistants include:

- freedom from sexual or romantic contact;
- terms and conditions of employment which limit the tasks expected of them;
- awareness of intellectual property rights with respect to data and their interpretation; and
- accurate attribution of authorship.

The research tradition demands that researchers should:

- never fabricate or knowingly misinterpret data or conclusions;
- publish findings as widely as possible;
- never publish findings in a selective way which gives a misleading impression; and
- always acknowledge material knowingly gleaned from other sources.

The provision for research students should include:

- training for students and supervisors;
- procedures for the appointment of suitably qualified supervisors;
- the specification of the roles and responsibilities of all concerned;

- the specification of levels of support to which students are entitled;
- the specification of how students' progress will be monitored;
- an introduction to the resources and facilities available for research activity;
- procedures for conversion to a higher or lower qualification;
- grievance and appeal procedures; and
- policies ensuring freedom from exploitation or harassment.

Staff development may be needed to help staff meet these raised expectations. Expectations related to teaching and administration may need to be modified. Structured mentoring systems and training may help lecturers develop the necessary skills and outlets.

Entry for the Reflective Diary

Write about your feelings about research and its importance to you as a lecturer.

Write about the factors which discourage you from research and publication:

e.g., time management;
lack of ideas;
lack of confidence;
lack of expertise; and
scale of the data you would need to collect.

Create a personal publication plan that would include action to overcome these problems.

Notes
Annotated List of Suggested Reading

Deakin University (1982) *The Action Research Reader*, Victoria, Deakin University Press.
This book probably includes everything you might want to know about action research. It is very long, but fortunately it is clearly laid out so you can dip into it for the historical background, theoretical framework, case studies of practice, political implications or whatever. If you manage to read it from cover to cover, you have more stamina than I have.

Ranson, S. (1992) 'The management and organisation of educational research', *Research Papers in Education*, 8, 2, pp. 177–98.
This is a report of an ESRC funded project that examined how university departments of education develop their research profiles. Ranson's style is coherent and readable. The first eleven pages provide a clear account of aspects of good practice in establishing a research culture. Although the report relates particularly to education, most of the findings would be of interest within any subject department.

References

ASHCROFT, K. (1988) 'The history of an innovation' *Assessment and Evaluation in Higher Education*, 12, 1, pp. 37–45.

ASHCROFT, K. and FOREMAN-PECK, L. (1994) *Managing Teaching and Learning in Higher Education*, London, Falmer Press.

ASHCROFT, K. and GRIFFITHS, M. (1989) 'Reflective teachers and reflective tutors: School experience in an initial teacher education course', *Journal of Education for Teaching*, 5, 1, pp. 35–52.

ASHCROFT, K. and TANN, S. (1988) 'Beyond building better checklists: Staff development in a school experience programme', *Assessment and Evaluation in Higher Education*, 13, 1, pp. 61–72.

BRITISH EDUCATIONAL RESEARCH ASSOCIATION (1992) *Ethical Guidelines for Funded Research*, London, BERA.

CARR, W. and KEMMIS, S. (1986) *Becoming Critical: Knowing through Action Research*, London, Falmer Press.

CAMPBELL, D.T. and STANLEY, J.C. (1963) *Experimental and Quasi-Experimental Designs for Research*, Chicago, Rand McNally.

DEAKIN UNIVERSITY (1982) *The Action Research Reader*, Victoria, Deakin University Press.

ELLIOTT, J. (1991) *Action Research for Educational Change*, Milton Keynes, Open University.

ELLIOTT, J. (1993) 'Towards a methodology of insider research', invitational seminar at *Oxford University*, November.

FURTHER EDUCATION FUNDING COUNCIL (1993) *Circular 93/28. Assessing Achievement*, Coventry, FEFC.

HIGHER EDUCATION FUNDING COUNCIL FOR ENGLAND (1994a) 'HEFCE provides stability and secures foundation for future expansion', *HEFCE News*, 5, March, pp. 1–2.

HIGHER EDUCATION FUNDING COUNCIL FOR ENGLAND (1994b), 'Measures on greater accountability for research funds introduced', *HEFCE News*, 5, March p. 3.

HIGHER EDUCATION FUNDING COUNCIL (1994) *1996 Research Assessment Exercise*, Bristol, HEFCE, Scottish Higher Education Funding Council and Department of Education Northern Ireland, June.

HIGHER EDUCATION QUALITY COUNCIL (1994) *Checklist for Quality Assurance: A Briefing Paper from the Higher Education Quality Council*, London, HEQC.

RANSON, S. (1992) 'The management and organisation of educational research', *Research Papers in Education*, 8, 2, pp. 177–98.

SCHON, D. (1983) *The Reflective Practitioner*, London, Jossey-Bass.

STENHOUSE, L. (1975) *An Introduction to Curriculum Research and Development*, London, Heinemann.

Chapter 11

Conclusion

The last few years have seen a shift in perspectives on quality. This shift has included a movement from focusing on the needs of the institution and the subject to a focus on multiple perspectives and interest groups. Thus institutions are more and more interested in the perspectives of students, employers, the community, and most especially the Government as expressed through funding bodies. At the same time, what has been assessed has changed. We used to look primarily at the process of teaching. Now the focus is increasingly on learning. The process approach has largely given way to an approach based on outputs. These outputs are sometimes complex, such as student learning, and sometimes oversimplified, such as some numerical performance indicators.

The results of quality assurance and assessment are put to multiple purposes, to determine resource allocation, to inform recruitment decisions, to inform course and staff development and to drive down the unit of resource. We must not fool ourselves into thinking each of these foci, purposes and perspectives is not value-laden or that these values are necessarily compatible.

I have argued that the way through the quality jungle, towards moral and educational defensibility and real educational worthwhileness, is through a process of critical analysis. I have argued that this analysis should be supported by a clearly articulated set of educational values and a rigorous evaluation of the long- and short-term consequences of action in the light of evidence, in order to develop a theory of quality in practice. This process requires qualities of openmindedness and responsibility and that you become involved in the management of your institution. The principled involvement of educationalists and students is the best guarantee that instrumental solutions to difficult institutional circumstances are examined. It is this involvement in the real world, with real dilemmas, that is required for the maintenance and enhancement of quality and academic standards.

The definition of quality varies depending on the perspective and interests of the person who examines it. Even the same viewpoint can yield different and contradictory models of quality. For example, the Conservative Government of the 1990s sought to define quality in terms of comparative performance tables, setting certain performance scores of individual institutions against a context of 'national average achievement' (FEFC, 1993a). Achievement in education was defined in terms of qualifications and test results. Within further and higher education, it also included career destinations of full-time students.

At the same time, the Government, under the auspices of the FEFC, had set up a Quality Assessment Committee with a more sophisticated definition of quality which takes into account quality control mechanisms within the institution, examination and validation through external bodies and external assessment of processes such as management, teaching and learning. Performance indicators included student achievement, choice and diversity, the scholarship and competence of lecturers and the support available for teaching and learning (see, for example, FEFC, 1993b). The institutional aims and strategic plan were the starting point for such an assessment.

Many institutions have made great progress to achieve a sound level of quality assurance. As late as 1992, Devlin (1992) found the majority of institutions of further education (82 per cent) which he surveyed within Northern Ireland had no quality assurance systems. Managers and lecturers have made this a priority, but even so, it is unlikely awareness of quality systems among staff is high.

A number of questions and issues relating to quality assurance systems have been identified within this book. Some of these relate to those identified by Cameron (1980). They include the value-laden decisions which have to be made about the level of information that will be required and the foci which are chosen for assessment (for instance, educational values or economy). Questions as to whether the focus is on input, process or outcomes are partly political issues, including the extent to which the criteria of effectiveness are explicit, the reference points involved, who sets the agenda and in whose interests. The way these issues are resolved will depend on the openness of the management system. There are varying models possible and these will result in different people acting as the motivator for the monitoring systems, doing the monitoring and being monitored. Questions about how data relating to quality are collected, processed and used relate closely to issues of control and empowerment. Probably the most fundamental issue, which will affect every question and policy that is eventually pursued, relates to decisions about whose purposes and interests are to be furthered. These important questions about ownership and control suggest an analysis of the strengths and weaknesses of top–down and bottom–up approaches to quality, the costs and benefits of different systems, and the technical adequacy of the measures used.

Issues of quality control and accountability have had fundamental effects on the process of strategic planning. As institutions achieve more control over their own affairs, the strategic plan has moved away from a 'wish list' presented to the local authority, towards a disciplined system of prioritization and negotiation. If the process has been effectively managed, the result should reflect the values of the institution and the needs and interests of various parties to the educational process. It will be organized and realistic and take into account money, time, expertise and values.

Thus, quality in teaching and learning is not separate from other systems in the institution. It depends upon your involvement in financial, administrative and quality assurance systems. Without this involvement, you are relying on others to ensure that educationally defensible solutions to problems are pursued and that you and your students will have an appropriate learning environment. The process of involvement which I hope this book has encouraged, may enable you to develop confidence, develop key skills and make closer links across the institution and with your students and the wider community.

References

CAMERON, R. (1980) 'Critical questions in assessing organisational effectiveness', *Organisational Dynamics*, Autumn.

DEVLIN, G. (1992) 'The Northern Ireland further education quality assurance survey', *Mendip Papers. No. 045*, Blagdon, Staff College.

FURTHER EDUCATION FUNDING COUNCIL (1993a) *Council Report. No. 11*, 23 December, FEFC.

FURTHER EDUCATION FUNDING COUNCIL (1993b) *Circular 93/28: Assessing Achievement*, Coventry, FEFC.

Index

academic: board 13, 28
  freedom 4, 206
  quality assurance systems 65
    mechanisms 51
  standards 26
accommodation: for students 76
accountability 18, 20, 217
  and assessment 127–8
  and course design 145–6
  of executive system 31
  and funding 158
  in research activity 209
  in staff appraisal 42
accreditation: and course design 140
  national system 140
action research 198
admissions: and courses 144–5
  procedures 10, 68–9, 182–4, 189
advertising: and marketing 187–8
aims: in course design 142–4, 152
application: for teaching posts 87–8
appointment: of staff 87–9, 105
appraisal: student 9
  system 9, 51
  see also staff appraisal
assertiveness techniques 104
assessment, of needs: in course design
  140, 145
assessment: criteria 116–18
  of competence 109, 124–6, 132, 133
  and enhanced learning 112
  formative 112, 114–15, 118, 119, 132
  forms of 116–18, 133
  models of 9, 126
  practices 110
  principles of 112–13
  purposes of 113–16, 132
  of quality 9, 11, 15–19, 35–6, 45, 77,
    109–35, 216
  quality assurance in 127–9, 133, 134
  and reflective practice 126–7
  resources 20–3

schemes 112
self- 9, 16, 18, 117
summative 112, 114, 117–19 *passim*,
  132
timing and clustering of 115–16
assessors: internal 128
  work-based 125

behavioural objectives 55
bidding, for funds: competitive 155
  principles of 162–7, 170
  and teaching quality 155
bids 165–6
  and intermediate targets 164
British Educational Research Association
  (BERA) 193, 201
British Standard 5750 21, 36
budgetary control: and efficiency
  158–9
business planning: need for 159–62,
  171

careers guidance: for students 75–6
CD Rom: use in research 208
change: effective 106
  implementing, stress of 104–5
  process 9
Charter for Higher Education 61
charters: for student support 61–2, 79
class size 52–5, 57
committees: layers of 28–9
  and lecturers 30–1
  models of 30
  processes of 28–9, 36
  system, role of 31, 36
communication skills 5, 11
community: local, links with 186–7
  rights and quality in Higher
    Education 63
competence-based: models of learning
  73
  qualifications 110, 124, 125, 137

Printed in the United Kingdom
by Lightning Source UK Ltd.
125165UK00002B/94/A